Teaching Every Student

in the Digital Age

Universal Design for Learning

David H. Rose and Anne Meyer

with Nicole Strangman and Gabrielle Rappolt

Association for Supervision and Curriculum Development ➤ Alexandria, Virginia USA

®

Association for Supervision and Curriculum Development
1703 N. Beauregard St. • Alexandria, VA 22311-1714 USA
Telephone: 1-800-933-2723 or 703-578-9600 • Fax: 703-575-5400

Web site: http://www.ascd.org • E-mail: member@ascd.org

Printed in the United States of America.

ASCD Product No. 101042

ASCD member price: $22.95   nonmember price: $26.95

s5/2002

Library of Congress Cataloging-in-Publication Data
Rose, David H. (David Howard)
    Teaching every student in the digital age : universal design for
learning / by David H. Rose and Anne Meyer with Nicole Strangman and
Gabrielle Rappolt.
        p. cm.
Includes bibliographical references and index.
    ISBN 0-87120-599-8 (alk. paper)
    1. Individualized instruction. 2. Education technology. 3.
Cognitive styles. 4. Children with disabilities—Education. I. Meyer,
Anne, Ed. D. II. Title.
    LB1031 .R67 2002
    371.39'4—dc21
                                                    2002001336

07 06 05 04 03 02   10 9 8 7 6 5 4 3 2 1

Teaching Every Student
in the Digital Age
Universal Design for Learning

105134

Acknowledgments

THE AUTHORS WISH TO THANK ELIZABETH A. MURRAY AND BRIDGET DALTON FOR their help in writing this book and Brenda Matthis and Linda M. Butler for their careful management of the writing and production process. Further, we gratefully acknowledge the valuable contributions to researching, writing, and producing this book from Linda V. Beardsley, Ann Brennan, Bernice Cheung, Kristen Cohen, Michael Cooper, Chuck Hitchcock, Richard M. Jackson, Alan S. Leney, Grace J. Meo, James Moore, Ron McAdow, Leslie O'Callaghan, Lucinda M. O'Neill, Donna Palley, Nancy Schick, Sheara Brand Seigal, Sheela Sethuraman, Ada Sullivan, Roxanne Ruzic, and our developmental editor, Joyce McLeod.

We are tremendously grateful to the following individuals, foundations, and organizations who contributed funds that made realization of this book possible: Ruth M. Epstein, Katharine Graham, Elizabeth Lorentz, Elizabeth E. Meyer, Robert C. Seamans Jr., Doris and Simon Scheff, Campbell Steward, Arthur K. Watson Charitable Trust, George J. Gillespie Charitable Trust, Foundation Cariñoso, Island Fund of the New York Community Trust, LD ACCESS Foundation, Inc., Pinky Foundation, Sidney & Judith Kranes Charitable Trust, and the National Center on Accessing the General Curriculum (NCAC), a cooperative agreement between CAST and the U.S. Department of Education, Office of Special Education (OSEP), Cooperative Agreement No. H324H990004. (The opinions expressed herein do not necessarily reflect the policy or position of the U.S. Department of Education, Office of Special Education Programs, and no official endorsement by the Department should be inferred.)

Preface

THIS BOOK IS THE RESULT OF 15 YEARS OF THOUGHT, RESEARCH, AND DEVELOPMENT conducted by the Center for Applied Special Technology (CAST) and a number of collaborating individuals, schools, districts, and states. CAST was founded in 1984 with a mission to develop and apply technologies that would expand learning opportunities for individuals with disabilities. Our premise was clear: Students with disabilities should be equipped with particular technologies—new tools and approaches—that would help them access a print-based curriculum.

In the years since CAST's inception, however, we have undergone a Copernican shift toward a new position: *the use of technology to transform the nature of the curriculum itself.* In the rapidly expanding capabilities of digital content, tools, and networks, we see the possibility of conceiving, designing, and delivering a curriculum that will accommodate widely varying learner needs. Essentially, this will transfer the burden of adjustment from students to the materials and methods they encounter in the classroom.

Background

The path to CAST's new viewpoint began to emerge more than a decade ago. In 1989, we created Gateway Stories (see Figure P.1) and Gateway Authoring System, a series of electronic books with numerous built-in options for students with disabilities. Students with learning disabilities could opt to have text read aloud; students with physical disabilities could navigate text with a switch attached to the computer; and students with low vision could have the book's controls (such as page turning) read aloud. Each setting was optional, making it possible to customize the books for each user. In addition, both Gateway Stories and Gateway Authoring System included templates for creating additional books with the same easily customized features.

—FIGURE P.1—
GATEWAY STORIES

Reprinted by permission of the authors from *The Goat, the Moat, and the Apple Tree*. Copyright © 1990 by Robert Brooks, Richard Wanderman, and Patricia Buchanan.

From this selection screen, users can click on an image to select one of four stories.

Contributing to CAST's receipt of the 1993 *Computerworld* Smithsonian Award for Innovation in Education and Academia, Gateway Stories proved to be intriguing and helpful, not only for our intended users—students with disabilities—but also for students just learning to read, those who spoke English as a second language, and those who simply found it engaging.

Suddenly, the light dawned! We realized that barriers to learning are not, in fact, inherent in the capacities of learners, but instead arise in learners' interactions with inflexible educational materials and methods. The flexibility we were able to build into digital "books" could be used to make all curriculum adjustable so that one electronic edition could meet the needs of extremely varied learners. Further, the benefits of customization would be available not only to students with disabilities, but to *every student*.

Thus began CAST's commitment to Universal Design for Learning (UDL). Universal Design for Learning is a research-based set of principles that together form a practical framework for using technology to maximize learning opportunities for every student. UDL principles draw on brain and media research to help educators reach all students by setting appropriate learning goals, choosing and developing effective methods and materials, and developing accurate and fair ways to assess students' progress.

Content and Format

The book is divided into two sections. The first addresses the concept of Universal Design for Learning; the second addresses the practical application of UDL in the classroom. Each chapter opens with a summary of key ideas and a graphic organizer that illustrates how the concepts fit together.

We have also decided to represent this book through a companion Web site (http://www.cast.org/TeachingEveryStudent, shown in Figure P.2). In our view, publishing this work in both traditional form and an online version is the best way to make the material accessible to the maximum number of readers and to accommodate the growing, changing nature of the concept, resources, and examples of UDL. The online version also offers readers the opportunity to give us feedback and exchange ideas with one another. Finally, publishing an electronic version seems the most appropriate way to demonstrate the flexible, interactive nature of networked digital materials.

On the *Teaching Every Student* Web site, hosted and maintained by CAST, you will find the text of this book and an expanding set of related Web links, organized into the following categories:

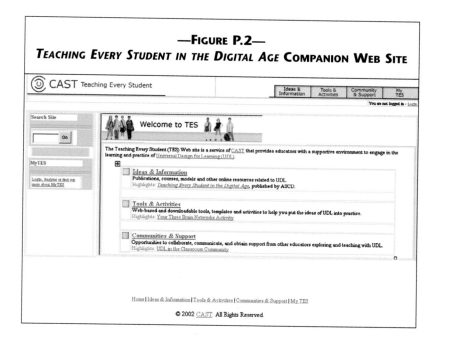

—FIGURE P.2—
TEACHING EVERY STUDENT IN THE DIGITAL AGE COMPANION WEB SITE

➤ **Resource Links** connect to collections of information and materials such as curriculum resources and online sources for digital text and images.

➤ **Background Knowledge Links** connect to related content such as more in-depth information, interviews with experts, and glossaries.

➤ **Example Links** connect to examples of concepts or techniques in use, such as videos or pictures from classrooms, ways to use software or Web sites, and student case stories.

➤ **Activity Links** connect to interactive experiences that offer you the opportunity to learn more through experimentation and practice.

➤ **Forum Links** connect to online discussions of key topics.

➤ **UDL Classroom Template Links** connect to forms and graphic materials that support classroom implementation of UDL. Some of these templates are also available in the Appendix (see page 176).

As you read the print version of this book, you will encounter references in the margins to each of these kinds of Web links (identified with the symbol in Figure P.3 and a short caption). These form a core set of resources that CAST will enhance and expand over time. We plan to build an extensive library of models and examples of UDL in action, developing momentum and a shared vision of UDL that will help educators and learners meet the myriad challenges they face.

Throughout the book, we name and discuss a number of teachers and students. These individuals are composites inspired by those with whom we have worked. The exception is Donna Palley, whom you will meet in chapter 1 and learn more about in chapter 8. Her work implementing UDL in the Concord, New Hampshire, school system is very real—and it is ongoing. Because this work requires the full concentration of Concord personnel, Donna and her colleagues cannot accept telephone calls or e-mail messages directly. Instead, we invite you to visit the *Teaching Every Student* Web site, where you will find a variety of lessons and implementation examples from Concord and from other CAST research sites. In addition, we hope you will participate in the site's online forums, where you can pose questions for us and for the personnel in Concord. We look forward to ongoing discussions on the concept and practice of UDL.

—FIGURE P.3—
WEB LINK INDICATOR

Web Link

PART 1

Universal Design for Learning:

The Concept

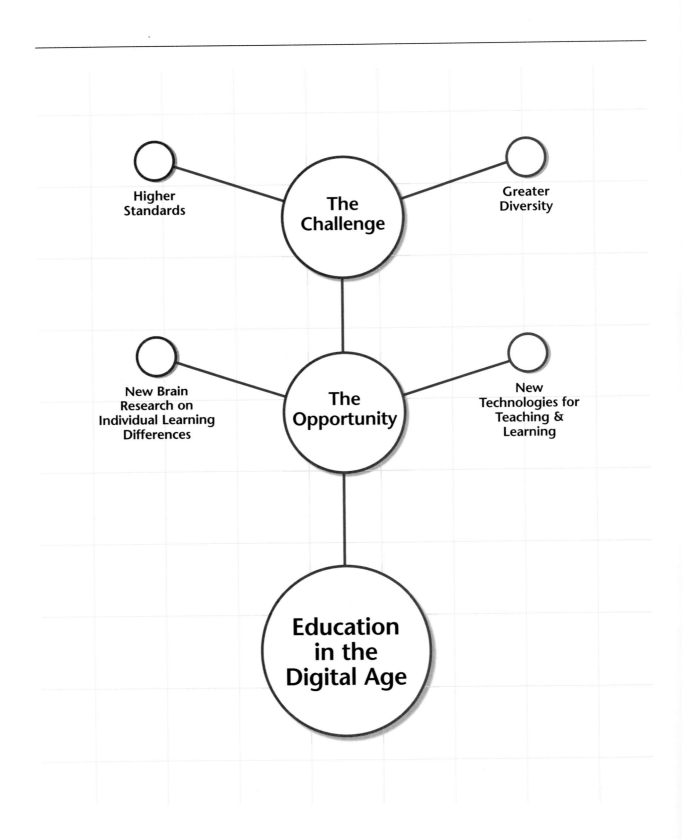

Education in the Digital Age

This chapter introduces the concept of Universal Design for Learning, a framework that can help you turn the challenges posed by high standards and increasing learner diversity into opportunities to maximize learning for every student.

KEY IDEAS

➤ In a time of greater student diversity, increased emphasis on standards and accountability challenges teachers to help all students achieve.

➤ New insights into the learning brain shed light on learner differences and effective uses of technology.

➤ UDL seizes the opportunity brought by rapidly evolving communication technologies to create flexible methods and materials that can reach diverse learners.

➤ Instilling flexibility into methods and materials maximizes learning opportunities not only for students with identified disabilities, but for all students.

➤ UDL is not "just one more thing;" it is an integral component of improving student learning, compatible with other approaches to education reform.

Hatching baby chicks is a regular part of the 2nd grade curriculum in the Concord, New Hampshire, public school system. But this year, instead of writing reports about the activity, 2nd graders are expressing what they are learning in many different media: creating clay sculptures, drawing and coloring pictures, recording the chicks' sounds, and writing text. Some students are using computers as they draw, record, or write; others use paper or conventional recording devices. At the end of the project, all work will be digitized and incorporated into the class "Chicks" Web page.

In a neighboring Concord high school, students with widely varying skills read *The Catcher in the Rye* in English class. The book is available in both traditional paperback form and as digitized text, which the computer can read aloud at varying rates. Prompts embedded in the digital version offer support for reading-comprehension strategies such as predicting, questioning, and summarizing. Some students take advantage of those supports, others use the digital version without supports, and some students opt for the printed text.

The students' assignment is to choose a chapter from *The Catcher in the Rye*, synthesize the important elements, tie these elements to their own lives, and present their ideas to their classmates. How they choose to fulfill this assignment is up to them. Students create videos, posters, written papers, oral reports, and collages. One student, a recent immigrant to the United States, is concerned that her English isn't fluent enough for an oral presentation. Her teacher helps her develop an animated scene on the computer using a software package called Hollywood (see Figure 1.1).

The student carefully writes each character's part, and when it is her turn to present before her classmates, she shows the animation with just a few words of explanation.

At another school in the district, parents, teachers, and students volunteer in Concord's Scanning Center, where they digitize printed text, including materials from the regular education curriculum and special project-based content. The newly created resources—ranging from texts that can be read aloud by computers to multimedia science experiments—are placed in a digital library, where they are available to all district personnel. Throughout the year, individual teachers access the materials and customize them to meet the needs of individual students. Some teachers in the Concord system will not even consider using a unit of

—**FIGURE 1.1**—
SCENE FROM A STUDENT'S
ANIMATED PRESENTATION

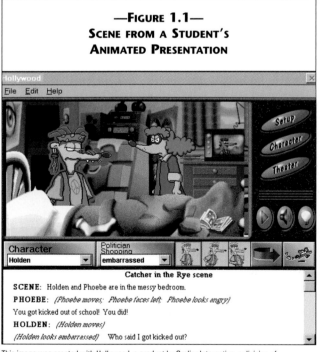

This image was created with Hollywood, a product by Grolier Interactive, a division of Scholastic Inc.

curriculum unless it is available in digital form.

These public schools in Concord, New Hampshire, share a district-wide commitment to maximizing every student's opportunity to learn by building flexible curriculum methods and materials. Their objective is to provide

➤ Carefully conceived classwide learning goals, inclusive of all students.

➤ Individualized approaches for reaching those goals, including customized supports that change as learners progress.

➤ Assessments that measure ongoing progress and provide teachers and students with useful feedback.

Concord's model for change is Universal Design for Learning, a research-based set of principles that forms a practical framework for using technology to maximize learning opportunities for every student. UDL actualizes the opportunities inherent in two great challenges facing today's educators: the challenge of learner diversity and the challenge of high standards.

Web Link

EXAMPLE:
A school leader describes the importance of digitized curriculum materials at *http://www.cast.org/ TeachingEveryStudent/ digitizedcurriculum*

The Challenge: Learner Diversity and High Standards

Cultural, educational, and legal changes have significantly altered the mix of students in regular education classrooms. Today's typical classroom might include students whose first language is not English; students who are not reading on grade level; students with behavioral, attentional, and motivational problems; students from varied cultural backgrounds; and students classified as gifted. In addition, there are students with particular needs, such as limited vision, motor disabilities, emotional difficulties, speech and language difficulties, and learning disabilities.

At the same time, increasing emphasis on learning standards places greater responsibility on teachers and administrators to ensure that each of these students reaches the highest levels of achievement. The Individuals with Disabilities Education Act (IDEA) Amendments of 1997 (text available at http://www.ideapractices.org/), preclude a separate educational agenda for students with disabilities and hold teachers responsible for ensuring that these students demonstrate progress within the general

Web Link

RESOURCE:
Most state and national standards are available online; you will find convenient links at *http://www.cast.org/TeachingEveryStudent/standards*

education curriculum. The Amendments indicate that high expectations and attention to access, as well as participation and progress within the general curriculum, are critical for improving outcomes for students with disabilities. Most of us would agree that these factors are critical for *all* learners.

The challenge posed by greater diversity and greater accountability is to enable students with widely divergent needs, skills, and interests to attain the same high standards. To transform the pressures of diversity into opportunities for all learners, we apply insights about learners who don't "fit the mold" to helps us create flexible curricula and tools that will work more effectively for everyone. In this way, the challenges we face as educators inspire us to reconsider the way curriculum is designed and the way schooling is conducted.

The Opportunity: New Brain Research and New Technology

Historically, most ideas about individual learning differences have been based on the assumption that the brain is roughly the same all over and that its different parts are essentially indistinguishable with respect to their roles in learning. This idea bred a decidedly one-dimensional view of learning and intelligence, as represented by measurement concepts like a single IQ score. In contrast, more recent theories, such as Multiple Intelligences theory (see Gardner, 1993), are consistent with what we are now discovering about the learning brain—namely that students do not have one global learning capacity, but *many multifaceted learning capacities*, and that a disability or challenge in one area may be countered by extraordinary ability in another.

Further, and of particular note for our purposes, the evaluation of ability is often confounded by the means and medium used to conduct the evaluation. For example, a person who appears learning disabled in a print-bound, text-based environment may look extraordinarily skilled in a graphics- or video-based environment.

Fortunately, technological advances have equipped educators with tremendous new instructional resources in the form of computers and digital media. New technologies offer us the opportunity to respond to the multifaceted individual differences in our student population by providing more varied media, tools, and methods. Because of their inherent flexibility, digital technologies can adjust to learner differences, enabling teachers to (1) differentiate problems a student may have using particular kinds of learning media from more general learning problems and (2) draw upon a student's other strengths and interests that may be blocked by the exclusive use of printed text.

Insights from recent brain research and the power of new technological tools combine to help meet the challenges posed by learner diversity in a time of heightened emphasis on standards, in the framework we call Universal Design for Learning.

UDL: The "Intersection of Initiatives"

> The concept of UDL is the intersection where all our initiatives—integrated units, multi-sensory teaching, multiple intelligences, differentiated instruction, use of computers in schools, performance-based assessment, and others—come together.

This statement comes from Donna Palley, Special Education Coordinator/Technology Specialist for the Concord, New Hampshire, school system (and the driving force behind Concord's UDL initiative). Her words capture our vision of UDL as an approach that ties together the work of other educational researchers and reformers who advocate a break from the traditional classroom model—that of a teacher standing up in front of rows of students to deliver "truth" and later using a test to check whether "truth" sank in. The traditional model has always posed problems for some students, and with increasing diversity, the number of students who fail to thrive in this environment is on the rise.

Among the educational approaches UDL supports is *differentiated instruction* (see Tomlinson, 1999a, 1999b), wherein teachers individualize criteria for student success, teaching methods, and means of student expression while monitoring student progress through ongoing, embedded assessment. UDL is also compatible with the concepts of *teachers as coaches or guides* (see O'Donnell, 1998), *learning as process* (see Graves,

1983, 1990), *cooperative learning* (see Johnson & Johnson, 1989, 1999; Marr, 1997; Wood et al., 1993), and *demonstrating learning in a wide variety of media* (see Sizer, 1992a, 1992b, 1996). All these approaches represent aspects of a model where learners actively construct meaning and teachers participate and support learning rather than impart knowledge.

In his book *Avatars of the Word*, James Joseph O'Donnell speculates on what the real roles of educators will be in an information-rich world:

> [It will be] to advise, guide, and encourage students wading through the deep waters of the information flood. [Educators] will thrive as mentors, tutors, backseat drivers, and coaches. They will use the best skill they have . . . to nudge, push, and sometimes pull students through the educationally crucial tasks of processing information: analysis, problem solving, and synthesis of ideas. These are the heart of education, and these are the activities on which our time can best be spent. (O'Donnell, 1998, p. 156)

This is the vision that connects Universal Design for Learning to other educational reform. Instead of being "just one more thing," the UDL framework provides a way to make various approaches to educational change more feasible by incorporating new insights on learning and new applications of technology.

The materials and methods teachers use can either present students with barriers to understanding or enhance their opportunities to learn. By developing and applying UDL, we can minimize barriers and realize the promise each student brings to school. The task for educators is to understand how students learn and use the technology available in this digital age to provide selected supports where they are needed and position the challenge appropriately for each learner. In this way, we can engage more students and help every one progress.

➤ ➤ ➤ ➤ ➤

In the next chapter, we look at new knowledge about the learning brain and consider how it can illuminate and refine teachers' understanding of differences among students.

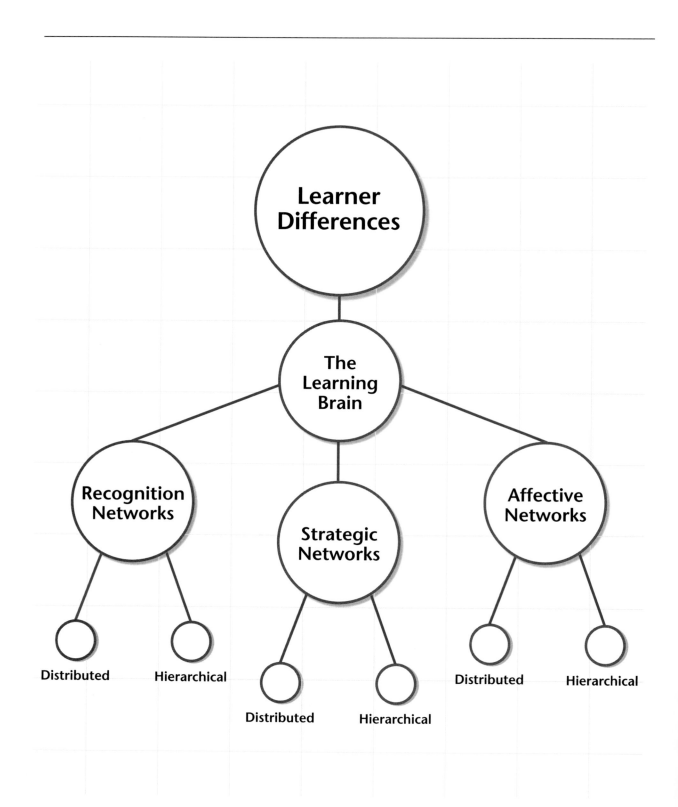

What Brain Research Tells Us About Learner Differences

2

In this chapter, you will learn how familiarity with brain research can help you understand your students better.

KEY IDEAS

➤ Learning is distributed across three interconnected networks: the *recognition* networks are specialized to receive and analyze information (the "what" of learning); the *strategic* networks are specialized to plan and execute actions (the "how" of learning); and the *affective* networks are specialized to evaluate and set priorities (the "why" of learning).

➤ Learners cannot be reduced to simple categories such as "disabled" or "bright." They differ within and across all three brain networks, showing shades of strength and weakness that make each of them unique.

The brain, the most powerful learning tool that a student brings to the classroom, is highly complex and something of a mystery. In recent years, scientists have made unprecedented progress toward unlocking the secrets of how our brains learn, driven in part by remarkable new technologies and techniques for imaging the brain's activity.

Scientists are using this new knowledge to address many questions that concern educators, students, parents, and policymakers:

➤ How does the brain work during learning?
➤ Under what conditions do we learn best?
➤ Why do some people learn differently from others?
➤ Is everyone's brain built the same way?

Web Link

BACKGROUND KNOWLEDGE: Neuroscience for Kids, a Web site for students and teachers, includes a concise and informative overview of brain imaging techniques. *http://faculty. washington.edu/ chudler/neurok.html*

Even when scientists explore learning directly, the educational significance of scientific research is rarely self-evident. In this chapter, we forge connections between neuroscience and the classroom by interpreting brain research from an educational perspective. We show how this research can illuminate and refine our understanding of differences between learners. These insights help us understand our students better and tailor learning experiences in ways that will maximize their opportunities to progress.

Understanding the Learning Brain

Most pictures of the brain show only the tissue visible on the surface—the deeply fissured and folded gray matter called the *cortex*. The complex organization and unique structure of this tissue gives it a central role in learning. Cortical tissue features astonishing connectivity: The approximately 1 trillion neurons in the cortex are linked by approximately 10 trillion connections, creating an incredibly dense network. Similar to a telephone or computer network, these multifaceted connections help individual parts of the brain communicate flexibly and along multiple pathways, regardless of whether they are close to each other or on opposite sides of the brain.

Within this large network, many smaller networks are specialized for performing particular kinds of processing and managing particular learning tasks. Three primary networks, structurally and functionally distinguishable but closely connected and functioning together, are equally essential to learning. We identify these networks by terms that reflect their functions: the *recognition*, *strategic*, and *affective* networks. The activities of these networks parallel the three prerequisites for learning described by the Russian psychologist Lev Vygotsky (1962): recognition of the information to be learned; application of strategies to process that information; and engagement with the learning task. In brief:

➤ *Recognition networks* are specialized to sense and assign meaning to patterns we see; they enable us to identify and understand information, ideas, and concepts.

➤ *Strategic networks* are specialized to generate and oversee mental and motor patterns. They enable us to plan, execute, and monitor actions and skills.

➤ *Affective networks* are specialized to evaluate patterns and assign them emotional significance; they enable us to engage with tasks and learning and with the world around us.

These three neural networks work together to coordinate even simple acts like signing a birthday card for a friend. Through recognition networks, we understand the concept of a birthday and identify the card, the pen, our hands as we write, and our signature. Through strategic networks, we set our goal of signing the card, form a plan for picking up the pen and moving it to produce our signature, monitor our progress, and make small course corrections, such as reducing the size of the letters if we begin to run out of space. Affective networks connect us to our feelings for our friend, motivate us to sign the card, and keep us on task.

These three networks share two common characteristics that have particular significance for learning: (1) Processing is *distributed* laterally across many brain regions operating in parallel (enabling, for example, simultaneous processing of color and shape); and (2) Processing is *hierarchical,* enabling simultaneous processing of sensory information entering low in the hierarchy ("bottom-up") and contextual influences entering high in the hierarchy ("top-down").

Although all brains share these general characteristics, individual brains differ substantially—a point that bears critical implications for teaching. Understanding the specialized functions of the recognition, strategic, and affective networks can help us appreciate the unique strengths and weaknesses of individual students. Let's take a closer look at each of the networks.

Recognition Networks

Located in the back of the brain, as shown in Figure 2.1, recognition networks enable us to identify and interpret patterns of sound, light, taste, smell, and touch. These networks enable us to recognize voices, faces, letters, and words, as well as more complex patterns, such as an author's style and nuance, and abstract concepts like justice.

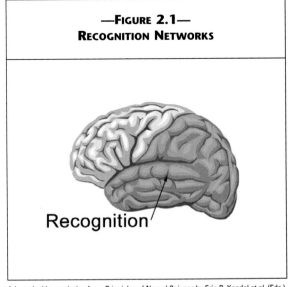

—FIGURE 2.1—
RECOGNITION NETWORKS

Recognition

Adapted with permission from *Principles of Neural Science* by Eric R. Kandel et al. (Eds.). © 2000 by The McGraw-Hill Companies.

This schematic drawing of the lateral surface of the human brain shows the regions primarily responsible for recognition.

—FIGURE 2.2—
"THE UNEXPECTED VISITOR"

Reprinted by permission of the publisher from *Eye Movements and Vision* by Alfred L. Yarbus. © 1967 by Plenum Publishers, Inc.

—FIGURE 2.3—
A CHAIR

Reprinted by permission of the publisher from *Eye Movements and Vision* by Alfred L. Yarbus. © 1967 by Plenum Publishers, Inc.

Take a look at the picture in Figure 2.2. Instantly, you probably recognize many of the objects depicted—people, furniture, doorways. If asked, you could identify *parts* of these objects, such as eyes, table legs, or doorknobs. Some of these objects are partially hidden; others are at odd angles or clustered in poor light, yet your recognition networks are so powerful that you have no difficulty determining what these objects are.

We can do more than just recognize *many* objects at essentially the same time; we can also recognize the same object in a number of different ways. For example, even out of context you can recognize the shape in Figure 2.3 as a chair. This is remarkable, given that this particular representation does not show the features usually associated with chairs, such as four legs and a seat. And chances are you can recognize it not only as *a* chair, but also as *the* chair from "The Unexpected Visitor" picture in Figure 2.2. Your recognition networks enable you to distinguish this specific chair from all the other chairs you have ever identified. Without articulating it, you also recognize the chair as a member of the category "furniture."

Recognition, which seems simple, is actually an incredibly complex feat. As scientists identify the salient characteristics of recognition networks, we understand more clearly how recognition actually works.

Recognition Processes Are Distributed

How does the brain accomplish the complex work of recognition in just a fraction of a second? Positron Emission Topography (PET) scan images give us some important clues. In Figure 2.4, we see a PET scan of the brain in the act of recognizing one set of words under two different sensory conditions. The same words have been presented *orally* to the brain pictured on the left and *visually* to the brain pictured on the right.

These contrasting images illustrate the fact that visual stimuli are recognized in one part of the cortex and auditory stimuli in another (Kandel, Schwartz, & Jessell, 1991). In other words, the general task of recognition is distributed across different areas, each specialized to handle a different component of recognition. (From this point on, we will refer to these specialized areas of the brain as "modules.") Distributed processing is not limited to differences between distinct sensory modalities, such as vision and hearing. The subprocesses within each sense modality are also distributed. For example, visual recognition is distributed across at least 30 different modules, so that elements like vertical lines, diagonal lines, color, and motion are all processed in physically discrete areas of the brain (Gazzaniga, 1995; Mountcastle, 1998; Roland & Zilles, 1998; Zeki, 1999).

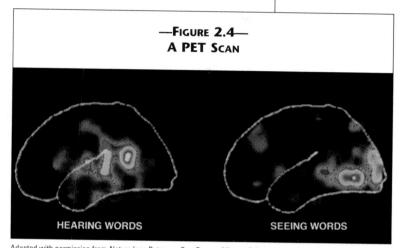

—FIGURE 2.4—
A PET SCAN

HEARING WORDS   SEEING WORDS

Adapted with permission from *Nature* (see Petersen, Fox, Posner, Mintun, & Raichle, 1988). ©1988 by MacMillan Magazines, Limited.

An analogy may clarify how distributed modular specialization works. Think of the brain as a kitchen full of food processors. Imagine that all the processors are the same basic make and model, but each comes with a specialized attachment for blending dough, shredding cabbage, or performing another specialized task. Although each processor performs the same general function, their *output* is as different as piecrust is from coleslaw. By keeping a kitchen full of processors, a chef needn't switch the blade for each new task or worry about getting cabbage in the piecrust! In the brain, distributed processing provides a similar advantage. All the modules have the same basic structure, but the tissue in each region is fine-tuned to process one type of input extremely efficiently. This works more effectively than would "all-purpose" brain tissue that would have to adapt to each new task.

Recognition is quick and efficient because all the modules are working in parallel. Through parallel processing—the simultaneous performance of multiple tasks by interconnected modules—our brains process and pool information that is distributed throughout our recognition networks, all in less than half a second. The brain's modules are interconnected through multiple pathways, enabling visual, auditory, olfactory, and tactile recognition to influence one another. This accounts for the interesting observation that an auditory or tactile stimulus can bias our interpretation of a visual pattern (see Martino & Marks, 2000).

The distributed nature of recognition has profound implications for individual differences. If recognition were the product of one homogeneous area of brain tissue, recognition abilities would vary from person to person in only a limited number of ways. Differences in recognition would have global effects. For example, if an entire modality, like vision, were the product of one subnetwork, any difference would affect vision as a whole. But because recognition is actually a coordinated act of many different modules, each very small component of recognition has the potential to exhibit person-to-person differences. The differences between us may affect one module, and therefore one aspect of recognition, or many modules, and therefore many aspects of recognition.

Recognition Involves Bottom-Up and Top-Down Processing

We have learned that individual aspects of patterns, such as color, shape, orientation, and motion, are processed in parallel by separate pathways within the recognition networks. Each of these pathways is organized into a hierarchical continuum, containing some brain regions that are highly complex, some that are comparatively simple, and others that are somewhere in between.

Let's continue to use vision as an example. As visual sensory information we take in though our eyes departs from our retinas, it travels up through an increasingly complex hierarchical network, eventually reaching the visual cortex. This is called "bottom-up" processing, and it is part of the way we extract visual details from an image such as "The Unexpected Visitor." This type of processing is responsible for identifications based on particular sensory features, meaning the quality of sensory input is very important. Poor lighting, low-quality photocopies, or mumbled speech can all impede bottom-up processing and make everyday recognition tasks difficult.

Just as important as the information flowing up the hierarchy of recognition structures is the information that travels down the hierarchy. To facilitate the recognition of details, our brains make use of higher-order information, such as background knowledge, context, and the overall pattern. When examining "The Unexpected Visitor," you applied knowledge about the kind of room the scene is set in (gleaned from bottom-up recognition of the room's more visible objects) to help you identify other objects that are difficult to recognize based on visual detail alone.

Bottom-up and top-down recognition processing both play critical roles in learning. Consider learning to read: The common assumption used to be that reading was mainly a bottom-up activity, wherein letters are recognized by their features, synthesized into words and sounds, and then analyzed for meaning. But research has shown that it is easier and faster to recognize letters in the context of words than it is to recognize them in isolation. This phenomenon, termed the *word superiority effect* (Adams, 1994), occurs because familiarity with the larger pattern (the word) constrains the bottom-up process of individual letter recognition and leads a reader to rely more on his or her expectation of what letters will come next and less on the actual visual features of those letters. That's why proofreading is so difficult. We miss errors because our word expectations are so powerful that they influence how we see the individual letters. Use of context and meaning to predict what is coming next is another familiar example of the top-down processing used in reading.

Because smoothly functioning recognition networks take advantage of both top-down and bottom-up processes, teaching to *both processes* rather than focusing exclusively on one or the other is the wisest choice. A positive example is the recent truce in the "phonics wars." Most programs have now adopted a form of reading instruction that incorporates both the top-down whole language method and bottom-up phonics. This balanced approach is consistent with the way the learning brain works.

Individual Differences in Recognition Networks

Although human brains all share the same basic recognition architecture and recognize things in roughly the same way, our recognition networks come in many shapes, sizes, and patterns. In anatomy, connectivity, physiology, and chemistry, each of us has a brain that is slightly different from everyone else's.

Web Link

ACTIVITY:
This online activity demonstrates the "word superiority effect"—how our brains use context to help recognize visual patterns:
http://coglab.wadsworth. com/experiments/ WordSuperiority/index. html

Web Link

EXAMPLE:
Individual differences
that affect learning are
apparent in brain
images such as those
available at
*http://www.cast.org/
TeachingEveryStudent/
brain*

PET scan images, such as those shown in Figure 2.4, usually represent averages across individuals. These averages highlight commonalities between individuals but obscure the fact that each individual brain actually reveals a unique pattern of activity. For example, most people, when they recognize an object visually, show increased activity in the back part of their brains; however, the exact magnitude, location, and distribution of that increased activity varies quite a bit. The active area of the cortex may be larger or smaller, more localized to the right or left hemisphere, or more widely or closely distributed. These variations undoubtedly manifest in the way people recognize things in the world—their recognition strengths, weaknesses, and preferences.

The distributed nature of processing in the brain leads to myriad subtle differences in recognition between individual learners. Unlike the global notion of ability suggested, for example, in a Stanford-Binet IQ score (see Thorndike, Hagen, & Sattler, 1986), learners' abilities are multifaceted. When two students perform the same academic task, the patterns of activity in their brains are as unique as their fingerprints. The uniqueness may not be visible in the overall level of brain activity, but rather lies in the pattern of activation: how the activity is distributed across different brain regions. For this reason, no one measure of brain activity—and no one learning score or variable—differentiates or describes individual learners in any meaningful way.

Traditional views of disability, also based on an implied assumption of unitary brain functioning, suggest that a person either does or does not belong to the category "disabled." New understanding about the distributed nature of neural processing shows that abilities in many domains fall along a very large number of continua. Further, the importance of a particular strength or weakness depends upon what is being asked of the learner. This is why, for example, a youngster with perfect pitch who has difficulty recognizing letters is seen as disabled, but a child who is tone deaf but can read words easily is not.

Specific differences in the recognition networks of individual learners range from the subtle to the profound. The recognition cortex in Albert Einstein's brain was disproportionately allocated to spatial cognition (Harvey, Kigar, & Witelson, 1999). He had difficulty recognizing the letter patterns and sound-to-symbol connections required for reading, but he was a genius at visualizing the deepest fundamentals of physics.

Awareness of these differences across his recognition networks could have helped Einstein's teachers shape instruction that would both capitalize on his spatial genius *and* support his areas of weakness.

Classroom Examples: Differences in Recognition

Although all three brain networks—recognition, strategic, and affective—are involved in learning any task, curricular teaching goals and methods tend to cluster into broad types that coincide with each network. For example, subject-verb agreement, the causes of The War of 1812, the structure of the atom, and the nuances of Dostoyevsky's style are all *patterns* to be recognized; these things are the "what" of learning.

Traditionally, when teachers teach these kinds of patterns, they tend to present them in one way for the entire class. But the overt and subtle differences in how students best recognize patterns suggest that more varied means of presentation can reach more students. Being aware of the distributed nature of recognition processes and the combination of top-down and bottom-up processing can help teachers understand individual learners better and shape instruction and assessment accordingly.

In the examples that follow, we illustrate classroom applications of these concepts and introduce you to some of the students and teachers we will use as examples throughout the book.

Meet Mr. Costa . . . and Sophia

In a suburban middle school outside of Philadelphia, Mr. Costa's 7th grade English students show widely varying talents and difficulties. He is working with the technology specialist to develop flexible approaches to accommodate these learner differences. One student in particular he finds both challenging and inspiring.

Sophia, a soprano in the school's top singing group, is legally blind but has significant residual vision. She cannot sight-read music, but she has such a good ear that she is able to learn her parts quickly. The rest of the group depends on her as one of its most talented and consistent members.

Although Sophia reads Braille well, she prefers to use a desktop magnifier to read printed text. This technology worked well for her in the self-contained classrooms of elementary school, but it is proving awkward in middle school, where she must move the magnifier from class to class. Furthermore, the magnifier does not allow Sophia to skim and scan text;

as a result, she is having a tough time staying on top of the increasing volume of reading assignments.

Mr. Costa understands that Sophia's visual acuity is only one small part of her recognition capacity. Equally important is her good ear for music; this ability to differentiate patterns in sound also enables her to understand and use language effectively.

In the middle school environment, barriers for Sophia include

• Heavy emphasis on printed text.

• Increasing use of other visual materials.

• The need to move from class to class, which makes the magnifier technology awkward or impossible to use.

Instead of regarding these barriers as Sophia's problem, Mr. Costa and Sophia's other teachers seek new ways to present content that will make learning more accessible to her, and in the process, offer new options for others in the class. Their approach relies on making text and images available in digital form and via a network, which will allow supports such as text-to-speech translation, voice recognition, and on-screen text and image enlargement to be readily available in classrooms throughout the school.

Meet Ms. Sablan . . . and Paula

Ms. Sablan, an experienced 3rd grade teacher, has a particularly diverse class this year, increasing the challenge she feels to help all her students develop strong literacy skills before they move on to 4th grade.

Paula is a particular concern. Despite excellent single-word decoding and spelling, Paula's reading comprehension is poor. She has difficulty grasping meaning from connected text, and her limited fluency suggests that she has trouble using context to predict words and ideas as she reads. Paula also tends to miss many of the subtle cues carried by tone of voice and other vocal nuances; she interprets spoken language very literally and misses the intended humor in the things her classmates say. As a result, many of Paula's peers see her as rather odd. Fortunately, Paula is able to connect with some of her classmates through a shared love of bike riding, and she has found opportunities to join in with others by participating in the school's weekend cycling club.

Considering Paula's recognition strengths and weaknesses, we can see she is highly skilled at bottom-up processing—synthesizing *parts,* such as the letters and sounds that make up words. But she has trouble with top-down processing—connecting what she is learning to other knowledge and understanding content and context of both written text and spoken language.

Ms. Sablan knows that efficient recognition involves both top-down and bottom-up processing, and she wants to help Paula build her ability to use context and prior knowledge when reading. She decides to reduce Paula's focus on word decoding and instead help Paula to develop explicit strategies for understanding the content of what she reads.

The power, flexibility, and speed of recognition networks are critical to how humans experience the world and are thus worthy of the attention of teachers and curriculum designers. As teachers, understanding the pattern of strengths and weaknesses within a learner's recognition networks can help us individualize the kind of challenge and support we provide, thus maximizing every student's opportunity to learn.

Recognition represents one way of "knowing" the world: building factual knowledge and relating new information we encounter to what we already know. Traditional curricula focus primarily on recognition, at times overlooking the other kinds of "knowing" served by strategic and affective networks. And yet these networks are no less important to effective learning.

Strategic Networks

It is through strategic networks that we plan, execute, and monitor our internally generated mental and motor patterns—actions and skills as diverse as sweeping the floor, deciding a chess move, or choosing a college. During some activities, such as playing sports, orchestrating an April Fool's joke, or composing an essay, we may be conscious of applying strategy. What most of us do not realize is that conscious or not, strategy is involved in essentially *everything* we do.

The strategic components of everyday tasks serve to illustrate the centrality of strategy for cognition and learning. Take another look at "The Unexpected Visitor" (Figure 2.5). Try to identify the *type of room* in which the scene is set.

Most likely you glanced at the image and had no trouble determining that it shows a living room or a parlor. Without being aware of it, you relied on your strategic networks to figure this out. You identified the goal of the task, came up with a plan to achieve it, executed that plan, and

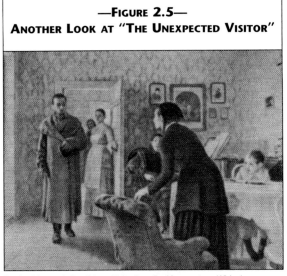

—FIGURE 2.5—
ANOTHER LOOK AT "THE UNEXPECTED VISITOR"

Reprinted by permission of the publisher from *Eye Movements and Vision* by Alfred L. Yarbus. © 1967 by Plenum Publishers, Inc.

—FIGURE 2.6—
EYE MOVEMENTS: THREE VIEWING STRATEGIES

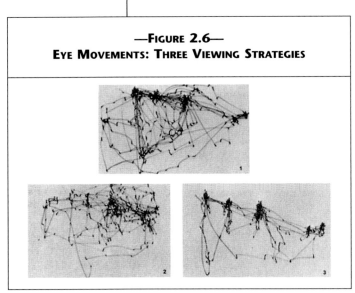

Reprinted by permission of the publisher from *Eye Movements and Vision* by Alfred L. Yarbus. © 1967 by Plenum Publishers, Inc.

evaluated its outcome, all the while avoiding distractions that might carry you off track. This underlying strategy is evident in Figure 2.6, which shows eye movements of someone examining "The Unexpected Visitor."

Notice that Figure 2.6 shows three eye movement maps. Each reflects the same individual looking at the same image, yet the patterns of movement are different. Why? The answer is *different goals*. First, the viewer was told to look at the image, but was given no specific instructions about what to look for (map 1, at the top of the figure). Second, he was instructed to identify the *ages* of the people in the picture (map 2, at the lower left). Third, he was asked to determine what the people in the picture were doing before the visitor arrived so unexpectedly (map 3, at the lower right). Each instruction required a different viewing strategy, and each new strategy resulted in a different pattern of eye movement.

As this example shows, even a simple action like searching a picture involves a multistep strategic process:

➤ Identify a goal.
➤ Design a suitable plan.
➤ Execute the plan.
➤ Self-monitor.
➤ Correct or adjust actions.

Skilled readers use this kind of strategic process whether they are reading to locate a particular fact, skimming to get the "gist," or relishing the literary language. Remarkably, our brains can plan, organize, and monitor patterns of action such as these, often while just barely engaging our conscious minds and usually while we are doing other things. How do our brains do this? The answer is that strategic networks operate in the same highly efficient fashion as recognition networks do.

Strategic Processes Are Distributed

The neural networks responsible for generating patterns of mental and motor action occupy their own unique territory, located primarily in the part of the brain called the frontal lobes (see Figure 2.7). Research into the effects of selective damage to the frontal lobes has revealed that like recognition, the ability to think and act strategically is distributed across specialized modules

Neurological and brain imaging studies tell us that within the frontal lobes, the prefrontal cortex oversees complex strategic capacities and is critical for identifying goals, selecting appropriate plans, and self-monitoring. If we were to show "The Unexpected Visitor" to a person with damage to this area of the brain, a map of his eye movements might not reveal the distinctive tracing patterns shown in Figure 2.6. Instead, the map might show random movements, indicating a focus on seemingly unrelated details. Even if this viewer's eye movements did suggest some kind of plan, he would not be able to alter this plan in response to unexpected variables, such as a change of instructions. For example, a directive to figure out the visitor's age and another to speculate on the prior activities of the woman in the foreground might produce no difference in pattern.

The pattern of activity distributed across the modules of the frontal lobes shapes how we plan and execute actions. These modules function in parallel, enabling us to perform highly complex actions with ease. Consider, for example, what's involved in playing the organ. If it were not for parallel processing within strategic networks, organists would never be able to simultaneously coordinate not one but several different keyboards and numerous pedals and switches!

Strategic modules, although operating in parallel, are also interdependent. The connections between modules enable modules doing

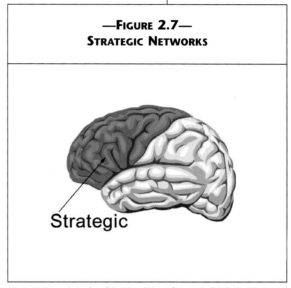

—FIGURE 2.7—
STRATEGIC NETWORKS

Strategic

Adapted with permission from *Principles of Neural Science*, by Eric R. Kandel et al. (Eds.). © 2000 by The McGraw-Hill Companies.

This schematic drawing of the lateral surface of the human brain shows the regions primarily responsible for strategy.

Web Link

BACKGROUND KNOWLEDGE:
School yourself in Brain Injury 101 at The Brain Injury Association of Washington's site: *http://www.biawa.org*

different things to influence one another. In fact, elements of our plans-of-action that come later in a series can influence those that come before (Fowler, 1981). This is why, for example, you will pick up a bowling ball one way if you intend to bowl the ball yourself and another way if you intend to hand it to a friend. Similarly, when we speak, separate but connected modules process syllables and words simultaneously, so that the pronunciation of any syllable or word is highly influenced by those that follow it. That's why prerecorded "voices" like the automated flight-arrival information broadcast in airports sound so odd to us: Both the words and sentences are spliced together from prerecorded individual sounds, and each sound is articulated the same way regardless of the linguistic context. Cursive writing provides yet another example: When we write, we form individual letters differently depending on which letters precede and follow them.

As teachers, being mindful of the parallel nature of strategic processing can help us better understand individual learners and design optimal supports for each. For example, school requires students to learn discrete strategic skills (such as listening, extracting relevant information, and writing down the information) and to execute these skills simultaneously (as when taking notes in class). From what we know about strategic networks, we can appreciate that these patterns of actions are not "built" by putting together a step-by-step sequence. Different layers of an action are added on at the same time and mutually influence one another. For this reason, skill instruction is often more effective when the various components of the process are learned simultaneously rather than one at a time (Gopher, 1996). Thus, a tennis instructor may model the whole serve and encourage the learner to try it out, only analyzing individual steps (ball toss, backswing, step forward, swing, and follow-through) when particular aspects must be corrected. Likewise, each subcomponent of a task like writing an essay makes the most sense to our students if it is taught in the context of the whole task.

Strategy Involves Bottom-Up and Top-Down Processing

Like recognition modules, strategic modules form part of a two-way hierarchical pathway. Neural signals travel from higher-order regions in the cortex down to the spinal cord, where the neurons that innervate muscles are found, enabling internally driven strategies ("I will pick up this pencil") to influence how we act on—and in—the world (picking up the pencil). Modules specialized to carry out different steps within a skills sequence reside at different levels along that path.

The top of the hierarchy orders the steps, "commands" our muscles to act, and keeps track of whether or not the goal is reached, modifying the plan as needed. As actions are practiced and perfected, they require decreasing amounts of monitoring from the top. Anyone who knows how to touch-type will remember that as a beginner, you had to rely heavily on conscious monitoring capacities to check finger placement and letter sequence. With practice, though, the pattern of movements necessary to hit the right keys became automated, requiring little if any conscious monitoring.

The top-down flow of information in strategic networks makes intuitive sense. We can understand that top-down processing enables us to carry out a plan formed high up in the neural hierarchy. When we as teachers express goals clearly, give verbal instructions, or offer models for students to work from, we are supporting students' top-down processing by stressing the importance of strategic skills and encouraging students to be guided by clear goals and plans.

Within strategic networks, information travels not only down from the cortex to the muscles, but also up from the muscles to the cortex. One source of bottom-up strategic pathways is the cerebellum, the cauliflower-shaped structure located at the back and base of the brain, overlaying the brainstem (see Figure 2.8). Pathways from the cerebellum to strategic modules in the cortex serve an important role in learning skills and strategies. The cerebellum takes sensory feedback, which clues it in to how actions are being executed, and compares it to other signals that convey the actions we intended. Then, through these bottom-up projections, the cerebellum informs our strategic networks about whether our actions are "on target." Although this is best described for motor patterns, bottom-up processing operates in a similar way to refine mental patterns. It works much like a thermostat, but regulating skills and strategies rather than temperature.

Thus, to acquire skills, students need support for both top-down and bottom-up strategic processing. They learn best when they have not only good instruction and good models but also plenty of opportunities to practice and to receive ongoing, relevant feedback. The kinds of models and supports most suitable for individual learners depend on the students' particular strategic strengths and weaknesses.

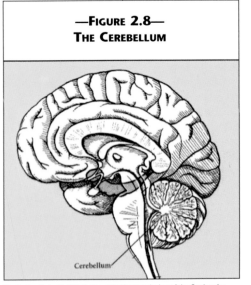

—FIGURE 2.8—
THE CEREBELLUM

Cerebellum

Illustration by Lydia Kibiuk. Reprinted by permission of the Society for Neuroscience.

Individual Differences in Strategic Networks

The distributed organization of strategic networks introduces a level of complexity that would not exist in a homogeneous network in which all tissue looks and acts the same and a deficit in one part of the network has the same effect as a deficit in another. In reality, deficits and strengths can affect very specific aspects of strategic skills. For example, a student may be skilled at making a plan but have difficulty self-monitoring when executing the plan. Another student might be an expert at finding information, but have difficulty organizing and keeping track of that information. Recent brain imaging experiments provide a novel illustration of individual differences in strategy. When two people are confronted with the same problem but solve it using different cognitive strategies, the brain images reveal two very different patterns of activity (Burbaud et al., 2000).

Differences in strategic networks manifest themselves in various ways in the classroom. For example, learners differ dramatically in their abilities to acquire and automate pattern-based routines such as forming letters, typing, spelling, and multiplying. Learners also differ in their ability to enact higher-level strategies such as planning, organizing, monitoring progress, devising alternative approaches, and seeking help when they need it. For example, students with executive-function disorders (disorders affecting reasoning, logic, hypothesis-testing, and similar high-level abilities) can have difficulty at all levels of reading. When decoding words, they may make impulsive guesses rather than apply their phonics knowledge or search for context cues. When reading a paragraph, they may fail to use organizing strategies to help them focus on the key points.

Variation within students' strategic networks also influences their abilities to use different kinds of learning tools. Students with motor difficulties may be marginally able or unable to use a keyboard or a mouse, to scan a line of text, or to turn the pages of a book. Speech difficulties may impede oral presentations, and students with language and learning difficulties may find that they expend so much energy attending to the mechanics of producing written text that they have difficulty communicating effectively in that medium. These are just a few of the obvious examples; often the strengths and weaknesses in strategic networks are more subtle.

Variations in the degree of bottom-up and top-down processing influence how students acquire skills. We have all seen students with the uncanny ability to watch someone else do something and then do it almost perfectly the first time; this is an indication of strong top-down strategic processing. On the other hand, we also know students who seem to learn best by doing; these are the students who achieve expertise only after lots of practice and feedback—an indication of strong bottom-up strategic processing. Awareness of these subtle differences can help teachers design optimal strategic teaching for different kinds of learners.

Classroom Examples: Differences in Strategy

Understanding the way strategic networks function and the differences in students' strategic networks is a useful guide when teaching skills and strategies such as predicting, summarizing, and determining the steps needed to solve a problem or write an essay. Differences in strategic skills manifest as preferences, proclivities, or significant strengths and weaknesses. The following set of classroom examples illustrates some of these differences.

Meet Mr. Mitchell . . . and Jamal

Mr. Mitchell teaches 5th grade in an urban Chicago school. This year's class is the largest he's ever taught, and it includes several students with disabilities. One of his students is Jamal, a young man with cerebral palsy. Jamal is an enthusiastic student and well on his way to becoming an expert on military tanks and submarines. From his home computer, he has found and collected hundreds of photos, stories, and Web sites devoted to this weaponry. Jamal speaks slowly but intelligibly. He uses a wheelchair for mobility and a variety of assistive technologies to help him operate his computer. Although Jamal cannot write or draw with pen and paper, he has learned to do these things with the support of a computer equipped with an expanded keyboard and a voice recognition system.

Jamal is integrated into Mr. Mitchell's classroom for all academic subjects. Science and social studies particularly engage him, and he uses his strong strategic skills (such as his ability to seek, locate, and save information) to good effect in these classes. But Jamal's motor difficulties affect the pace of his work. He is keeping up, but barely—challenged by the large amounts of required reading and writing. Despite his interest and abilities, Jamal must invest tremendous effort to avoid falling behind, and at times, he becomes discouraged.

Jamal's story to date is one of strategic success, but he works slowly and the academic demands he faces will only increase as he progresses from grade-to-grade. Realizing that Jamal's motor difficulties are a potential threat to success, Mr. Mitchell plans to scaffold Jamal's areas of difficulty and draw upon his particular strategic strengths. Among other things, Mr. Mitchell will make sure assigned text is available in digital form so that Jamal can navigate it on the computer with keyboard or voice-activated commands. He will also make sure Jamal has access to computer-based drawing and composition tools rather than just pencil and paper. Mr. Mitchell hopes these methods will help Jamal stay engaged and enable him to develop new ways to manage his increasing workload.

Meet Ms. Chen . . . and Charlie

Ms. Chen has taught 6th grade in rural Iowa for three years. One of her major goals for this year is to find a way to adapt her techniques and materials so that she can reach all students in the class, who range from "highly focused" to "highly distractible."

Ms. Chen describes Charlie as a constant source of classroom energy. He dives headlong into activities, jumps out of his seat to answer questions, and constantly seeks new things to do and join. He finishes few of the things he starts. When boredom descends or something new comes up, Charlie quickly abandons his task, regardless of whether it is complete. This is true not only for extended projects, such as a science fair experiment or a book report, but also for short-term tasks like looking up a word in the dictionary. Unless Ms. Chen or one of Charlie's parents structures him closely, he rarely completes his schoolwork. He also forgets his homework and textbook nearly every day, and despite his enthusiasm, he is rarely ready to begin an activity with the rest of the class.

At first glance, it seems that Charlie's problem is distractibility. However, Ms. Chen has found that if she minimizes external distractions, Charlie will create his own. Further, when engaged in an activity that interests him, like a Nintendo game or a certain school project, he can focus for long periods of time. Ms. Chen realizes that she needs to help Charlie develop strategic skills, particularly the ability to plan, self-monitor, and complete tasks.

These classroom examples illustrate the multiple and varied influences of strategic networks on students' performance. Understanding the many facets of strategic learning, the approaches most suited to supporting strategic networks, and the patterns of strength and weakness in different students can help shape instruction to support every learner's unique needs.

Affective Networks

Learning requires interaction with the external world-with varied materials, tools, people, and contexts. But different students experience the same situations in very different ways. A well-known poem by e. e. cummings illustrates this idea:

maggie and milly and molly and may
went down to the beach (to play one day)

and maggie discovered a shell that sang
so sweetly she couldn't remember her troubles, and

milly befriended a stranded star
whose rays five languid fingers were;

and molly was chased by a horrible thing
which raced sideways while blowing bubbles: and

may came home with a smooth round stone
as small as a world and as large as alone.

For whatever we lose (like a you or a me)
it's always ourselves we find in the sea.*

With the closing line "it's always ourselves we find in the sea," cummings summarizes a principle long known to poets and now confirmed by neuroscientists: What individuals "see" is determined partly by their own internal state—a melting pot of emotions, needs, and memories. Each girl in the poem experiences the beach in her own distinctive manner.

To illustrate this further, let's return to "The Unexpected Visitor" (see Figure 2.9). Look at the picture again and note what grabs your attention. A variety of factors determines what attracts your eye and how long you inspect the image. There's your emotional state, your familiarity with the picture, your interest (or lack of interest) in the content or form, and your state of energy or fatigue, to name just a few. More generally, we can say that your memory, personality, motivation, mood, interest, and biological state all influence how you interact with the picture.

—FIGURE 2.9—
"THE UNEXPECTED VISITOR"

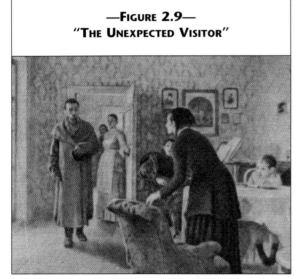

Reprinted by permission of the publisher from *Eye Movements and Vision* by Alfred L. Yarbus. © 1967 by Plenum Publishers, Inc.

Of course, these kinds of characteristics and states vary tremendously across viewers. A psychologist might attend to the expressions on the people's faces, while an interior designer might take note of the room's décor. The mother of a toddler might be drawn to the child seated at the table, whereas a musician might first notice the piano. If asked to comment on the state of mind of those in the picture, each viewer would offer a unique perspective.

The power of affective variables to influence what we see and how we interpret the environment is exploited in the Rorschach, a projective test used by psychologists. The inkblot in Figure 2.10 is not from the Rorschach itself, but it presents a similarly ambiguous image.

Clearly, inkblots are not representational images. Still, most people, when asked to describe what they see in an inkblot, find figures, animals, or objects. By collecting many responses, researchers develop norms based on what people without emotional disturbances are likely to find in these patterns. (Because the strong emotions experienced by people with affective disorders tend to significantly influence what they see in the outside world, they tend to register unusual responses on tests like the Rorschach.) By examining a patient's responses across many different stimuli and looking for commonalities and patterns, psychologists can deduce a patient's fears, preoccupations, and desires.

To some extent, the entire world is a Rorschach. At any instant, multiple facets of the environment compete for our attention. These demands require not only that we recognize objects and formulate strategies, but also that we evaluate their significance and importance to ourselves. *How* we do so largely reflects our own emotions and motivations.

Emotion, like recognition and strategy, belongs to circumscribed networks within the brain. Recognition networks help us to identify objects, such as coffeepots and cars, and strategic networks enable us to act on these objects—

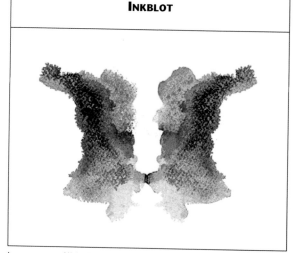

—FIGURE 2.10—
INKBLOT

Image courtesy of Helge Malmgrem, Department of Philosophy, Göteborg University, Sweden. Reprinted with permission from the HTML version of *Moving Toward the Other*, a poster presented at the "Tucson III" conference, April 27–May 3, 1998.

reaching to pour, turning to steer. Affective networks attach emotional significance to these objects and actions, influencing in a third way what we see and do.

Like recognition and strategic networks, affective networks are extremely efficient. Murphy and Zajonc (1993) have demonstrated that our brains can evaluate the importance of an object within just a quarter of a second! In spite of their complexity, affective evaluations are performed rapidly and effectively. How is this so?

Affective Processes Are Distributed

Intuitively, emotion seems to be a more complex and elusive phenomenon than recognition or strategy. However, the neural processing of emotion occurs in a very similar way. Affective networks are made up of many specialized modules, located predominantly at the core of the brain and associated with the limbic system (Damasio, 1994). Some of these modules are visible in Figure 2.11. Because affective networks are distributed across many modules, learners exhibit many differences along many

Web Link

BACKGROUND KNOWLEDGE:
The connection between thinking and feeling is the subject of this text interview with neuroscientist Joseph Ledoux. Online at *http://www.edge.org/ 3rd_culture/ledoux/ ledoux_p1.html.*

—FIGURE 2.11—
AFFECTIVE NETWORKS

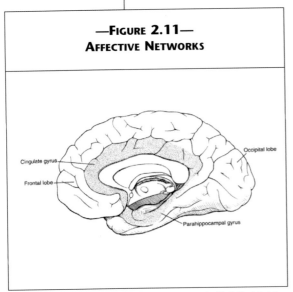

Reprinted with permission from *Principles of Neural Science*, by Eric R. Kandel et al. (Eds). © 2000 by The McGraw-Hill Company.

This medial view of the brain shows the limbic lobe, site of the affective networks. The limbic lobe includes primitive cortical tissue (stippled area), the frontal lobes, and underlying cortical structures (hippocampus and dentate gyrus, not shown).

continua that influence their motivation to learn and their subsequent and ongoing engagement with learning tasks.

Evidence of the distributed nature of affective networks comes from the selective deficits that result from disease or damage in specific locations within the brain. Some patients can express emotion but cannot recognize emotion in other people's faces or voices. Others show the reverse deficit: They can read emotional responses of others but they cannot express emotion themselves. These two types of deficits are linked to brain damage in different, specific locations (DeKosky, Heilman, Bowers, & Valenstein, 1980; Heilman, Scholes, & Watson, 1975). What this research tells us is that we use different parts of our affective networks to recognize emotion and to express emotion. Further, the subprocesses involved in recognizing emotion, like being able to interpret facial expressions and speech for emotional content, are each handled by different areas.

It should come as no surprise that affective networks operate in parallel. They process different kinds of emotional information simultaneously and communicate closely though myriad interconnections to create a whole affective impression. When students watch a teacher during a lecture, they process the expression on her face and the emotion in her voice at the same time. Further, because the brain modules are interconnected, the teacher's facial expressions influence how the students interpret her voice (de Gelder, Bocker, Tuomainen, Hensen, & Vroomen, 1999).

Affect Involves Bottom-Up and Top-Down Processing

As with the other two networks, the modules that make up affective networks are hierarchically organized, and the information travels in both bottom-up and top-down directions. Bottom-up connections in affective networks ensure that we are emotionally responsive to the outside world. Information travels from the sensory organs (such as the eyes and ears) up the hierarchical continuum. When it reaches the apex of the pathway—the limbic cortex—we "feel" emotional reactions.

We respond to emotionally reactive stimuli, such as scary faces, even when we are not consciously aware of them (Murphy & Zajonc, 1993). Before we even identify a sound or shape, our nervous system may initiate physiological responses such as an adrenaline rush, muscular contractions, and increased blood pressure—our bodies' physical manifestations of fear. This purely unconscious emotion reflects a second type of bottom-up processing, in which information travels only partway up the hierarchy, stopping short of the cortex (LeDoux, 1998). This type of processing gives rise to a cruder emotional response, one that may or may not be appropriate to the given situation.

Here's an everyday example that illustrates bottom-up affective processing. Suppose you are walking in unfamiliar woods and detect a sudden movement in your peripheral vision. Almost before you become aware of the disturbance, your eyes leap to focus on the source, and your body prepares for fight or flight. Seconds later, you identify the source of the sound: a harmless robin. Your initial responses to the noise—the physiological changes, the protective hunching of your body, and covering your head with your arms—are part of a crude defensive instinct mediated by rapid bottom-up processing. A full second may pass before your conscious awareness of fear coincides with a more analytical look at the source of the noise, so that you can decide what to do. In this case, you probably chuckle over your reaction and walk on.

Of course, instinctual emotional responses can be counterproductive. Extreme nervousness before a presentation, a recital, or an athletic competition can overwhelm and distract us, diminishing the effectiveness of our performance. Affective top-down processing helps us consciously calm ourselves through a variety of techniques such as breathing, refocusing attention, and visualizing success. Without top-down emotional processing, we would be vulnerable to intense, overblown emotions of all kinds and unable to practice the self-restraint needed to keep ourselves on task. Teachers can take advantage of top-down processing to help alleviate the negative emotion students may have learned to associate with schoolwork.

Individual Differences in Affective Networks

Because affective networks work in roughly similar ways across many individuals, we can make some fairly solid generalizations about how people respond to particular situations. Upon the death of a loved one we become sad; startled by a sudden loud noise or dangerous animal we become surprised and scared. However, human beings are not emotional clones. When confronted with the same life event, different people exhibit different kinds and intensities of emotion. In study after study, scientists have shown that people can be sorted into "high" and "low" emotional responders based on their patterns of self-reported emotion, changes in facial expression, or autonomic reflexes (Asendorpf, 1987; Carels et al., 1999; Cole, 1996; Dimberg, 1990; Larsen, 1987). Even animals display this variability (Adamec, 1991; Kalin, 1999; Kalin, Shelton, & Davidson, 2000).

It is easy to spot the outcomes of affective variability. The next time you find yourself in a doctor's office waiting room, take note of the other patients. Some will start to show signs of agitation the minute their appointment time has come and gone. Others will simply sit back and sigh; they might become upset only if the wait continues for an extended period. Still others will appear to simply accept the situation; they will remain relaxed and calm no matter how long the delay persists.

We might like to think that our emotional tendencies are acquired traits and therefore entirely controllable. However, brain research has revealed that some affective characteristics are strongly associated with measurable neurological differences. For example, functional brain imaging techniques have revealed that people suffering from clinical depression exhibit a characteristic asymmetry in the brain (Bruder et al., 1997; Tomarken, Davidson, Wheeler, & Doss, 1992). Depressives tend to have abnormally high resting brain activity in right-hemisphere affective networks. People suffering from panic disorder also show increased resting activity on the right side of the brain, but in different affective modules from those who are depressed (Reiman, et al., 1984).

Affective differences exert powerful influences on learners' ability to engage with learning and to progress. In studies of highly successful adult dyslexics, Rosalie Fink (1995, 1998) conclusively demonstrated the very significant positive impact affect can have on learning. The individuals in her study overcame severe deficits in recognition and strategic skills by virtue of their deep engagement with and interest in particular subject matter. Strong positive affect made the critical difference in their learning outcomes.

Conversely, and as more commonly noted, affective problems also interfere with learning in various ways. One of the reasons students with severe affective disorders related to childhood depression or abuse are often vulnerable to reading failure is because strong affective influences can derail the work of recognition and strategic networks (see Gentile, Lamb, & Rivers, 1985; Kinard, 2001). Students preoccupied with emotional concerns may have little attention left over for schoolwork. In addition, students with a history of learning problems often become discouraged about their own abilities and withdraw effort from learning tasks. Still others may learn to associate negative feelings with certain subjects or media.

Understanding affective issues can help teachers support all learners more appropriately. Of the three learning networks, affective networks are perhaps intuitively the most essential for learning, yet they are given the least formal emphasis in the curriculum. All teachers know how important it is to engage students in the learning process, to help them to love learning, to enjoy challenges, to connect with subject matter, and to persist when things get tough. When students withdraw their effort and engagement, it is tempting to consider this a problem outside the core enterprise of teaching. We believe this is a mistake. Attending to affective issues when considering students' needs is an integral component of instruction, and it can increase teaching effectiveness significantly.

Consider these differences: Some students prefer to read in a quiet environment; others are comfortable reading in the middle of noisy activity. Some like the predictability of reading familiar stories multiple times, whereas others find rereading boring. Some students like the structure of being told what books to read and when to read them; others thrive on choice and independence. In addition, of course, there is huge variation in the type of content that interests different learners. All these preferences factor in to why students whose skills and achievement levels appear very similar on a test may react—and perform—very differently to particular assignments.

Classroom Examples: Differences in Affect

Although the students we've met so far in this chapter illustrate issues related primarily to recognition or strategic networks, each also raises an important affective angle. Sophia's love of music and poetry, Jamal's fascination with military tanks and subs, Charlie's deep concentration when playing Nintendo, and Paula's pleasure in riding bikes with other children all provide "hooks" for building engagement and learning. Positive emotion helps to motivate students just as negative emotion impedes progress. The teachers and students in the next two classroom examples illustrate both sides of the coin—how affective issues can sometimes be the root of both learning difficulties *and* learning solutions.

Meet Mr. O'Connell . . . and Miguel

Mr. O'Connell is a 4th grade teacher in a San Diego suburb. He is juggling a classroom full of diverse students facing all kinds of learning challenges, but he's particularly concerned about Miguel, for whom emotional factors have become a big issue.

Miguel has struggled with reading and math basics throughout his schooling, but with support from his family and adjustments to his assignments, he has progressed well. But recently Miguel's world has been thrown into turmoil by his parents' divorce and a grandparent's illness. Now his attention in class has started to wander, and his performance is on the decline. Mr. O'Connell recognizes that Miguel's academic problems are probably related to the boy's confusion and anxiety caused by events at home.

There is a bit of encouraging news: The art teacher reports that Miguel has started to produce detailed and skillful art projects and seems, in that subject, to be deeply engaged. Bearing this in mind, Mr. O'Connell plans to explore ways of bringing art into other subject areas to capitalize on the one area where Miguel shows interest and enthusiasm.

Meet Ms. Abrams . . . and Kamla

Ms. Abrams, an experienced 6th grade teacher in a mid-sized K–8 school in New York City, describes Kamla as a student who relates well to her peers, respects her teachers, and adores sports. But Kamla's long-term struggle with academics seems to have dampened her enthusiasm and energy for schoolwork. Two years ago, in the 4th grade, Kamla's decoding deficits led to her classification as a "slow reader," although no specific disability was identified.

Now, in Ms. Abrams's classroom, Kamla continues to struggle with reading and writing. When asked to write an essay, she squirms in her chair, holding her pen awkwardly and moving her paper all over the desk. Reading is a similar struggle, although Ms. Abrams has noticed Kamla seems to enjoy articles and books about sports. Ms. Abrams suspects that this is partly because Kamla feels no pressure to complete this kind of reading within a time limit and partly because the sports topics feed Kamla's interests. Otherwise, Kamla's discomfort extends to most classroom assignments, and overall, she appears disengaged from learning.

Kamla's focus on the basketball court contrasts markedly with her lack of engagement in the classroom. She is a talented athlete who practices her sport diligently and enthusiastically. Her commitment in this area testifies to her ability to persist and to work hard in the service of something she loves to do.

Ms. Abrams puzzles over how to draw upon this affective strength to build a connection to academic learning. In personalizing instruction for Kamla, Ms. Abrams hopes to overcome the negative associations Kamla has formed with traditional academic tasks. She decides to bridge Kamla's interests in sports to academic tasks in hopes of generating some of the same enthusiasm, interest, and persistence so apparent on the basketball court.

It is evident to Mr. O'Connell and Ms. Abrams that supporting the affective aspects of learning is as important as supporting recognition and strategy. Of course, Miguel's and Kamla's difficulties are not purely affective, but rather result from interactions between all three learning networks. Attention to all three networks is critical for understanding individual needs and strengths and for determining individually appropriate teaching methods and materials.

Implications for Educators

Brain imaging technologies and neural networks are certainly not the first things that jump into most teachers' minds on the way to school each morning. But you do not need to have a degree in neuroscience to reap the benefits of understanding the learning brain. The fundamental nature of the recognition, strategic, and affective networks form a framework we can use to analyze our students' individual strengths and weaknesses and understand their individual differences.

Web Link

ACTIVITY:
Use the three brain networks to analyze individual differences at *http://www.cast.org/ TeachingEveryStudent/ networks*

One of the clearest and most important revelations stemming from brain research is that there are no "regular" students. The notion of broad categories of learners—smart, not smart, disabled, not disabled, regular, not regular—is a gross oversimplification that does not reflect reality. By categorizing students in this way, we miss many subtle and important qualities and focus instead on a single characteristic.

The modular organization of learning networks and the highly specialized subprocesses within networks mean that each student brings a unique assortment of strengths, weaknesses, and preferences to school. In our classroom examples so far, we have focused on characteristics within a single brain network in order to highlight the impact of issues within each network. This is *not* a recommendation to focus on one network alone for any given student. In fact, patterns of strength and weakness across all three networks interact with the teaching and learning environment in ways that can either bring about progress or frustration. Sometimes a problem in one area can receive so much attention that other issues are missed. For example, students with learning disabilities are often mistakenly thought to have problems only with recognizing words. But as our final classroom example of this chapter illustrates, most learning disabilities actually involve all three learning networks.

Meet Mr. Hernandez . . . and Patrick

Mr. Hernandez teaches 6th grade in a middle-class suburban neighborhood. One of his new students this year is Patrick, "a good kid," albeit one who doesn't seem terribly invested in his schoolwork. According to Patrick's elementary and early middle school teachers, he is a "classic dyslexic, with atrocious spelling, missed vowels, and disjointed thoughts." Despite tutoring and other special supports, Patrick continues to have difficulty reading and writing.

Mr. Hernandez spends the first few weeks of the semester identifying Patrick's strengths and weaknesses across all three networks. He notes that Patrick's learning issues are more complex than his individualized education plan (IEP) indicates. In addition to problems with recognition-based skills in reading and writing, Patrick demonstrates some strategic issues. Specifically, he's easily distracted and has difficulty self-monitoring, causing him to lose track of his goal midway through an activity. Further, Mr. Hernandez notes that although Patrick is generally cheerful, he has become accustomed to failure. In fact, Patrick's identity seems in some ways tied to being a poor student. From time to time, he jokes about his poor grades in a seemingly proud way and seems largely unwilling to invest effort in schoolwork. These behaviors clearly signal affective concerns that should be addressed.

Mr. Hernandez considers the best approach for supporting Patrick's learning based on his broader understanding of Patrick's strengths and weaknesses. He decides to address the affective side first, knowing that if Patrick is not motivated to achieve academically, his progress on all fronts will be limited. Mr. Hernandez will try capitalizing on Patrick's strong interest in baseball to fashion some early writing and math assignments around that subject. He also plans to support Patrick's reading and writing mechanics so that difficulties there don't interfere with his ability to produce good work.

New insights into the learning brain help educators understand how learners differ and give us ideas about how we might better promote their learning. **UDL Classroom Template 1**, available in the Appendix (p. 178) and online, will guide you through the development of your own Class Learning Profile—a compendium of your students' strengths, weaknesses, and interests across the three brain networks.

➤ ➤ ➤ ➤ ➤

Educators hoping to get the most accurate picture of students' capacities must also carefully consider the materials and tools available to them in the classroom. It is in the intersection of student characteristics and the tools they use that students' abilities are actually defined. In the next chapter, we examine the media and tools of teaching.

Web Link

CLASSROOM TEMPLATE:
The **Class Learning Profile Template** helps you evaluate learner needs and strengths in light of the three brain networks at *http://www.cast.org/ TeachingEveryStudent/ learnerneeds*

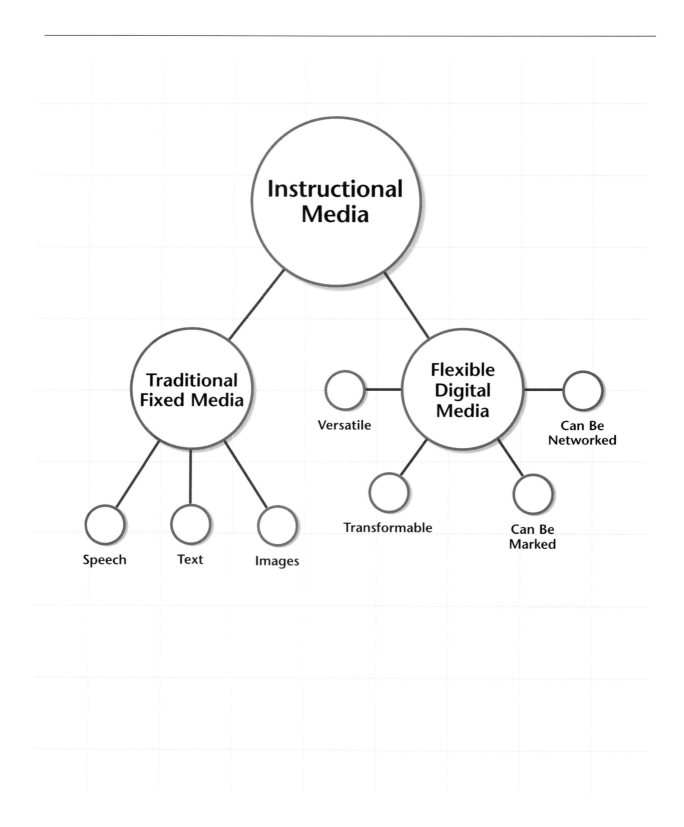

Why We Need Flexible Instructional Media

In this chapter, you will learn how the qualities of various instructional media (text, speech, images, and digital media) affect their accessibility to students and see why flexibility in media is the key to providing instruction that reaches more students, more effectively.

KEY IDEAS

➤ Learners' capacities are not inherent; capacities are defined by the interplay between learners' abilities and the tools they use.

➤ Traditional classroom materials and media, like books and speech, come in "one size" for all, but they do not fit everyone. Inflexible media actually create barriers to learning.

➤ New classroom media, like digital text, sound, images, and the World Wide Web, can be adjusted for different individuals and can open doors to learning.

Traditional media for teaching—speech, text, and images—are so ingrained in our methods and curriculum that we rarely pause to consider their use. Instead of thinking carefully about which medium to use in a given situation, we usually select what we have chosen in the past or what is convenient now.

What few of us recognize is that these media have very different things to offer. The inherent communicative strengths and weaknesses of speech, text, and images determine their suitability for different instructional purposes. As teachers, when selecting a medium for teaching, we should consider its appropriateness for the particular content or activity. But the selection process does not stop there. We also need to weigh the characteristics of our students. Each individual's facility with a medium is a function of the proclivities, strengths, and weaknesses of their learning networks and the particular demands each medium makes on these networks.

This analysis is not usually a part of how we understand and appraise our students' capacities, how we teach, and how we evaluate learners' progress. Unwittingly, we have allowed traditional media to shape these practices. Instead of considering students individually, we operate on a one-size-fits-all mindset. When we set goals, we often tie them to particular media without considering alternatives. When we evaluate children's abilities, it is often on the basis of their performance within a single medium. We categorize as disabled those students for whom a printed textbook, a lecture, a chart, or a videotape is difficult or impossible to use. We then prescribe for them special goals, teaching methods, and materials—often with a remedial focus. Students are assessed according to standards and standardized tests with little regard for how the chosen medium affects their learning or their ability to demonstrate that learning.

This situation has developed in part because traditional instructional media and materials are inflexible and not amenable to individualization. New electronic media offer the opportunity—and we believe, the obligation—to re-examine old assumptions about teaching media and tools and reconsider their impact on learners.

The first half of this chapter focuses on traditional fixed media: speech, printed text, and still or video images (as opposed to their new digital counterparts). We outline the nature of each as a means of communication, discuss advantages and drawbacks, show how each places certain demands on learners' brain networks, and explain how each interacts with individual differences. In the second half, we focus on digital media, highlighting their inherent wealth of flexibility and illustrating how this flexibility provides teachers a new and better approach to understanding and addressing learner differences.

Traditional Instructional Media

Go back to Mississippi, go back to Alabama, go back to
Georgia, go back to Louisiana, go back to the slums and
ghettos of our northern cities, knowing that somehow this

situation can and will be changed. Let us not wallow in the valley of despair. I say to you today, my friends, that in spite of the difficulties and frustrations of the moment, I still have a dream. It is a dream deeply rooted in the American dream.
I have a dream that one day this nation will rise up and live out the true meaning of its creed: "We hold these truths to be self-evident: that all men are created equal."
I have a dream that one day on the red hills of Georgia the sons of former slaves and the sons of former slave owners will be able to sit down together at a table of brotherhood.

Web Link

EXAMPLE:
Hear, see, and read Dr. King's "I Have a Dream" in audio, video, text, and still pictures at
http://www.cast.org/TeachingEveryStudent/Mlk

Most of us easily recognize this passage as text from Dr. Martin Luther King's "I Have a Dream" speech (1963, p. 219)—if not immediately, then surely when we read the familiar words, "I have a dream." We would recognize the passage even more quickly if we could hear Dr. King's voice or see the scene on videotape or on the World Wide Web.

Although one might argue that the literal content of "I Have a Dream" remains the same whether it is presented as text, speech, or image, it is clear that each medium produces a qualitatively different effect. The textual version of Dr. King's speech contains the words, powerful and evocative. The audio offers vocal cues—intonation, pauses, volume, and pitch—tools this eloquent orator used very skillfully to convey the meaning of his message. The video version adds to the vocal cues a variety of visual ones. There are Dr. King's gestures and facial expressions and the environmental context—the large, responsive audience and the majestic setting on The Mall in Washington, D.C. (see Figure 3.1).

As this example suggests, the particular qualities of speech, text, and images differentiate their respective communicative power and

—FIGURE 3.1—
"I HAVE A DREAM"

© AP/Wide World Photos. Used with permission.

influence their suitability for various expressive purposes. Each medium's characteristics drive how the brain understands it and how effective it can be in instruction. Understanding the differences among the traditional classroom media can help teachers select the most appropriate means to present different content and tasks. Explorations into speech, text, and images can provide a better understanding of students' learning strengths and weaknesses. They reveal that barriers to learning do not necessarily lie within a student's physiological or psychological makeup, but rather occur at the intersection of the task, the student's strengths and weaknesses, and the instructional media and tools used to present that task.

How We Process Sound

Many of the distinctive qualities of speech relate to the physics of sound. Sound is a forceful, physical medium. Any disturbance that vibrates air— an explosion, a plucked guitar string, or the movement of a cricket's legs— creates a traveling wave of energy. The brain's recognition networks contain specialized modules for processing sound, located within the auditory cortex. When a wave of energy reaches our ears and the air pressure pounds on our eardrums, the energy is transformed into patterns of nerve impulses that the processing modules within our auditory cortex recognize as sound.

Here is a key point. The patterns of vibration that reach our ears are transient. For example, as you pronounce the word *permanence*, the first syllable, "per," is gone before you pronounce the second syllable, "ma." You can record sound to review later, but when you play it back, it's transient again. Although a digital recording, such as the one illustrated in Figure 3.2, might enable you to "see" a segment of a sound wave, interpreting that segment requires specialized expertise. It's just not possible to generate a true "still shot" of sound. In fact, time is inseparable from sound because the brain responds to the number of waves *per second*. A word spoken, a car horn, and a sonata are all

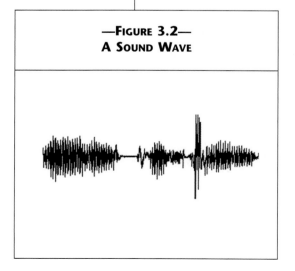

—FIGURE 3.2—
A SOUND WAVE

patterns in time, which cannot be frozen and examined. Sound perception is thus intimately connected to transient sequences in time—and thus to memory.

Think of speech as a particularly rich subcategory of sound. Human vocal chords generate extremely complex patterns, and the ability to recognize the source of these sounds (the particular vibration patterns of the sender) and the meaning of vocalizations is one of our most remarkable traits.

Qualities of Speech

The qualities of speech vary with its context. We speak very differently in conversation than we do when we are performing in a play, making stump speeches on the campaign trail, testifying in court, telling a bedtime story, or presenting a unit in the classroom. A good way to examine speech as a communicative medium is to consider it in the context of public speaking, a much-studied form of speech. The two major recommendations you will find in most popular guides to speechmaking highlight the medium's chief strength—its versatility and expressive power— and its chief limitation—the demand it makes on the audience's memory.

Advantages of speech. Perhaps the most basic rule of public speaking is *never read your speech.* The arguments mostly boil down to a single point: Reading text makes a presentation less natural-sounding, and therefore, less effective.

Natural speech works better because of its enormous expressive power. It offers a wonderfully rich vocal orchestration that enables us to express meanings clearly and energetically, beyond what words and syntax alone can convey. With our voices, we can vary intonation, pace, volume, and pitch to emphasize significant points, clarify intent and point of view, sharpen impact, provide background and emotional tone (such as sarcasm or irony), and even alter meaning. When we speak directly instead of reading text, we also tend to emphasize or clarify our words through physical cues, such as facial expression, gestures, motion, and posture. Speech is also interactive in that we can alter our tone, expressions, and gestures based on our audience's responses.

Limitations of speech. The second basic rule for speechmaking is *keep it brief.* In *Say It in Six* (Hoff & Maguire, 1996), the authors argue somewhat hyperbolically that you should never use more than six minutes to say *anything*. Other oratory experts concur that short and concise is best, but allow that a major speech could run as long as 18 to 20 minutes.

This call for brevity relates to speech's major limitation: its transience. Speech requires our listeners to remember, and it is easy to overload a listener's memory with a long, complex presentation . . . or even a long, complex sentence. Speech's transience and reliance on audience memory is also the reason why expert public speakers use techniques designed to reduce memory load and increase power. For example, Dr. King's "I Have a Dream" speech uses the technique of repetition to great effect. His repeated use of those four famous words provides the structure, rhythmic power, and emphasis that ultimately make the speech more memorable.

Both major characteristics of speech—its rich expressiveness and its transience—are experienced differently by different listeners. In order to find out why and how, we need to explore what understanding speech requires of the brain's recognition, strategic, and affective networks. Of course, speech is a medium used by both teachers and learners in the classroom. For the sake of brevity, we take the standpoint of the learner, focusing on the demands of understanding speech, rather than those of generating it.

Understanding Speech: The Role of Recognition Networks

Spoken communication conveys a sequence of shared-meaning elements that we call words. In the act of understanding speech, recognition networks rely on distributed, parallel processing to interpret many kinds of complex stimuli, while simultaneously processing individual sounds, words, phrases, and intonation. Of course, understanding speech requires both bottom-up processing—interpreting meaning from the flow of sounds—and top-down processing—using prior knowledge and context to predict what words will come next and to make sense of what we are hearing. To clarify how recognition networks process speech, let's first explore the steps required to recognize words and phrases.

Recognizing words requires a complex set of steps including hearing and differentiating individual sounds (also called *phonemes*) and attaching meaning to words. In speech, phonemes are uttered in rapid sequence. Understanding spoken language requires the ability to hear and distinguish these sounds rapidly to segment the stream of aural input into the words to which we can then attach appropriate meaning.

Barriers to understanding speech include hearing impairments and difficulty segmenting speech-sounds quickly. Research has shown that some children cannot process spoken language quickly enough to segment normal speech into phonemes. It's only when the speech is slowed dramatically (using a computer) that these children can learn to segment speech into the individual sounds that make up words (see Tallal et al., 1996).

Semantic recognition—the ability to attach meaning to individual words—is another critical part of understanding language and another place where barriers may arise. Some of the words we hear cannot be defined based solely on how they sound. The word *rock*, for example, can mean a type of music, a geological formation, or something we do to soothe a baby. Although most of us can easily assign meaning to the word *rock* in context ("I stubbed my toe on that rock"), some individuals are unable to connect these words to their meanings—although they can accurately hear and repeat spoken words. This dissociation reflects the fact that recognition networks have two ways of extracting meaning, each one vulnerable to individual differences. They operate in a bottom-up fashion to use phonemic information to recall meaning but when definitions are ambiguous, they must process in a top-down fashion, using contextual information derive meaning (see Federmeier, Segal, Lombrozo, & Kutas, 2000; Ward, Stott, & Parkin, 2000).

As we can see, the task of recognizing spoken words is a complex combination of bottom-up and top-down processing. But recognizing single words is just a tiny fraction of what we must do to interpret speech, which is long strings of words combined into phrases and sentences. We take for granted the understanding of grammar and syntax we apply when we speak and when we listen, and we usually are not aware that we must apply this knowledge to interpret even simple sentences. Difficulties using grammatical constructions can appear independently of other language problems in a disorder called *agrammatism* (Nadeau, 1988).

Visual cues are also very important for understanding speech because they convey meaning that the bare bones of speech simply cannot express. Facial expressions and gestures provide emphasis, context, and significance to verbal communications. If a student standing outside of the room were to overhear his teacher say to his parents, "Your son is a real trouble-maker," he might become very concerned. However, he probably wouldn't be concerned if he could see his teacher's amused and benign expression—a cue that would help him recognize her joking tone.

Because people who are blind cannot access visual cues, they sometimes miss key facets of spoken conversation. This is also a problem for people with damage to certain parts of recognition networks in the brain's right hemisphere who, although able to see, cannot interpret emotions via facial expressions (see DeKosky et al., 1980). Students with attention deficits may also sometimes fail to interpret visual cues—not because they are incapable of seeing or understanding them, but because they may not properly attend to them (Barkly, 1997; Lyon, 1994).

As this discussion illustrates, understanding speech places extensive demands on a listener's brain. In a classroom context, students must recognize sounds, words, and a variety of aural and visual cues simultaneously in order to attach appropriate meaning to the streams of speech coming from their teacher and their classmates. Thank goodness for parallel processing! But recognition networks are not working alone when students are interpreting spoken language. Listening to and understanding speech also requires us to act strategically and to stay focused and engaged. These are the domains of the strategic and affective networks.

Understanding Speech: The Role of Strategic Networks

It seems obvious that strategic networks, specializing in motor plans and actions, play an essential role in speaking. After all, we have to plan what we're going to say and go through the physical activity of producing speech. However, strategic networks' role in *listening* is not as immediately clear. Although in a conversation we often must prepare an answer or question while listening to someone speak, the listening itself seems effortless and unplanned. Listening to lectures seems even more passive. How much strategy could listening require?

In fact, listening requires heavy participation of the brain's strategic networks, in part because of the memory demands imposed by speech's transience. To gain meaning we must actively remember what we hear. And despite experts' advice that speechmakers "keep it short," we are often subjected to long speeches, particularly in academic settings! Organizing a long, continuous stream of speech into meaningful segments, placing these segments in context with prior knowledge, and engaging tactics to remember new concepts presented in the speech (taking notes, for example) are all strategic processes that are vital to understanding what we hear. A variety of brain imaging studies corroborate that what we call "active listening" is a significant act of cognition that engages modules throughout strategic networks (Gabrieli, Poldrack, & Desmond, 1998; Posner & Pavese, 1998; Smith, Jonides, Marshuetz, & Koeppe, 1998).

Differences in the ways our strategic networks operate manifest as functional differences in how well each of us can learn from information presented through speech. Students with executive-function disorders, students who have attention deficit hyperactivity disorder (ADHD), and students with other, subtler difficulties rarely have trouble *recognizing* speech as it is occurring. However, they often have trouble *understanding* speech because they cannot enact the strategies and skills necessary for active listening, learning, and remembering.

"Verbal working memory" is one strategic function fundamental to speech comprehension. Individuals with impaired working memory functions (for example, some individuals with epilepsy) may be fully capable of recognizing speech but nevertheless struggle to comprehend it because their frontal networks cannot "hold on" to spoken language long enough (Jambaque et al., 1993).

Concentration is another key factor. Understanding speech requires a listener to devote attention selectively and to screen out irrelevant stimuli. Various deficiencies in strategic networks affecting attention can seriously undermine speech comprehension. For example, some patients with Parkinson's disease—a condition characterized by degeneration of the frontal cortex—exhibit an impaired sentence comprehension that appears to be due to a loss of selective attention (Grossman, 1999).

It is interesting to note that students with strong strategic listening skills seem to be able to compensate somewhat for problems with speech recognition. A good memory can help a student retain information long enough to support comparatively slow recognition processes. Further, strong top-down strategic skills help learners predict, hypothesize, and fill in gaps in what they hear. In this way, both strengths and weaknesses in students' strategic networks affect how well they are able to understand speech.

Understanding Speech:
The Role of Affective Networks

The demands speech places on memory also call on affective networks. In order to remember what they hear, listeners must stay actively engaged while they listen. Following the advice of the experts, speakers sustain listeners' attention by appealing to their interests, fears, hopes, and senses of humor. Thus, the affective dimension of language—the emotional content that is carried by words, but is distinct from the words themselves—is important for a speaker to consider.

Because affective networks are distributed, different modules process the emotional content conveyed by intonation, facial expression, and gesture. Thus, different people may have trouble with different aspects of the affective processing of speech. For example, neurologist and author Oliver Sacks describes a patient who could understand words perfectly but could not decode the expressive character of speech. When listening to someone speak, she was unable to discern an angry tone from a cheerful or sad one. This meant that unlike most people, she could not rely on affective cues to clarify ambiguous sentences and therefore, had to insist that those around her use unambiguous words. Strict adherence to "proper words in proper places" was the only way she could understand what a speaker intended to say (Sacks, 1985, p. 79).

Damage to speech recognition networks can disrupt the ability to distinguish the speaker's tone of voice (sad, angry, happy) while sparing literal word comprehension (Tucker, Watson, & Heilman, 1977). These kinds of selective deficits further illustrate the distributed, modular nature of language processing. Individuals differ in their ability to employ and interpret these emotional cues, just as they differ in their ability to understand semantic content or to apply strategies for listening and remembering.

Students with emotional difficulties (whether these difficulties have resulted from situational issues or inherent traits) can find listening very challenging. Emotional difficulties alone may impede a student's ability to use information conveyed through speech, in part because the feelings themselves can demand students' attention and make it difficult to concentrate on other matters.

As this discussion has outlined, speech, a seemingly simple medium that most of us take for granted, requires highly complex, rapid processing on the listener's part. With access to nearly a dozen separate channels of communication, including words, gesture, intonation, facial expression, pitch, volume, and pauses, speakers can convey their ideas with great intensity, sharp clarity, and strong emphasis. Because meaning is conveyed through several channels simultaneously, speech supports great subtlety and nuance, much like a complex piece of music. Expression or intonation can contradict words, creating irony or humor. Alternately, expression and intonation can reinforce words, creating emphasis and clarity.

The richness and power of speech make it an excellent medium for communication and teaching. This richness requires extensive processing by the three modular, interconnecting networks in the brain, and learners present myriad subtle strengths and weaknesses as listeners. However, the transience of speech that's inherent in the way we process sound presents a variety of challenges and potential barriers to learners. As teachers, when we are aware of these barriers, we can adjust our teaching methods and materials to support every student's learning. This may involve supplementing speech with other traditional media when conveying concepts or applying the power of digital media to provide additional support.

With the fundamental qualities of speech established, let's move on to text and images, the two other traditional classroom media. Although each offers its own advantages and challenges for students, both depend on the processing of light.

How We Process Light

Perceiving visual media like text and images requires us to process light. Like sound, light is an invention of sorts, a perception our nervous system creates from traveling energy waves. Specialized cells in the retinas of our eyes absorb electromagnetic energy waves and convert them into a neural signal that our brains interpret as light. Using light, we are able to identify shape, color, depth, and motion—all critical for recognizing the world visually.

Although both sound and light are linked to traveling energy waves, the two kinds of waves are fundamentally distinct. Whereas sound is inherently mechanical, the product of energy created and propagated by movements and vibrations, light measures the electromagnetic energy reflected by an object—something less physical, more passive (Bregman, 1990). This might seem like a rather arcane point, but these differences factor in perception. For example, if we witness a rockslide, both sound and light contribute to our impression, but the sound has a tremendous affect, conveying a physical sense of moving masses hitting the ground. Compared to sound, light affects most of us less palpably, physically, and emotionally. Think about how silent movies seem less gripping than films with sound effects and music.

At the same time, light provides a more durable record than sound. The sound of a rockslide is created by the physical impact of rocks hitting each other and the ground, sending up vibrations that last only a few seconds. However, we can *see* the fallen rocks on the ground long after the noise has faded away. Whether you look at an object now or five hours from now, it will still be visible.

The visual cortex of the brain is specialized to process light. Cells in the visual cortex are selectively wired to cells in lower-order structures that conduct visual signals, newly converted from electromagnetic energy. Various parts of the visual cortex receive different patterns of input, reflecting their specialized roles in discerning features such as object motion, shape, and color. In addition, certain kinds of visual stimuli, such as letters and faces, are processed in separate regions. For example, processing modules important for reading text are specialized to recognize types of lines—diagonal lines, vertical lines, and curved lines. Modules important for decoding images are specialized to recognize color, texture, and form. Features of different sorts are extracted in parallel, endowing our visual systems with remarkable speed and efficiency.

We now have a basic idea of how light, and therefore the visual input, is processed by the nervous system. To read text and interpret images, we grapple with the strengths and limitations of the visual medium—and we bring our own unique brain networks to the task.

The Qualities of Text

Because printed text is so central to our culture, learning to read and write is the primary focus of the early school years. Teachers tend to relegate communication in all other media—even speech—to peripheral status. Because text is so powerful and so ubiquitous, we rarely pause to consider its limitations and the way those limitations affect learners. Analyzing the qualities of text can help us make wiser choices about when to use this medium.

Advantages of text. Whereas oral language is a "presentational" medium, text is truly a "representational" one. That is to say, text can be viewed as a *re*-presentation of spoken language in a new format—a format that overcomes transience, the major liability of spoken language. Text reduces the memory demands of spoken language by providing us with a lasting record. This advance has served humanity by scaffolding cultural memory across time, enabling us to maintain historical records without continuous oral repetition. Text also permits us to reach a mass audience dispersed in both time and space.

The act of creating text also helps us in a variety of ways. Once written, notes can be revisited at any time (provided they are not lost) and even passed on to another. We can create text to support memory, attention, or even comprehension. Text also helps us stay on course during our work. Think of the checklists we make to track our progress through a series of tasks.

The permanence of text supports a fidelity not possible with speech. This feature is inordinately valuable—whether the text is a legal document or a love letter. Not only can text maintain an accurate record of past events, it can also help us communicate information *more exactly* in the present. We can prepare a communication on paper, then read and revise the text to make sure we include all the necessary information. The exact record text provides lets us first convey complex concepts, such as philosophical arguments or historical interpretations, which in turn can be reread, reexamined, and reconsidered.

Limitations of text. Although text has many advantages, it has significant limitations, too. The most obvious drawback of text as a communication tool is that it lacks the inherent expressiveness of speech. The text version of Dr. King's speech accurately reports his words, but there's no question that the emotive qualities and impact are diminished on the page.

Text is also bound by a large number of conventions that writers must follow and readers must understand. For example, various kinds of printed documents are presented differently. A novel is generally formatted in single columns, with chapter titles in large type and content presented on sequential pages. In contrast, a newspaper presents text in small columns with headings above stories. Several newspaper stories might begin on the same page and conclude on different pages. Each of the many presentational forms of text—novels, poems, newspaper articles, and reference books—requires readers to approach it in a certain manner. For example, narrative and expository texts are designed to be read from start to finish, in a linear, logical order (Bolter, 1991; McLuhan, 1994; Meskill, 1999). Reference books like dictionaries and thesauruses are designed for selective consultation and require the reader to apply prior knowledge of the rules of alphabetization. Thus, the conventions of textual communications convey information outside of the words themselves that is nevertheless essential to finding the words' meaning. Such conventions can be enormously helpful and supportive, offering structural cues that direct reading. But for some learners, these conventions are difficult to grasp and use.

All students do not experience the advantages and limitations of text in the same way. The reason relates to how text engages the three brain networks. Here, for the sake of brevity, we focus on what is involved in reading text, rather than producing it. Reading engages multiple areas in all three networks. The involvement of myriad individual processing modules within recognition, strategic, and affective networks leads to innumerable differences between learners' strengths and challenges in learning to read and in reading well.

Reading Text: The Role of Recognition Networks

Reading is a difficult task—and really a compilation of many tasks. Decoding text requires students to recognize several levels of complex patterns (letters, letter-sound correspondences, words, phrases, and sentences) and a variety of forms (essays, newspaper stories, poems). This requires the coordinated action of many different recognition modules. Because individual differences can crop up in any of these modules, learners' abilities to read are subject to various subtle or profound barriers, beginning at the letter level.

You might think that recognizing letters would be a challenging task, especially considering that each letter in the alphabet can appear in different fonts, sizes, colors, and styles. However, most people find letter recognition easy. This facility is due to the modularity and efficiency of our visual recognition networks, which divide and distribute the task of identifying letter features, processing them rapidly in parallel and combining the information very quickly. Still, some students have trouble identifying letters and confuse similar-looking or similar-sounding letters, even late in the process of learning to read (see Roswell & Natchez, 1977).

Making the connections between letter forms and letter sounds is much more complex and can be much more problematic. Although the English alphabet has only 26 letters, it has twice that many distinctive sounds. To represent all the sounds in our language, we use combinations of letters (called *graphemes*), based on complex correspondence relationships. The letter *A,* for example, represents a wide range of sounds as in *law, play*, and *cat.* Just as understanding the meaning of a spoken word may require semantic context, letter-sound relationships depend heavily upon letter context. Unlike the simple correlation of letter shape to letter name, (which is primarily, if not entirely, a "bottom-up" process), aligning letters with their sounds requires top-down processing. Readers must apply conventions based on the placement of a letter in the context of its surrounding letters to be able to differentiate, for example, the *A*-sound in *rat* from the *A*-sound in *rate.*

These sound combinations represented in text are also essential to determining word meaning. Just as many spoken words sound the same but mean different things, many written words *look* the same but have different meanings, requiring yet another level of contextual, top-down processing. For example, you have to know the semantic context of the word "read" before you can pronounce it or identify its tense. ("Yesterday Boris read his spy orders; tomorrow, Natasha will read the secret code.")

Brain imaging techniques are beginning to help researchers understand the relationship between modular recognition networks and various kinds of reading difficulties. For example, researchers have found significant differences in the brain activation of dyslexic and nondyslexic readers, indicating among dyslexics "a disruption within the neural systems serving to link the visual representation of the letters to the phonological structures they represent" (Shaywitz et al., 1998, p. 2640). These studies indicate an impairment of the module that links letters to sounds. As another example, students with autism are often "gifted" in recognizing the patterns of letter-to-sound correspondences and single-word decoding that comprise the early stages of reading. However, difficulties understanding what they read coincide with problems with other kinds of contextual, top-down processing. Thus, differences in recognition ability can splinter across many separate aspects of recognition and across individuals.

In sum, recognizing text is a complex, multi-dimensional process that places a variety of demands on learners' recognition networks. Readers must recognize letter forms, letter-sound correspondences, words, sentences, and larger units of meaning. Each of these tasks requires rapid, automatic processing and interconnections between a large number of neural modules.

Reading Text: The Role of Strategic Networks

Many noneducators fail to realize that recognition is just one of several elemental facets of reading. Strategic networks are also involved at all levels of reading, even decoding, although this is so primarily when children are learning or struggling to read. Strategic networks are most significantly involved in comprehension, which is not simply a matter of "recognizing" the meaning of text, but also involves constructing that meaning through interpretation and analysis.

This construction is an active process. Reading for meaning requires us to set goals (try to find out who shot President Lincoln, enjoy a good story, or learn the molecular structure of an organic compound); create and execute a plan to achieve those goals; generate hypotheses and test them against textual cues; constantly monitor what is being read and compare that to prior knowledge; reread when comprehension falters; and evaluate whether a goal has been achieved. Research confirms that skilled readers adapt their pace and approach according to their purposes and the types of texts they are reading (see McGann, 1991).

Separate modules within a strategic network manage the various elements of reading, and problems can occur at any part of the process. Difficulty setting goals, understanding purpose, interpreting structural cues and meaning within text, connecting prior knowledge with new content, monitoring progress, and remembering concepts are among the many weaknesses based in strategic networks. Further, when decoding is not automatic, the brain recruits strategic networks into the work of analyzing words—a process that sidetracks a learner's ability to focus on constructing meaning.

Reading Text: The Role of Affective Networks

Affective networks provide an excellent illustration of how differently speech and text call upon and impact the nervous system. The energy of sound (and therefore speech) is directly "wired up" to affective networks in our brain cortex and limbic system, exerting an emotional impact that enhances and in some cases alters the meaning of a visual stimulus. For example, think of a scene from the movie *Jaws*. The camera is panning across the harbor at sunset . . . and the recognizable "shark theme" is rising on the soundtrack. Now imagine the same scene without sound, or accompanied by serene classical music, a soothing romantic song, or blaring rock music. This exercise shows us how much of a visual experience's emotional content can be conveyed through sound.

Text employs various methods and conventions to try to replicate the emotive power of speech. These include punctuation (compare *Mom lost the car keys!* with *Mom lost the car keys?* and *Mom lost the car keys.*), and descriptive parts of speech, like adverbs ("Sure!" he said *mockingly* or *angrily* or *hopelessly* or *hurriedly* or *boldly* or *balefully*). Spacing and visual variations such as boldface and underlining are additional ways of representing emotion on the printed page. But none of these visual conventions connects directly to the nervous system. To access emotion through text, readers must interpret these cues and conventions and "add back," if you will, the expressive nuance of speech and sound. This requires top-down affective processing—using context to infer the correct emotional tone. Good readers can re-create the emotion an author embeds in text, but gleaning text's emotional content can be a challenge for poor readers who struggle to grasp the basic meaning of words. Because text does not have a direct route to emotion, it may be harder to engage students in text than in speech, leaving them vulnerable to outside distractions.

Difficulty understanding the emotions in text is only one part of the challenge for affective networks. A range of other challenges centers on

Web Link

BACKGROUND KNOWLEDGE:
Learn about the research-proven Reciprocal Teaching method developed by Anne Marie Palincsar at:
http://www.ncrel.org/ sdrs/areas/issues/ students/learning/ lr2recib.htm

Web Link

EXAMPLE:
Experience the power of sound in video at *http://www.cast.org/ TeachingEveryStudent/ sound*

students' experiences with the process of reading and their interest in the content presented. For students who have trouble reading, negative associations with text can build to the point where they no longer invest effort, convinced that they will fail. Students can also be turned off by reading if they continually encounter texts that are not relevant to them.

Thus, individual differences in affective networks can shape students' understanding of text and their engagement with the content. Being aware of text's demands on affective networks and being sensitive to students' individual differences can help teachers provide appropriate choices of reading matter, build supports to engage students, and use other media constructively.

Our exploration of recognition, strategic, and affective networks and how they are recruited by the task of reading provides us with additional insight into the potential advantages and limitations of text as an instructional medium. Recognizing patterns in text, enlisting and applying various interpretive strategies, and engaging with the process and content of reading are all highly complex acts involving modules in all three networks. Each part of the process is susceptible to individual differences, whether these are talents or difficulties. For example, although text reduces the memory demands posed by speech and offers visual organizational cues such as white space, formatting, and headings, the need to decode and to understand and apply those cues causes new and different barriers for many students.

When teachers get to know their students' strengths and weaknesses in recognition, strategy, and affect, they can make better choices about when and how to use text. Understanding the critical role of brain networks in reading and the different ways in which their performance can be derailed also helps teachers to be conscious of the choices they make when setting goals and selecting materials and methods for different learners.

The Qualities of Images

Consideration of images—their strengths and weaknesses as a communication medium and the demands they place on learners—rounds out our discussion of traditional fixed instructional media. Still images are a longstanding component of instruction, but one that has usually been relegated to a lesser role. However, images' increasing cultural prevalence through television, magazines, movies, and, of course, computers, are making them more important in classrooms.

Advantages of images. The major point of contrast between still images and language is that language communicates linearly and sequentially, whereas images communicate everything at once. Images offer immediacy and they capture the entirety of a view. Novelist Mark Helprin expresses a similar viewpoint through one of his characters:

> Paintings . . . (are) so easily apprehensible. They're present all
> at once, unlike music, or language, with which you can lie to
> the common man merely because he may not remember
> what has just been and cannot know what is coming. . . .
> Painting is tranquil and appeals directly to heart and soul."
> (Helprin, 1991, p. 284)

This quote highlights another important advantage of images: their ability to convey emotion and feeling more directly than text can. Images' directness and ability to present all their information simultaneously makes them excellent choices for portraying mood, capturing relationships, making comparisons, and understanding parts versus wholes. Finally, representational images don't require decoding because they convey information literally. Viewers need not follow a particular path when looking at the elements in an image; they can choose the order of inspection.

Limitations of images. Although images can be used to simplify complex information (e.g., a visual display of data or a diagram of the water cycle), sometimes they are governed by conventions that can be quite complex, requiring training and practice to interpret. Further, images are not ideal for conveying conceptual, philosophical, and abstract information—anything below the surface or above the instance. Their ability to explain, clarify, ask questions, speculate, negate, or convey inner thoughts and emotion is inferior to language in many cases (Stephens, 1998). Of course, there are exceptions. Think about how powerfully expressive pictures of the American flag can be: the flag raised at Iwo Jima, the flag burned in protest, the flag brandished by an Olympian, or the flag flying over the rubble of the World Trade Towers.

Images also make unique demands on the nervous system. Let's touch briefly on some of the different processes involved in understanding images to highlight barriers some learners may face.

Understanding Images: The Role of Recognition Networks

Interpreting images requires visual acuity and the ability to recognize the parts in relation to each other—in size, depth, movement, and many other ways. Because different visual features are processed in different parts of the visual system, some aspects of an image can be accessible to an observer, while others may not be.

For example, studies have shown that particular brain lesions can impair the ability to analyze parts of a picture, but not the ability to understand the picture's *gestalt*—the overall idea it's communicating. Other damage can disrupt the ability to perceive shape, but not color (Zeki, 1999). These specific deficits are not unlike those we observed with spoken language, as when a person with a particular language disorder might have difficulty understanding word meanings but can interpret emotional tone or vice versa. These insights make it clear that images, like other media, are processed in parallel by multiple modules within recognition networks.

Understanding Images: The Role of Strategic Networks

Understanding an image requires the analysis of parts and wholes. Individuals create viewing strategies according to their own purposes and the nature of the image itself. Images used to convey complicated concepts make additional demands, requiring skilled interpretation based on the knowledge of graphic conventions, such as placing the most important elements at the center of the page, or organizing the various elements in ways that draw the eye and encourage it to linger.

Just as learners can be distracted when processing text, they can mistakenly focus on an image's unimportant elements. Strategic networks help viewers determine what is important and focus their attention where it is most productive. Skilled viewers are much more successful because they apply top-down processing: Their inspection is more firmly anchored to the meaning or knowledge they seek, and they are skilled at tying what they see to what they already know.

Understanding Images:
The Role of Affective Networks

Affect is also crucial to deciding the important elements of images and understanding them. A viewer's individual emotional preoccupations may steer him away from his intended viewing strategy or prevent him from receiving the message the image's creator intended. On the other hand, a lack of emotional engagement may prevent a viewer from looking closely at an image or may block the viewer's comprehension of the image's emotional content. However, affect is not always negative. Positive affective engagement may feed an individual's interest—and persistence—in working with images.

Compared to speech and text, images offer a partially overlapping but unique set of advantages and limitations for teachers and learners. Images share the directness and emotive power of spoken language and the permanence of text. Unlike either of these media, they present everything at once rather than sequentially, giving viewers the opportunity to examine the information in images in their own preferred sequence. Barriers to understanding images can occur in any or all brain networks and include among other things, inability to see the images, difficulty with systematic examination and interpretation, or simple lack of interest. Considering the purpose of a particular lesson and the strengths and weaknesses of a student can help teachers evaluate the appropriateness of using images for teaching and student expression.

Overcoming the Limitations of
Traditional Media

Thus far, we have provided an overview of how speech, text, and images each present a unique profile of strengths and weaknesses not experienced equally by all individuals. In the classroom, each medium poses barriers for some students, while offering particular opportunities to others. None works optimally for every student or for every situation, which means that several media options should be available.

Unfortunately, many classrooms continue to be dominated by a single medium—usually printed textbooks. This dominance prevents teachers from reaching all students and instead forces them to cater to those who find text accessible and create barriers for those who do not. There are further consequences. Even students able to access text are missing out because we know that there are other media more suitable for communicating particular kinds of material. Finally, students' preferences and proclivities for *certain* media and tools can play an important role in deepening their engagement and enhancing their success, even if they are capable of using a variety of media.

What is the alternative? Is the answer simply for teachers to incorporate more text- and image-based instruction? To make multiple presentations of the same content—using text for some, speech for others, and images for still others? This just isn't very feasible. Collecting and maintaining a sufficiently varied assortment of traditional media that would allow us to create an optimal instructional environment for every student in every unit of curriculum would be incredibly costly, consume too much space, and create nearly insurmountable logistical problems. No, *more* media is not a reasonable alternative. Teachers don't need more media; what we need is *better* media.

Fortunately, we don't have to wait for better media to come along. Digital media—available now—can help overcome the limitations of traditional instructional formats.

The Power of Digital Media

Although digital media also represent information through text, sound, and images, the similarities to traditional media end there. By virtue of one essential feature—*flexibility*—digital media surpass traditional media in their ability to meet diverse students' varied needs in a variety of instructional contexts. This flexibility is inherent in the way digital content is stored and transmitted.

Over the last six thousand years, we humans have invented a wonderful array of storage mechanisms for our communications, ranging from stone to parchment to vinyl. Most of these techniques are an application of the same basic concept: Information is stored by taking a direct or encoded representation (a letter, an image, a sound) and physically embedding it in a medium (paper or vinyl), where it becomes permanent.

In digital media, content is stored in an entirely different manner. Rather than being embedded in a physical medium, the information is transformed into something abstract (bytes: ones and zeroes), which can then be presented in almost any medium and quickly transferred from one medium to another.

Consider the familiar image of DaVinci's *Mona Lisa* (see Figure 3.3). A conventional print reproduction stores the masterpiece (paint permanently embedded in canvas) in a similarly fixed format: as ink permanently set on paper. A digital reproduction stores the *Mona Lisa* as a set of numbers in a computer. When these numbers are "read," the image is re-created on the computer screen. But unlike the paint-on-canvas version or the ink-on-paper version, this image of the *Mona Lisa* is not permanently fixed in this one format and location. On the contrary, you could display the same content on your 14-inch computer monitor, a 40-foot video screen in Times Square, a Web page in Singapore, or a Palm Pilot.

Moreover, the digital *Mona Lisa* is malleable: The whole image can be made darker or lighter, the greens subdued, or the edges sharpened. Parts of the image can be transposed or deleted, duplicated and recombined (as was the case with the image in Figure 3.3.) What once was permanent can be altered, removed at will, or restored—multiple times.

Digital media offer a remarkable, almost paradoxical, set of features. They can save text, speech, and images reliably and precisely over time, and yet they offer tremendous flexibility in how and where those text, speech, and images can be redisplayed. The same content that is irrevocably fixed in a traditional medium can be flexibly accessed in a digital medium and changed or adapted. This is very useful to a

—FIGURE 3.3—
A DIGITALLY-MANIPULATED *MONA LISA*

Photograph by Martin Kausal. Reproduced with permission.

teacher with a diverse classroom. Four aspects of digital media's flexibility are particularly beneficial for classroom application: versatility, transformability, the ability to be marked, and the ability to be networked. Let's examine each in turn.

Digital Media Are Versatile

Unlike a printed book, which can present only text and images, digital media can display content in many formats—text, still image, sound, moving image, combinations of text on video, sound in text, video in text, and more. Compared to print—and indeed, to any traditional medium—this versatility is astonishing. What's most exciting is that it offers users the chance to work in a preferred medium or interact with multiple media simultaneously. In a digitally equipped class studying Dr. King's "I Have a Dream" speech, for example, a student with reading problems, a student with a preference for visual material, and a student who loves to read could access the material as speech, video, and text, respectively. Or they could access it as video *and* text or text *and* speech.

Digital Media Are Transformable

Because the display instructions are separable from the content itself, digital media allow the same content to be displayed in multiple ways. Web pages are a familiar example. Various users accessing the same Web page can alter how the site's content is presented; they can change the appearance of text or images, adjust sound volume, turn off graphics, and so forth simply by selecting a different browser, changing browser settings, or using a different computer. We call these kinds of adjustments "within-media transformations," because they adjust the way something is presented without changing it to another medium. That is, a loud or a soft sound is still a sound; large or small text is still text.

With digital media, "cross-media transformations"—transformations from one medium to another—are also possible. Speech recognition software, which automatically translates spoken language into text, is one example. Text-to-speech software, which transforms text into speech, is another. These tools can now be embedded into Web browsers and other software programs via translation algorithms so that the transformation from one medium to another can take place automatically and just in time—right when users want to access the material.

The capacity to transform digital content, both within and across media, is a powerful asset. Using within-media transformations, students who have trouble seeing small text can increase its size; those who have trouble understanding speech can slow the speech down or increase its volume. Using cross-media transformations, a teacher can set up a computer to read words aloud on demand for a student with dyslexia. These are just a few examples of the almost endless possibilities for application.

Digital Media Can Be Marked

Hypertext markup language (HTML) is a code for constructing Web pages. HTML allows a Web page designer to "mark up" text, tagging different structural components such as the title, subheadings, or main body. Newer markup languages, like XML, provide an increasing variety of "tags" and even give designers the ability to invent their own tags. Once content is marked, a Web page designer can direct the display of the different components (put all text marked as headers in a 12-point Helvetica font, for example).

The advantage of these marking tools is that they allow teachers and students (with only a small amount of training) to flexibly alter content to accommodate needs or preferences. If you wanted to use a particular text to teach your students about literary devices, you could mark all the sentences containing similes and set them to be displayed in boldface type. A Latin teacher could mark the text to italicize all words that have Latin roots. Students trying to understand a detailed piece of text could mark it to underline all the summary sentences as a way to keep track of the most important information.

What differentiates the marking ability available with digital media from that used with traditional media (a textbook and a highlighter pen, for example) is that with digital media, markups can be shown or hidden, amended, expanded, or deleted. The same store of information can be marked in different ways for different students. It can also be unmarked and re-marked to suit the evolving needs of any particular student.

Digital Media Can Be Networked

The fourth great advantage of digital media is that it's possible to link one piece of digitally stored content to another. This "networkability" allows digital media to incorporate embedded hyperlinks to all kinds of learning supports—from direct access to dictionaries and thesauruses, to prompts that can support reading comprehension, to supplementary content that builds background knowledge, to electronic notepads or visual organizers. Networkability makes possible rapid navigation between a word and its definition, an image and its description, a video and it caption, or a text passage from Robert McCloskey's *Make Way for Ducklings* and an audio file of real ducks quacking. All these things are possible with multimedia packages and a local network of rich digital resources. And if the network includes the World Wide Web, educators and learners gain access to all this and more—widely varying and continually updated materials, not to mention the perspectives and contributions of diverse experts, mentors, and peers from all over the world.

The Web is itself an excellent illustration of the four flexible characteristics of digital media. Its strengths parallel those of neural networks. Like neural networks, Web information is distributed across many different locations and interconnected via a dense collection of links. From any networked computer, there is near-immediate access to information elsewhere in the network. Even with billions of Web sites, the Web is far less complex and infinitely less intelligent than a human brain. Nevertheless, compared to traditional media, it has capabilities that are a much better match for the potential and diversity of the human learner.

Implications for Educators

With a better understanding of new and traditional media and how individual brains interact with each, teachers can reevaluate how they teach, how students learn, and how best to use various tools and techniques to individualize these processes. As our discussion of the three brain networks and individual differences makes plain, no single traditional instructional medium format works for all students. And although it is possible to remove barriers and expand access to learning by offering content in a variety of media, the fixed nature of speech, text, and images makes this an impractical, unviable option for most educators.

The flexibility of new media opens new doors to diverse learners. Digital capacity to combine and transform text, speech, and images leads to a more diversified palette for communication—one that can accommodate the varied strengths and weaknesses of each medium and every brain.

Digital media also has the potential to transform the learning process. The hegemony of printed text has already disappeared in high-impact fields like advertising, entertainment, and communication, but in education, its dominance remains. In the years ahead, however, it is clear that text-only instruction will give way to a more deliberate application of multimedia. Instructional designers will use digital tools to tailor media to the task, to different kinds of learning, and to different kinds of students, reducing the barriers and inefficiencies inherent in one-size-fits-all printed textbooks. New expertise in the representational and expressive qualities of each medium and the new blends that will evolve will help educators reach a broader spectrum of students with a broader spectrum of knowledge.

Students with various kinds of disabilities are likely to be the earliest and most obvious beneficiaries. Media such as talking books, descriptive videos, and American Sign Language (ASL) tracks vastly increase both access and learning opportunities. Using digital tools actually changes those students' capacities and makes them far more capable. An extreme example is a student with severe physical and language disabilities who, independently, might be able to communicate only by indicating *yes* and *no*. With a computer and the right software tools, this student can be on an equal footing with others.

The incidental but equally important beneficiaries of new digital media for teaching will include teachers and students of subjects like math, music, geography, and physics—subjects that have never easily yielded their magic through linear text. Ultimately, the new media will benefit all learners.

➤ ➤ ➤ ➤ ➤

Incorporating digital media into the classroom is an important step that requires thoughtful consideration. Accessing their flexibility requires a shift in how educators think about instruction. CAST's intent is to help teachers understand the process of integrating digital media into the curriculum to engage diverse learners in meaningful educational progress. Our framework, Universal Design for Learning, provides guidance for that process. In the next chapter, we define UDL in more detail and explain its three guiding principles.

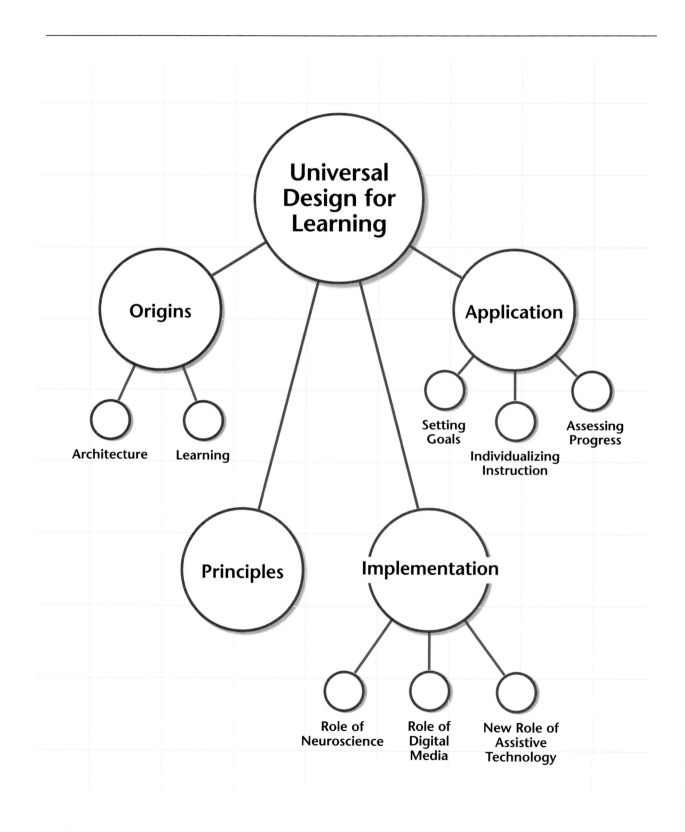

What Is Universal Design for Learning?

In this chapter, you will learn about the theory of Universal Design for Learning and how it can help teachers meet standards yet still address the unique needs of every student.

KEY IDEAS

The key to helping all students achieve is identifying and removing barriers from our teaching methods and curriculum materials. Drawing from brain research and using new media, the UDL framework proposes that educators strive for three kinds of flexibility:

➤ To represent information in multiple formats and media.

➤ To provide multiple pathways for students' action and expression.

➤ To provide multiple ways to engage students' interest and motivation.

The three UDL principles, implemented with new media, can help us improve how we set goals, individualize instruction, and assess students progress.

This is a challenging time to be a teacher. New policies and changing demographics are making schools more diverse than ever. An increasing number of students with disabilities and learning differences are being educated in regular classrooms, and new policies are holding schools accountable for the progress of all learners. State and federal standards, together with a shift in how literacy is defined, are compelling teachers not only to cover large amounts of material but also to instill a deep understanding of this material. These days, we are demanding more of students than the acquisition of facts: We want them to ask questions, find information, and use that information effectively. We want them to *learn how to learn.*

In this chapter, we share our vision for a new approach to pedagogy that responds to the challenges of education today. CAST has drawn on the neuroscience of learning and the study of media to develop the concept of Universal Design for Learning. The central practical premise of UDL is that a curriculum should include alternatives to make it accessible and appropriate for individuals with different backgrounds, learning styles, abilities, and disabilities in widely varied learning contexts. The "universal" in universal design does not imply one optimal solution for everyone. Rather it reflects an awareness of the unique nature of each learner and the need to accommodate differences, creating learning experiences that suit the learner and maximize his or her ability to progress. UDL provides a framework that helps teachers differentiate their instruction through carefully articulated goals and individualized materials, methods, and assessments.

We begin this chapter by tracing the origins and development of UDL and addressing the important difference between *access to information* and *access to learning*. Next, we introduce the three basic principles of UDL and illustrate how—by applying insights into the brain and the strengths of new media—teachers can use these principles to inject flexibility into their classrooms.

The Origins of UDL

Universal Design for Learning is an extension of an architectural movement called *universal design*. Originally formulated by Ron Mace at North Carolina State University, the idea behind universal design in architecture is to create structures that are conceived, designed, and constructed to accommodate the widest spectrum of users, including those with disabilities, without the need for subsequent adaptation or specialized design.

Universal Design: Access for All

Before the universal design movement, architects rarely addressed the mobility and communication needs of people with disabilities. The results were buildings that were inaccessible to many. Legislation mandating universal access led to extensive retrofitting with ramps, elevators, talking signs, and other access devices. But retrofitting is expensive, often aesthetically disastrous (as illustrated in Figure 4.1), and usually inadequate in many ways.

Universal design provided a new and better approach. Architects realized that by considering the needs of their buildings' potential users at the outset, they could subtly integrate universal accessibility into the fabric of the building's design. Universal design challenges architects to innovate, often improving aesthetics and functionality. For example, the universally designed pyramid-shaped entrance to The Louvre, shown in Figure 4.2, embeds a sleek modern elevator within its spiral staircase.

As universal design's concept of access for all spread to areas such civic engineering and commercial product design, an unanticipated benefit became apparent: *Addressing the divergent needs of special populations increases usability for everyone.* The classic example is the curb cut. Originally designed to enable those in wheelchairs to negotiate curbs, curb cuts also ease travel for people pushing strollers or riding skateboards, pedestrians with canes, and even the average walker. Television captioning provides another example. When captioning first became available, it was intended just for hearing-impaired people, who had to retrofit their televisions by purchasing expensive decoder boxes to access the captions. Later, decoder chips were built into every television, making captioning standard and available to all viewers. This universal design feature now benefits not only the deaf, but also exercisers in health clubs, diners in noisy restaurants, individuals working on their language skills, and couples who go to sleep at different times. Further, as a built-in feature, access to television captioning costs a few cents rather than several hundred dollars.

—FIGURE 4.1—
ACCESS IN A RETROFITTED BUILDING

—FIGURE 4.2—
ACCESS IN A UNIVERSALLY DESIGNED BUILDING

Pyramide du Louvre, I. M. Pei, architect. Image reproduced with the permission of the Louvre Museum, Paris.

Web Link

BACKGROUND KNOWLEDGE:
The Center for Universal Design advocates principles that result in environments and products for all people. For more information about these ideas see *http://www.design.ncsu.edu/cud/*

Extending Universal Design to Learning

Universal Design for Learning extends universal design in two key ways. First, it applies the idea of built-in flexibility to the educational curriculum. Second, it pushes universal design one step further by supporting not only improved access to information within classrooms, but also improved access to learning.

Universal design in the curriculum. In the early 1990s, the staff at CAST was working with collaborating schools to adapt print-based curricula so these materials would be accessible to students with disabilities. The barriers inherent in printed textbooks had long excluded students with physical disabilities, students with visual impairments, and students with learning disabilities, among many others.

It seemed ironic to us that legislators and architects were working very hard to ensure that educational *buildings* were universally accessible, but no such movement pursued universal accessibility for the methods and materials used inside the buildings—*the curriculum*. From our work with individual teachers and learners, we realized that the concept of universal design could be applied to curriculum materials and approaches. We experimented with multimedia tools and created some learning materials with built-in options that made them more flexible than printed books.

Out of that work came the prototype for a new and flexible kind of electronic book that we later co-developed (with Scholastic Inc.) into the language arts curriculum called WiggleWorks. The books in the Wiggle-Works curriculum, all available on CD-ROM, have one distinguishing characteristic: They were developed from the start with features that allow them to be used by *all* kinds of students, including those with disabilities. Students with physical disabilities can turn pages and access controls with the touch of a key or a switch attached to the computer. Students with visual impairments can select large text with high contrast or opt to hear the text read aloud, navigating the program through buttons that "speak" their functions. This feature is also helpful to students who have difficulty decoding printed text.

Most important, the program's management system allows teachers and parents to "set up" the books to suit each learner's needs and preferences. Varied presentations of content and differing sets of supports are available for each student who signs in to the program. WiggleWorks is not a special education product, but a literacy program for all learners.

The built-in flexibility improves access and usability for all, making the program the first example of universally designed curriculum.

Access to information vs. access to learning. Non-educators often make the mistake of equating access to information with access to learning. In reality, these are two separate goals. In fact, increasing access to information can actually *undermine* learning because it sometimes requires reducing or eliminating the challenge or resistance that is essential to learning.

The distinction between access to information and access to learning is analogous to the kind of heavy lifting done by a professional mover versus that done by a body builder. The professional mover is interested in getting the sofa from point A to point B as quickly as possible and with the least wear and tear on his muscles. Therefore, he uses tools such as a dolly, a hydraulic lift, and a truck to help him do the job. These tools reduce the challenge of the work—a goal that suits the mover very well. The body builder has a different goal: increasing muscle. He seeks opportunities to lift weights, undertaking long workouts and increasing the weight as his strength improves. He uses tools that selectively support the muscles not being trained and increase resistance for those that are.

The goals of learners more closely resemble those of the athlete-in-training than those of the mover. UDL is predicated on that difference. As educators, our aim is not simply to make information accessible to students, but to make learning accessible. This requires resistance and challenge. Much as the body builder needs to know which muscle group requires strengthening before he can structure his training, the teacher needs to know the instructional goal in order to appropriately structure teaching. For example, if Kamla's teacher, Ms. Abrams, sets the goal of helping Kamla learn to decode text more fluently, allowing Kamla to use the computer's text-to-speech function on a reading assignment would undermine that goal rather than support it. However, if the goal were to help Kamla master the content within the text and build her enthusiasm for that content, then computer-supported reading would be an appropriate support.

Similarly, when Ms. Chen wants to work on Charlie's research skills, providing full access to the World Wide Web (and its endless diversions) could undercut this "distractible" student's learning rather than enhance it. To help Charlie focus on learning research skills, Ms. Chen might

Web Link

EXAMPLE:
Scholastic's Wiggle-Works, the first literacy program to incorporate UDL principles, was co-developed by CAST. To find out how young children benefit from this learning tool, go to *http://www.cast.org/ TeachingEveryStudent/ wiggleworks*

restrict his access to a particular set of articles and Web sites relevant to the task. By aligning Charlie's focus with his learning challenge, Ms. Chen increases his chances of success.

Thus, although access to content and activities is often essential for learning, access to information is neither sufficient for nor synonymous with learning. Knowing the instructional goal is essential for determining when to provide support and when to provide resistance and challenge. With this balance aligned appropriately, students gain access to learning. The UDL framework provides guidance for using technology to support that balance.

The Framework for UDL: Three Principles

Because all three brain networks are involved in learning, teachers cannot literally "teach to" students' recognition, strategic, and affective networks as separate entities. However, thinking about these networks individually helps us remember that learning is multifaceted and that barriers in the curriculum can arise in a number of places. Broadly speaking, we teach our students to

➤ Recognize essential cues and patterns.
➤ Master skillful strategies for action.
➤ Engage with learning.

A successful learning environment supports and challenges students in each of these arenas while minimizing barriers. And because no two students show the same patterns of strength, weakness, and preference within these domains, minimizing barriers requires highly flexible teaching strategies and materials. Accordingly, the UDL framework consists of three overarching operative principles, each formed to minimize barriers and maximize learning through flexibility. Each of the principles, listed in Figure 4.3, advocates a particular teaching approach for supporting learner differences in recognition, strategy, or affect.

The three UDL principles share one common recommendation: *to provide students with a wider variety of options*. To accommodate a broad spectrum of learners, universally designed curricula require a range of options for accessing, using, and engaging with learning materials. Like universal design in architecture, with its stairs, ramps, and elevators, these alternatives reduce barriers for individuals with disabilities but also enhance opportunities for every student.

Web Link

BACKGROUND KNOWLEDGE:
For addition material about Universal Design for Learning, see *http://www.cast.org/ TeachingEveryStudent/ UDL*

—**FIGURE 4.3**—
PRINCIPLES OF THE UDL FRAMEWORK

Principle 1: To support recognition learning, provide multiple, flexible methods of presentation.

Principle 2: To support strategic learning, provide multiple, flexible methods of expression and apprenticeship.

Principle 3: To support affective learning, provide multiple, flexible options for engagement.

Consider an example. Suppose Mr. Costa is teaching a civics unit on national elections and wants to convey the fundamental importance of voter participation. He chooses to use a chart—an ideal means of representation for some kinds of information and for some students, but a medium that presents learning barriers for other students. Obviously, a student who is blind cannot learn from a visual chart, nor can students who have difficulty discerning colors, interpreting keys and symbols, or deciphering the significance of spatial relationships between elements. For these students, charts actually present a barrier.

What could Mr. Costa do about that barrier? In this case, both his teaching goal and the barriers in the medium he has chosen (images) relate to *recognition,* the learning networks addressed by UDL Principle 1. Principle 1 recommends that the teacher provide multiple representations of the same information. A verbal description of the chart, a tactile graphic representation, or an e-text version read by the computer would all make the key concepts accessible to students who are blind or otherwise visually impaired. The verbal description would have the additional advantage of helping other students in the class by providing complementary information not contained within the chart and offering a different context and emphasis. This option would also help students who have difficulty interpreting graphically displayed data. These are just a few of the ways that providing two representations of the data instead of one allows Mr. Costa to create a richer cognitive learning environment for all his students.

UDL Implementation

The framework of UDL consists of instructional approaches that provide students with choices and alternatives in the materials, content, tools, contexts, and supports they use. But in addition to challenging teachers to be more flexible, UDL provides guidelines for creating flexibility that is both *systematic* and *effective*. These guidelines are derived from research on the learning brain and knowledge of the qualities of digital media. How do we use these fields of knowledge to develop systematic methods for increasing classroom flexibility?

The Role of Applied Neuroscience

Brain research provides a basis for determining the kinds of teaching and learning alternatives most useful for a particular student in a given circumstance. Insights about how the three neural networks function help us understand corresponding kinds of teaching and corresponding ways to individualize instruction for different learners.

Recall that the three networks—recognition, strategy, and affect—share several organizational features. Each processes information via distributed modules operating in parallel, using both top-down (contextual information from high in the hierarchy) and bottom-up (detailed information from low in the hierarchy) pathways. When we understand these features, we can identify several parameters that will help structure and simplify the selection of teaching and learning alternatives.

Building on the bottom-up nature of the learning networks (their reliance on detailed sensory information), we know we should provide students with sensory alternatives to ensure that those who have difficulty with one sensory modality (such as speech or sight) will not be excluded from learning opportunities. The verbal description of Mr. Costa's voter participation chart is a good example of a bottom-up sensory alternative. Similarly, bottom-up motor alternatives, such as special keyboards or voice recognition software, can ensure that students with physical disabilities will not be excluded from a particular learning task. This kind of alternative crosses modalities, offering students a completely different way to obtain or express ideas.

A second kind of alternative preserves the sensory or physical modality but provides *enhancement* to highlight certain information. Through these additions, we can scaffold students who have weaknesses that interfere with learning a task or who are novices in a particular domain. Returning to the chart example, Mr. Costa might provide an alternative version with the critical information circled or illustrated in a different color. This is an ideal scaffold for students who might have difficulty identifying key information in the larger context.

Recognition, strategic, and affective networks also use top-down processing to do their jobs. Therefore, a representation that provides additional context or background knowledge to help students constrain their search or action based on prior knowledge and expectation can be an equally powerful tool. Mr. Costa might build an electronic version of the voter participation chart, with hyperlinks to related information or to guiding questions that would direct students' interpretation. This kind of representation would be particularly useful to students with cognitive challenges that make it hard for them to remember information, students who lack the necessary background knowledge or have little experience interpreting charts, or students who can interpret the chart easily but desire more in-depth knowledge.

This short illustration shows that teachers' choices of media alternatives for particular tasks and students can be guided by an understanding of how the brain learns. Because UDL accounts for the organizational features and specialized learning in the three types of brain networks, it can guide flexible, individualized teaching.

The Role of Digital Media

In an ideal world, teachers might present information in a dozen different ways and offer students an equal number of options for expressing knowledge. But realistically, even the most creative teacher can only present one option at a time. And even if we did manage to use a variety of approaches and media to present concepts, our students would still need to practice those concepts and apply them on their own. The impracticality of using fixed materials such as printed textbooks to create a flexible learning environment is obvious. New digital media offer a much more feasible foundation for the UDL framework.

As we noted in chapter 3, the qualities of digital media most germane to education are their *versatility* (the ability to present information in any one of several media); their *transformability* (the capacity for content to be transformed from one medium to another); their *capacity for being marked;*

and their *capacity to be networked.* Teachers and students using networked digital materials can select the most suitable medium or use multiple media simultaneously. They can also convert material from one medium to another on the fly, modify the appearance of information within one medium, delve more deeply or connect laterally to other concepts through links, and communicate with many different people through networked computers. Let's revisit one of our example classrooms for an illustration.

Web Link

RESOURCE:
Electronic text repositories store and index public domain materials. Find a variety of sources for e-text and a tool, CAST's eText Spider, to help you locate particular works. Online at *http://www.cast.org/ TeachingEveryStudent/ spider*

Digital Media Applied

Ms. Chen's 6th grade class is studying Mark Twain's *The Adventures of Tom Sawyer.* The book is available both in a traditional print version and online at Project Gutenberg (http://promo.net/pg/). Ms. Chen has downloaded the digital version to the class computers. The content in the print and digital versions is identical, and students can choose the version they prefer.

The print version of *Tom Sawyer* offers many familiar advantages. Students can carry it around, mark it up to highlight important passages, make notes in the margins, and flip through the pages to look for particular sections. While reading, they know exactly where they are in the story and how many pages they have to go. Many students choose the print version, finding it easy to use.

Many, but not all. Ms. Chen's class includes one student who is blind, another who is physically disabled, and another who has been diagnosed with dyslexia. Several students speak limited English. For these learners, the print version is *not* easy to use; in fact it may be totally inaccessible. Other students in Ms. Chen's class whose reading is not fluent, who bring limited vocabulary and background knowledge to the story, or who are struggling with the literary concepts she is teaching find that although they can use the print version, it provides little support for their learning. For them, the print version is a hurdle, not a ramp.

How is the digital version different? It offers multiple ways of presenting the same content—effectively supporting the different recognition, strategic, and affective networks of different learners and providing them both access to information and access to learning.

Recognition support. The digital version allows Ms. Chen and her students to customize the text according to their needs and preferences. Web browsers and word processors make it easy to change text size or color to make it more visible. Screen reading software is available to read the text aloud or display the digital text through a refreshable

Braille device that provides a tactile representation of the story. The digital version can go beyond providing access, to also offer support for students with various recognition-based learning difficulties. There are a number of software programs (including TextHELP Systems Ltd.'s TextHELP, Kurzweil Education Systems's Kurzweil 3000, and CAST's own eReader, shown in Figure 4.4) that can present digital stories with supports for reading.

The eReader is a special Web browser that reads and highlights words, emphasizing the link between written and spoken language. Students can click on any word to hear its pronunciation or set up the program to read and highlight text sequentially—a word, a sentence, a paragraph, or a chapter at a time. Students can decide how fast the program reads and choose from a wide selection of voices.

When Ms. Chen plans how she will use the digital version, she considers her instructional goals. She wants her students to enjoy and appreciate the humor in *Tom Sawyer* and to study some of the literary techniques Twain uses. Reading mechanics is not her objective; therefore, she encourages struggling readers to use the eReader to get at the story's meaning and keep up with their classmates.

—FIGURE 4.4—
SAMPLE RECOGNITION SUPPORT IN CAST EREADER

Strategic support. Students with physical disabilities that prevent them from holding the book or turning its pages can navigate through the digital version, take notes, and generate their own text using alternative keyboards or programs that allow alternate means of navigating the digital text (examples include IntelliTools' Intellikeys-brand keyboard and overlays). Students with handwriting and spelling difficulties also find support for writing in the digital version of *Tom Sawyer*. For example, eReader offers a digital notebook next to the text itself, enabling students to copy passages and take notes while they read. Using programs that support embedded hyperlinks (such as Inspiration and HyperStudio), students can digitally record their own voices, draw, or write text comments. These digital tools provide media options for supported student expression.

Affective support. Finally, the digital version of *Tom Sawyer* offers multiple, flexible options for engaging students in the story. Because the story is in digital form, Ms. Chen can select from a menu of supports so that the level of challenge is appropriate for every reader. Links to background knowledge, vocabulary, and reading support can help students who struggle with the text in printed form and keep their frustration levels low. Interested students who want to know more can follow embedded links to other stories by Twain, related information about the time and setting of the story, and other material relating to Twain's writing technique. And Ms. Chen can also offer students varied choices of media for responding to the novel and creating their own compositions to demonstrate their knowledge. Students can create multimedia presentations using HyperStudio, design a Web page with links to related sites, devise a concept map, or write a paper.

As this example shows, digital media's versatility, transformability, and capacity for being marked and networked not only enhance the supportive power of learning media but also transform the learning enterprise itself. Flexible materials do not replace teachers, but they do extend our reach and make it easier for us to provide individualized learning supports and challenges for our students.

The New Role of Assistive Technology

Assistive technologies include tools such as *video enlargers* (tools that magnify printed text on a video monitor), *single ability switches* (tools that enable users to activate a mouse-click via different muscles such as an eyebrow or an elbow), and *alternative keyboards* (tools that offer alternative surfaces and "key sizes" for people who cannot use a standard keyboard). Although both UDL and assistive technology rely on new media to improve learning access, each assumes a very different role for curriculum.

The assistive technology model assumes that a printed curriculum is a given and provides tools to support individual access to it. Tools such as the video enlarger are not integral to the curriculum, but rather, are associated with the individual students who need them; they are simply means to helping these students overcome barriers in the curriculum. The assumption that students must obtain individual tools in order to overcome barriers in an inflexible curriculum is inherently antithetical to UDL.

To solve the same problems, UDL looks not to the student but to the curriculum itself. The underlying assumption is that by using flexible media, we can *embed options within the curriculum* so that it can be adjusted to meet the needs and preferences of each learner. This built-in flexibility reduces, but does not eliminate, the need for assistive technologies. Students with motor difficulties who access the computer via alternative keyboards or single ability switches will still need their tools. However, we believe the role of assistive technologies and the way people view them will shift as UDL curricula become more available.

As the concept of UDL gains acceptance, people will understand that assistive technologies are tools like eyeglasses and personal digital assistants that enhance personal effectiveness; they do not relegate their users to a separate category such as "disabled." Already, some of these devices, once solely linked to disability, are working their way into the mainstream community. For example, speech recognition technology is applied in voice-activated telephone directories, airline reservation systems, and banking systems.

As you can see, UDL has the potential to minimize the need for assistive technology and to maximize learning opportunities for all. We use the word "potential" deliberately, because the inherent flexibility of digital media does not guarantee that UDL will become real. Multimedia and the World Wide Web can be as inaccessible as print is. For example, image-based computer learning games are inaccessible to students who are blind; games that rely upon aural prompts and feedback without text equivalents are inaccessible to students who are deaf; and games that are text-based are inaccessible to students with dyslexia. To overcome these barriers, technology developers need to consciously apply UDL principles as they develop learning materials, and teachers need to select tools that have inherent flexibility.

UDL Application: Rethinking Our Practice

The UDL framework shifts educators' understanding of learner differences. It challenges us to rethink the nature of curriculum materials and endow them with the inherent flexibility necessary to serve diverse learning needs. UDL also opens the door for rethinking how we teach. With the option to individualize learning supports and focus the challenge differently and appropriately for each learner, teachers must be very clear about the learning goals they set for any given assignment or unit. Only when goals are clear can we select and apply flexible materials to support and challenge each learner. Similarly, clear goals help us focus our assessment of student progress in an accurate and useful way. The UDL framework can guide these three pedagogical steps, helping teachers to *set clear goals*, *individualize instruction*, and *assess progress*.

Setting Clear Goals

The first step, setting clear goals, seems on first glance to require little thought. After all, learning standards spell out what students need to learn, and curricula include summaries of the material to be covered. But looking through the UDL lens, we see that goals are often inadvertently embedded in the means for achieving them. Consider this goal: *Every student will be able to write an essay in cursive.* Though this degree of specificity would be quite unusual, the point is clear; as stated, the goal is so embedded in the method necessary to achieve it that many students could not possibly succeed. Those with physical disabilities, spelling and handwriting difficulties, and problems with organization could not even participate.

We can use the UDL framework to rethink this goal and analyze its true intent. Do we really care whether the essay is produced in cursive? Isn't organizing and composing the essay the real purpose? Once we clarify the overarching goal, we can reword it broadly enough to include all students, knowing that supports and scaffolds will be needed to help some students participate, and extra challenges will be needed to move other students to new levels. By simply removing express reference to the medium and stating the goal this way—*"Students will write an essay"*— we open the door for more students' participation and success. The clear goal helps teachers determine how to choose and apply the flexibility inherent in UDL learning materials. Chapter 5 provides a more detailed discussion of this topic.

Individualizing Instruction

The next step in paving every student's path to high proficiency is to provide instruction that helps each achieve classroom goals. Diverse digital tools and materials, with UDL flexibility built in, allow teachers to provide a degree of individualization impossible with traditional instructional materials. The instructional strategies articulated in UDL's three principles can help us make educated and scientifically grounded choices from the many alternatives available. We discuss this in depth in chapter 6.

Assessing Progress

Good pedagogy also includes effective and ongoing assessment, not only to measure a student's progress, but also to adjust instruction and to evaluate the effectiveness of methods and materials. Ongoing assessment enables teachers to ensure that the goals they have set and the methods and materials they are using continue to support students' progress. As you will read in chapter 7, UDL provides teachers with the tools they need to align assessment with each student's instructional goals, materials, and methods.

The Value of Universal Design for Learning

Universal Design for Learning provides a framework for individualizing learning in a standards-based environment through flexible pedagogy and tools. It challenges teachers to incorporate flexibility into instructional methods and materials as a way to accommodate every student in the classroom.

Within the framework of UDL, Sophia, who needs supports to overcome her visual deficits, and Paula, who has trouble with reading comprehension, could successfully read the same story using a software program that offers text-to-speech, images, and links to vocabulary and background knowledge. Charlie, who needs sequenced, structured support when working on a research project, and Jamal, who can manage the sequential steps in research but needs support for his fine motor disability, could conduct online research using the same program, but different supports. Kamla, whose interests lie primarily in sports, and Jamal, who is an expert on tanks and submarines, could pursue the same reading or math project in the content area of their choosing, thus adjusting for their individual affective networks.

In a traditional classroom, with traditional perspectives, methods, and tools, this type of pedagogical flexibility seems totally implausible. With the perspectives gained from brain research and the possibilities afforded by new media, UDL offers teachers a practical framework for injecting flexibility into the classroom. UDL does more than insist on flexibility; it provides teachers with the information and resources they need to achieve it.

The practices we recommend should be familiar to you, because these are the very same practices good teachers use when they can. The difference is that UDL, drawing on the versatility of digital media and its capacity to be transformed and networked, enables teachers to adjust instruction for the *whole class,* and not just for individual students. In this manner, it empowers us to teach *every* student, not just some.

➤ ➤ ➤ ➤ ➤

In the following chapters, Part II of this book, we explain how to apply the UDL framework to set goals, individualize instruction, and assess student learning in your own classroom.

Web Link

EXAMPLE:
Teachers describe the positive effects of applying UDL principles at
http://www.cast.org/ TeachingEveryStudent/ teacherUDL

PART II

Universal Design
for Learning:

Practical Applications

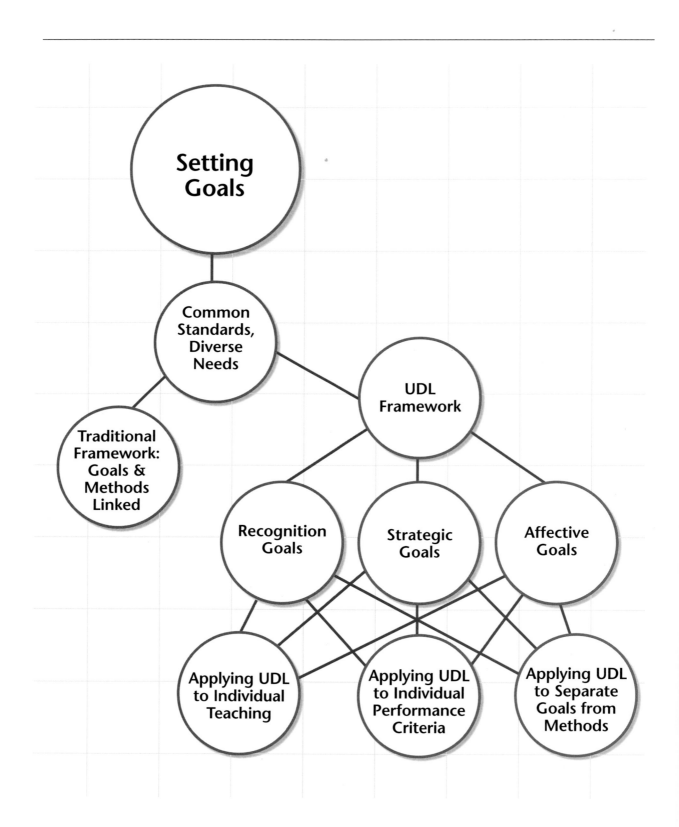

Using UDL to Set Clear Goals

5

In this chapter, you will learn how UDL can help resolve the apparent contradiction between standards and student diversity when setting goals for students.

KEY IDEAS

➤ Brain research supports the idea that clear goals are essential for learning, but teachers often lack clear goals for students, in part because our reliance on traditional, fixed media leads us to believe there is only one path to learning.

➤ We can apply what we know about the three brain networks and the nature of new media to separate goals from the means for achieving them, interpret standards for particular classrooms, and derive goals that all students can strive for.

➤ New Web-based software being researched at CAST is an example of a flexible tool that supports multiple pathways to common goals.

Common sense tells us that setting clear goals for students is the essential first step in teaching. Clear goals allow teachers to determine the best methods and materials for reaching our objectives and also enable us to establish appropriate criteria for assessing students' success.

Recent research on how goals are represented in the brain adds a strong neurobiological rationale for shaping and communicating clear goals to students. An everyday example highlights some key findings from this research: Suppose your goal is to drink a cup of coffee without spilling any on your clean shirt. How is this goal represented in the brain?

Earlier theory suggested that our brains specify goals as a precise sequence of muscle actions (first, extend the arm toward the cup; next,

87

open the fingers to grasp the handle; then close the fingers; and so forth). As it turns out, this is not how it works. See for yourself: Mentally set the goal of picking up a coffee cup and bringing it to your lips. Now do it. You found it routine, right? Put the cup back down, move twelve inches away from it, and attempt the same goal again. Again, it's routine, despite the fact that your muscles had to act in a slightly different sequence. Even if you placed a heavy weight on your arm, you would still have little difficulty smoothly adjusting your movements to retrieve the cup. It's difficult to reconcile this experiment with the idea that the brain represents actions with exactly specified muscle movements. If this were true, changing the necessary sequence of muscle actions would require a new mental representation, introducing a new challenge.

Neuroscientists now know that our strategic networks create internal plans based entirely upon the *goal* of an action (see Frith & Dolan, 1996; Funahashi, 2001; Levine et al., 1998). Following a plan that is based on an outcome—rather than one that is more concerned with the precise steps necessary to reach that outcome—is the surest way to preserve the outcome when external conditions change. For example, to attain the stated goal, "Drink some coffee," there are many options open to us, including reaching for a cup in any number of ways, leaning forward to use a straw, or sipping the coffee out of a spoon. In contrast, there are limited alternative pathways through which we might attain the goal, "Reach forward six inches, grasp the handle of the cup, tighten your grip, lift to your mouth, and drink some coffee." A goal this specific leaves little leeway to coffee drinkers. This raises an important issue: Goals that are too highly specified limit the possible strategies for reaching them, thus suppressing creative solutions and limiting the number of people who can even attempt to attain the goals.

Because strategic networks must understand the intended outcome of the goal in order to construct a plan of action, a fuzzy goal, or a goal confounded with the means to achieve it, leads to actions that lack focus. Without clear objective, it's difficult to gauge progress. In contrast, clearly communicated goals can support all three brain networks by helping students know what they are supposed to do, how to do it, and why it is important. Students who understand the goals of their schoolwork are more likely to stay focused, monitor themselves successfully, and derive satisfaction from their progress.

Setting clear goals and communicating them so that students understand them is neither as easy nor as widely practiced as we might think.
It requires that teachers overcome several challenges, the most important
of which is the apparent contradiction between standards and learner
diversity.

Common Standards, Diverse Student Needs

Any teacher will confirm that standards exert a powerful and controver-
sial influence on today's classrooms (O'Neil & Tell, 1999; Sizer, 1999;
Tomlinson, 1999a). Developed by national, state, and local curriculum-
writing groups and by subject area experts, standards aim to articulate the
knowledge, skills, and understanding all students should gain in a particular subject, with more specific benchmarks of achievement by grade
level. Standards express what schools value and, therefore, determine
what teachers teach and assess. To best serve our students, we need to
understand the strengths and limitations of standards as they are currently designed so that we may interpret and apply them effectively and contribute to their improvement.

First, the strengths. If properly constructed, standards can help us
realize the dream of learning for all (Schmoker & Marzano, 1999). Well-
designed standards focus primarily on "learning how to learn," calling for
students to gain knowledge, skills, and understanding. They leave room
for teachers to shape goals and to individualize the means for attaining
them. In other words, good standards represent the community's beliefs
about the knowledge, skills, and understanding that all students should
develop, but they allow that *how* and *to what degree* students develop and
demonstrate that learning can be as varied and creative as are the teachers
and students themselves.

However, many educators are concerned about the current design and
application of standards (see Dempster, 1993; Rosenholtz, 1991;
Schmoker & Marzano, 1999; Wolk, 1998). Howard Gardner and the
Project Zero group, in their work on teaching for understanding, warn
that standards that specify particular knowledge and skills can actually
lead teachers to decrease their focus on true understanding (Gardner,
1999). In such classrooms, students might acquire an impressive amount
of factual knowledge, but not understand the meaning and importance of

Web Link

FORUM:
Share your experi-
ences and opinions!
Join an online conver-
sation about standards
in diverse classrooms
at
*http://www.cast.org/
TeachingEveryStudent/
standardsforum*

what they have studied (Blythe & Associates, 1998). The kind of understanding standards usually fail to capture is articulated by David Perkins (1998) as "the ability to think and act flexibly with what one knows . . . more like learning to improvise jazz or hold a good conversation or rock climb than learning the multiplication table. . . ." (p. 43). Critics also point out that some standards prescribe too narrowly and specifically what students should learn. Such overly specified standards can lead to a host of problems: "one-size-fits-all" approaches, cookie-cutter curricula, "teaching to the test," and an increased need to cover large amounts of material instead of delving deeply into concepts.

We believe the key to reconciling standards with student diversity is a careful examination of the standards themselves—first to determine the true purpose of a particular standard, and then to separate that purpose from the methods for attaining it. If the goal statement reflects its true purpose, it can work for an entire class made up of diverse learners. The means, or approaches, can then be individualized.

The Problem with the Traditional Framework: Goals and Methods Linked

Partly because teachers have functioned for so many years with inflexible curriculum materials and methods, we tend to think narrowly about learner goals and the available pathways for their attainment. When goals are too tightly tied to methods, the logical result is that some students encounter barriers that prevent them from working toward these goals and others are not offered an appropriate level of challenge (Rose & Meyer, 2000).

Consider an analogy. Imagine a woodworking instructor is setting goals and performance criteria for a class of 30 students. One of the first goals he sets is *"Students will master cutting wood with a handsaw."* The performance criterion is for all students to use a handsaw to cut along a straight line drawn on a board. What is the likelihood that every one of the instructor's students will be able to achieve this goal?

The odds aren't very good. The wording of the goal confounds its objective with the means for attaining it, and the single performance criterion guarantees that while some students will be under-challenged, others will be over-challenged and have almost no chance of success. It's clear this goal could not be attained by a student like Sophia, who would have difficulty seeing a line drawn on a board, or by a student like Jamal, who lacks the physical ability to use a handsaw or to cut along a straight line. The goal would also be problematic for any student who fears being injured with sharp tools. Further, because students differ in coordination, strength, and physical ability, the single performance will be too high for some and too low for others.

The UDL Solution:
Goals and Methods Differentiated

If the woodworking instructor had only a handsaw and pencil (the woodshop equivalent of traditional, inflexible instructional media and materials), he might find it very difficult to shift set and reinterpret the goal so that all of his students could make progress. However, if he had a range of modern tools to work with (the equivalent of UDL's flexible media), he could broaden the goal from "master cutting wood with a handsaw" to "cutting wood" or "learning basic carpentry,"—two outcomes that better represent his true purpose. All students could work toward these broader goals, using whatever tools suit them best, and all could strive toward levels of competency that represent individual progress.

Like the woodworking instructor, teachers who have access to only a few tools and methods for teaching and assessing learners' progress naturally tend to define goals that are closely tied to methods. Consider this goal, set by Patrick's teacher, Mr. Hernandez, as part of a class research project: *"Students will collect information from a variety of books as part of their research."* In a traditional classroom, with only traditional fixed media available, Mr. Hernandez might logically conclude that Patrick couldn't work toward the same goal as his classmates because of his slow reading and tendency to be easily discouraged.

What if, in addition to books, the resources available to Mr. Hernandez's students included digital text with reading support, a variety of image-rich sources, videos, and scaffolds to help Patrick stay focused and organize his information? In this classroom, it would be clearer that the goal's true purpose—learning to collect and synthesize information—does not depend upon the use of printed text. Mr. Hernandez might restate the goal more generally: *"Students will collect information from a variety of sources."* This rewording separates the goal from the methods for attaining it, broadening the options for the entire class. Patrick, instead of having to lower his sights because of difficulty accessing a particular medium, could rely on scaffolds and supports to achieve the same goal as his peers.

UDL offers educators practical guidance for reconciling common standards with diverse needs. Remembering that our overarching intent is for each student to learn, we can use the UDL framework to

➤ Structure our analysis of the nature of a standard, goal, or unit of curriculum so that we can determine its true purpose, then separate the desired outcome from the means to attain it.

➤ Guide selection and assembly of flexible media and materials that can support diverse pathways to the goal for different students.

➤ Help us communicate goals and means to students so they know what they are doing, how they might do it, and why it is important.

Applying UDL to Separate Goals from Methods

The framework of the three brain networks guides interpretation of learning standards in two ways. First, by considering the wording carefully we can determine if the true purpose of the standard centers on learning information (recognition networks), learning skills or processes (strategic networks), or engagement (affective networks). When we can pinpoint the main focus of the goal, we can identify the aspects that must be held constant for all students. Second, and equally important for the process of individualizing instruction, knowing the real purpose of a goal helps determine where we can offer flexible options and where we can provide scaffolds without removing the challenge. Let's take a closer look at what's involved.

Determining Which Network is Central to a Standard

You may recall that setting goals and monitoring progress are the domains of strategic networks. Still, attaining any goal involves the whole brain. To illustrate, consider what is involved in attaining your goal of drinking a cup of coffee: Your *recognition networks* are in full gear, enabling you to identify the cup; its size, location, and heft; recognize the table and your hand; and monitor the changing location of your arm and hand as you reach for the cup. *Strategic networks* are centrally involved in setting the goal, initiating your reach, monitoring your progress, and making any necessary course corrections. Affect motivates you to lift the cup because you are curious about our experiment, thirsty, or tired and in need of caffeine.

Although pursuing goals involves the whole brain, most learning goals do tend to fall primarily into the domain of one brain network, one kind of "knowing." Some goals emphasize information and facts, the *"what"* of learning—the domain of recognition networks. Some goals emphasize skills and processes, the *"how"* of learning—the domain of strategic networks. Less common (but we believe, just as important) are the goals that emphasize the value and importance of ideas and connections to students' lives, the *"why"* of learning—the domain of affective networks. Determining which network is central to a standard is the first step in separating goals from methods. Below, we provide some general guidelines.

Recognition goals. Standards that ask students to identify "who, what, when, and where" prioritize the *learning of specific content.* This is the domain of recognition networks. Examples of such standards include

➤ Understands the genetic basis for transfer of biological characteristics from one generation to the next.[1]

➤ Knows the location of places, geographic features, and patterns of the environment.[2]

➤ Understands and applies basic and advanced properties of functions and algebra.[3]

Strategic goals. Standards that ask students to learn "how" to do something emphasize *skills and strategies*, the province of strategic networks. Examples of these standards include

➤ Demonstrates competence in general skills for reading a variety of literary texts.[4]

Sources: [1]Mid-Continent Research for Education and Learning (http://www.mcrel.org/). [2]National Geography Standards (http://www.ncge.org/publications/tutorial/standards). [3]National Council of Teachers of Mathematics (http://standards.nctm.org/). [4]National Council of Teachers of English (http://www.ncte.org/standards/standards.shtml).

➤ Demonstrates competence in the general skills and strategies of the writing process.[5]

➤ Understands the nature of scientific inquiry.[6]

Affective goals. Standards related to affect are still rather rare and are relatively easy to identify. Examples include:

➤ Students should enjoy, appreciate, and use mathematics, just as they should enjoy, appreciate, and use music, art, and literature.[7]

➤ Students will select a variety of materials to read for discovery, appreciation, and enjoyment, summarize the readings, and connect them to prior knowledge and experience.[8]

Determining a Standard's True Purpose

Knowing which network is most central to a particular standard helps us determine what its true purpose is. Only then can we know which aspects must be held constant if the standard is to be met and which aspects can be varied to support individual learning differences. Speaking very broadly, the following guidelines apply:

➤ For recognition goals, focused on *specific content*, that content is key.

➤ For strategic goals, focused on *a specific process or medium,* that process or medium is key.

➤ For affective goals, focused on *a particular value or emotional outcome*, that emotional outcome is key.

Considering Multiple Means to Goal Attainment

When the true purpose of a standard is understood, teachers can explore the various means students might use to attain that standard and various supports we might provide to help them do so.

Consider this standard: *"The student will demonstrate competence in the general skills and strategies of the writing process."* This standard focuses on *process* and is rooted in strategic networks. Because the content is not specified and is not key to this particular standard, we could increase students' engagement by encouraging them to select content that interests them and setting the challenge at individually appropriate levels.

Sources: [5]National Council of Teachers of English (http://www.ncte.org/standards/standards. shtml). [6]Mid-Continent Research for Education and Learning (http://www.mcrel.org/). [7]Electronic Learning Marketplace (www.elm.maine.edu/mlr/math.stm). [8]Madison Metropolitan School District Content Standards and Grade Level Performance Standards (www.madison.k12.wi.us/tnl/lang01.htm).

A tougher question is whether a teacher could be flexible about supporting the actual writing skills targeted in the standard. The writing process involves the ability to create a draft, elicit and use feedback, and revise and share one's work—processes that can be learned and practiced in numerous media, including text, sound, animation, images, and video. Although it is true that for students to attain this standard, they must ultimately be able to compose in text, we could scaffold their learning by encouraging composition and editing in these other media. Further, because this goal focuses on writing *process* and not writing *mechanics*, we could use text-related scaffolds, including speech recognition, word prediction, spell checking, and text-to-speech.

Here is another example: *"Students will identify and express the major causes of the United States Civil War."* This goal is content-specific—rooted in recognition networks—but both the means of obtaining the content and demonstrating knowledge are open to interpretation. Students could derive their understanding of the causes of the Civil War by exploring Internet sites, viewing appropriate videos (such as the 1990 series created by Ken Burns), reading text resources with or without support for decoding, visiting a museum, or interviewing Civil War experts in person or online. Moreover, we could allow them to demonstrate their knowledge in many ways.

When affect is more widely recognized as a critical component of learning, specific affective goals will become more commonplace. In fact, many teachers already pursue affective goals. For example, Mr. Hernandez placed the affective goal of recharging Patrick's emotional batteries front and center. Other goals became secondary as he supported and built on Patrick's enthusiasm. For some students, at some times, it may be more important to build engagement than to attempt to develop knowledge or skills. Balancing these three networks as we develop goals is in part a fine art.

Applying UDL to Reframe Standards as Clear Classroom Goals

Students' individual differences in recognition, strategy, and affect require that we set our goals carefully. As we have established, a goal that restricts students to one type of content or one method of expression is not likely to be attainable for the entire class. By reframing goals to allow for multiple media and means for expression and engagement, we can offer more palatable options for *all* students.

To illustrate the possibilities, consider the following example from the sport of high jumping. At one time, every high jump competitor used the same tried-and-true technique. Learning the sport of high jumping was a matter of mastering that particular technique—the goal had become confused with the means. However, Oregon athlete Dick Fosbury broke the mold with a new technique, despite attempts by his coaches to train him in the traditional method. In the 1968 Olympics, Fosbury startled the world by winning the gold medal with an idiosyncratic technique, shown in Figure 5.1, dubbed "The Fosbury Flop." The Flop enabled others to continue to break high jumping records, and it has since become the standard technique for jumpers everywhere.

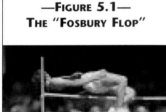

—FIGURE 5.1—
THE "FOSBURY FLOP"

© AP/Wide World Photos. Used with permission.

Dick Fosbury's unique strategic networks created a major innovation that benefited many other athletes as well as himself. Had he pursued the goal of mastering the traditional approach to high jumping, he would probably never have been more than a mediocre jumper, much less an Olympic champion and the catalyst for the revolution of the sport. Fortunately, his goal was to jump as high as he could, by whatever method worked!

There are two lessons to take from this example. First, it shows us again why it's wise to avoid too much specification when we set goals. Second, it points out that we should always consider whether particulars of expression, recognition, or affect are germane to the goals we set. If we give students appropriate latitude and supports to pursue goals in their own fashion, they can be both creative and successful.

For example, suppose Mr. Costa set the goal for everyone in his class to learn about culture in the United States by interviewing someone who emigrated to this country, writing interview notes on paper, reading about their interviewee's homeland, and writing a report. If Mr. Costa carefully considered the diversity of his students, he would realize that as stated, this goal excludes some. For example, Sophia's visual difficulties limit her ability to recognize visual content and to express herself on paper. Further, as specified, the task might not especially engage her.

By considering the UDL framework, Mr. Costa could keep the fundamental goal intact, but reframe it to accommodate different recognition, expression, and engagement networks in his class. He might modify the goal as follows: "Learn about culture in the United States by interviewing someone who emigrated to this country, *recording* the interview, and *collecting and presenting* information about your interviewee's home country and its culture." By removing specific mention of writing on paper, Mr. Costa gives his students more options. Sophia, for example, could collect her information through audiotape, read about her subject's homeland supported by digital text and text-to-speech software, and create an audiotape or a digital multimedia presentation in PowerPoint that could even include songs from both cultures.

As this example shows, with a diverse array of resources and a steady focus on the true goal, achieving flexibility in means and methods is relatively straightforward.

Using the UDL Framework to Individualize Scaffolds and Performance Criteria

Once a teacher has interpreted and refined the true purpose of a standard and reframed it as a classroom goal that allows for multiple methods, the next step is to set the level of challenge appropriately for individual students.

In order for learning to be successful, the performance criterion should relate to learners' particular recognition, strategic, and affective networks. If the demands on these networks are too great, students may become frustrated and are likely to learn little. On the other hand, a performance criterion that doesn't sufficiently tax these networks fails to provide the challenge necessary for growth. When students can complete tasks without thinking or working, boredom and disengagement are right around the corner. Vygotsky's (1962) concept of the zone of proximal development characterizes the ideal challenge as a level just beyond easy reach, but attainable with scaffolds or help from others. Faced with an insufficient challenge, students can complete a task without thinking or working; faced with too much challenge, students have little incentive to stay engaged.

Web Link

ACTIVITY:
For help using the UDL framework to derive teachable goals from curriculum standards, see the tutorial at *http://www.cast.org/ TeachingEveryStudent/ goals*

Research supports the positive effects of deep engagement that creates a sense of total involvement with a task. Csikszentmihalyi (1997) calls this state "flow" and explains that it's only possible when the level of challenge is just right:

> Flow tends to occur when a person's skills are fully involved in overcoming a challenge that is just about manageable. . . . When goals are clear, feedback relevant, and challenges and skills are in balance, attention becomes ordered and fully invested. Because of the total demand on psychic energy, a person in flow is completely focused. (pp. 30–31)

This state of flow is also noted by Malone (1981) in his studies of video games, in which the challenge escalates as players develop skill, so that they're always playing just above their current level of competence. The video game Lode Runner, for example, includes more than 100 levels, with each level slightly harder than the level beneath it. Mastery of one level opens the door to the next; the difference between successive levels is small, presenting a highly motivating challenge. This same kind of incremental challenge can foster engagement in the classroom. To adjust performance criteria appropriately, we should look to students' strengths and weaknesses in recognition and strategy, as well as their preferences.

So far, we have seen that deriving clear goals from standards requires teasing out the central purpose of a standard by separating the goal from the means for attaining it, restating the goal in a way that is attainable for all students, and then individualizing the pathways to the goal and performance criteria for measuring success. Let's see how one of our classroom example teachers might follow this process.

Setting "Universally Designed" Goals

Mr. Hernandez is faced with a new social studies standard calling for students to learn characteristics of the 50 states in the U.S. by studying one state in depth. The suggested benchmark for students at his grade level (6th grade) is that they be able to write seven paragraphs about that state. Mr. Hernandez's class includes one student designated as mildly mentally retarded, two brothers who recently arrived from Africa and speak very little English, a student who spends half of his day in a residential psychiatric institution, and two students with language-based learning disabilities (one of whom is Patrick).

To derive a clear goal from this standard that will be suitable for everyone in the class, Mr. Hernandez takes the following steps:

1. He identifies the standard's chief purpose. This one is designed to measure students' knowledge of specific content (U.S. states) and also their ability to carry out specific strategic processes: finding, organizing, and presenting information.

2. He derives a classroom goal that accommodates this focus: *"Students will collect and organize information about one state into a coherent presentation that must have some text but can also include images."*

3. He considers the barriers to recognition, strategy, and affect inherent in existing materials and tools and selects additional resources to help students overcome them. Because some of his students have difficulty reading printed text, he decides to make all textual resources available digitally and let students use software that reads the text aloud. He also provides materials at different reading levels.

4. He fashions the parameters of each student's assignment, the scaffolds available to each, and the performance criteria based on individual differences in recognition, strategy, and affect. For example:

• Students struggling with recognition barriers in traditional materials will use digital text materials with text-to-speech and collections of digital images, while those with recognition strengths will be encouraged to assemble their own resources.

• Students with strong writing skills will write a number of paragraphs about their state, with the option of including pictures and other media. Less adept writers will use on-screen templates to design presentations based primarily on pictures and sounds.

• Students who require greater challenge to get them engaged will be asked to create longer and more in-depth pieces and perhaps use a medium completely new to them. Students needing less challenge will be asked to create more modest pieces and will take advantage of templates and pre-assembled resources.

Although all Mr. Hernandez's students will be pursuing the same goal—researching, organizing, and presenting information about a state—the scaffolds and performance criteria are individualized for each student.

Communicating a Shared Understanding of Goals

In their work on teaching for understanding, Howard Gardner and the staff at Project Zero emphasize the importance of defining clear goals (which they call *throughlines*) and communicating them to students:

> Making these throughlines explicit for students helps to ensure that the students stay focused on developing the most essential understandings. By making such goals explicit for students, you give them the opportunity to monitor their own growth and the power to separate the relevant from the irrelevant, the useful work from the interesting-but-distracting work. (Blythe & Associates, 1998, p. 50)

Within a print-based curriculum, where the means to achieving learning goals are essentially the same for everyone (reading and writing), the need to articulate clear goals is less apparent than when multiple pathways are possible. However, in a UDL classroom, which offers diverse media, tools, and content, the need for clearly articulated goals is obvious. When students work with new tools and try new approaches, they need to know what they are trying to accomplish in order for the tools and approaches to have a positive impact on learning. Using a multimedia CD-ROM or the Internet just for the sake of using it won't help students progress. For students starting on the journey of developing skills with new tools and methods, knowing the destination is more important than ever.

Applying New Media to Support Clear and Appropriate Goals

CAST's research explores ways to build flexible scaffolds into learning tools and media so that diverse learners can *mindfully* pursue common goals. In CAST's eTrekker project, we developed a series of prototypes designed to support student inquiry and research on the Internet. The eTrekker prototype was conceived to help students with learning and organizational difficulties learn to search, evaluate, organize, and present information in the complex, distracting world of the Internet. Figure 5.2 illustrates one of the eTrekker prototype's designs, showing three functional regions on the main screen.

eTrekker is a step along the way toward developing a UDL tool that will help students keep their goals front-and-center and, at the same time, support varied recognition, strategic, and affective networks. The prototype shown is designed to help students define the goal of an Internet search before they get online. Once the student sets the goal, it will remain at the top of the screen throughout successive searches. In addition, eTrekker incorporates a variety of options that support students' differing pathways for learning.

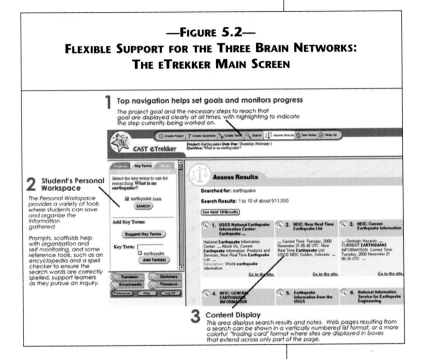

—**FIGURE 5.2**—
FLEXIBLE SUPPORT FOR THE THREE BRAIN NETWORKS: THE eTREKKER MAIN SCREEN

To support *multiple recognition pathways*, students can select

➤ A text or an image-based password.

➤ One of two formats for displaying search results.

➤ A text or speech presentation (listening via a screen reader or text-to-speech browser).

To support *multiple strategic pathways*, students can access

➤ Screen helps that divide the search process into visibly labeled and highlighted steps.

➤ A "breadcrumb trail" that records previous searches and results.

Finally, to support *multiple affective pathways*, students find

➤ A highly interactive digital environment.

➤ Open-ended choice of content.

➤ Playful language.

➤ Navigational landmarks.

➤ A simple, distraction-free layout.

How might teachers apply a tool like eTrekker in their classrooms?

eTrekker Application in the Classroom

Ms. Chen and Ms. Abrams have assigned a science research project with the following goal: *"Students will understand how to conduct inquiry-based research using a variety of source materials."* This is a process-oriented goal that allows for different content and media within the subject area of science. It requires students to make progress in the following strategic skills:

- Defining a research goal.
- Keeping that goal in mind throughout the project.
- Learning search strategies such as asking good questions, selecting key words, and finding relevant information.
- Monitoring their own progress.
- Finding sources of information.
- Evaluating the quality of information.
- Keeping track of information collected and returning easily to sources.
- Organizing and assembling the information into a meaningful presentation.

An electronic curriculum tool such as the eTrekker prototype can support these steps and processes by separating them in sequence, making them explicit, and providing scaffolds to reinforce student skills.

Ms. Chen's student, Charlie, and Ms. Abrams's student, Kamla, encounter different barriers when they begin this activity. Charlie has difficulty organizing and self-monitoring; he needs a lot of structure and direction during his search. Kamla is wary of text; she needs help staying engaged in the task and maintaining her confidence. Ms. Chen and Ms. Abrams could use eTrekker's inherent flexibility to provide individualized support to both Charlie and Kamla while each pursues the same goal.

eTrekker can provide the structure and direction Charlie needs in the form of

- An initial prompt to continue an old project or start a new one.
- A "Create Project" screen with a place to record important information (see Figure 5.3).
- Prompts guiding goal definition and expression.

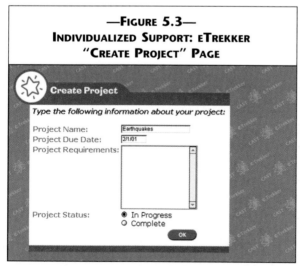

—FIGURE 5.3—
INDIVIDUALIZED SUPPORT: ETREKKER "CREATE PROJECT" PAGE

On this page, Charlie can create a project name and record important information, such as the due date and project requirements. This information helps him keep track of the purpose for his searches and the timetable of assignments. Charlie is further supported by prompts that remind him when he forgets to fill in all of the needed information.

- Step-by-step guides through the search process.
- A search term suggestion tool.
- Highlighted markers (status bars) at the top of the screen indicating the current stage of the search process (see Figure 5.4).
- A listing of search results by educational value.
- A note-taking tool.

With eTrekker, Kamla gets the supports she needs in the form of

- An alternative to the traditional textbook format.
- The option of a trading card search result display format (see Figure 5.5).
- A step-by-step structure that makes the search process less daunting.
- An automatic spell checker (see Figure 5.6).
- Screen reader compatibility that enables selected text to be read aloud.
- A dictionary, thesaurus, and encyclopedia.

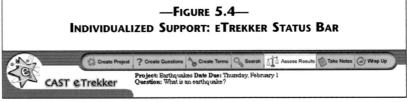

—FIGURE 5.4—
INDIVIDUALIZED SUPPORT: eTREKKER STATUS BAR

Wherever he is in the program, Charlie needs only to glance up at the top of the screen to be reminded of what project stage he's working on and what his project goal is.

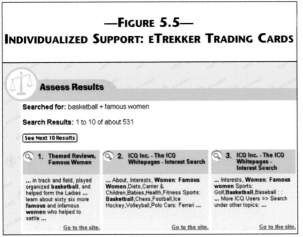

—FIGURE 5.5—
INDIVIDUALIZED SUPPORT: eTREKKER TRADING CARDS

Kamla can chose a "trading card" format for displaying the information she finds—tying the sports content to a sports format.

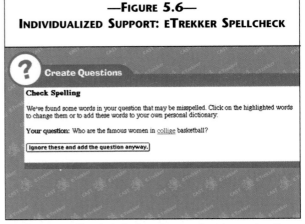

—FIGURE 5.6—
INDIVIDUALIZED SUPPORT: eTREKKER SPELLCHECK

Kamla gets spelling help before she searches, improving the likelihood of success.

Web Link

EXAMPLE:
Students benefit from a supported Internet search tool. See CAST's prototype at *http://www.cast.org/ TeachingEveryStudent/ search*

These classroom examples illustrate interactive media's potential to adjust to a variety of learners, providing the right degree of support and challenge. The eTrekker prototype typifies the promise of flexible, digital curriculum materials that will support multiple pathways to common goals, help teachers to individualize instruction and performance criteria, and ensure productive learning experiences for all students.

The Value of UDL in Goal Setting

When a goal is clear, our strategic networks can devise many different ways to reach it. For teachers, clear goals are the foundation for individualizing teaching. Goals specifying which aspects of instruction and assessment are central (and therefore, must be held constant) and which aspects are not central (and therefore, can be varied). Goals help students understand the true purpose of their efforts and what they need to do to make progress.

A common problem with current standards is that they are often stated too explicitly or confounded with the medium of presentation or expression—most often printed text. Broader, richer goals, such as helping students learn to think like historians or scientists, leave avenues open for the use of flexible tools and media capable of accommodating diverse learners.

The UDL framework provides a structure for reviewing and reinterpreting standards' fundamental purpose and deriving appropriate goals for individual students. Considering the three brain networks can help determine whether a goal is focused on information (recognition networks), on process (strategic networks), or on significance for students (affective networks). Of course, all learning requires the whole brain, and goals do cross boundaries, but thinking broadly in this way helps us understand and refine our priorities, making learning goals clearer for teachers *and* students.

With the goal stated clearly and separated from the methods, teachers can use flexible media to individualize means, scaffolds, and performance criteria to suit individual students' recognition, strategic, and affective networks. This variability helps teachers to focus the challenge at the right level and on the right content or skill targeted by the goal, freeing students from the confines of inappropriate media and materials.

➤ ➤ ➤ ➤ ➤

The next step in paving all students' path to high proficiency is to provide them with instruction that helps them achieve the goals. In the next chapter, we show how to use digital tools and materials—the heart of the UDL classroom—to individualize materials and methods.

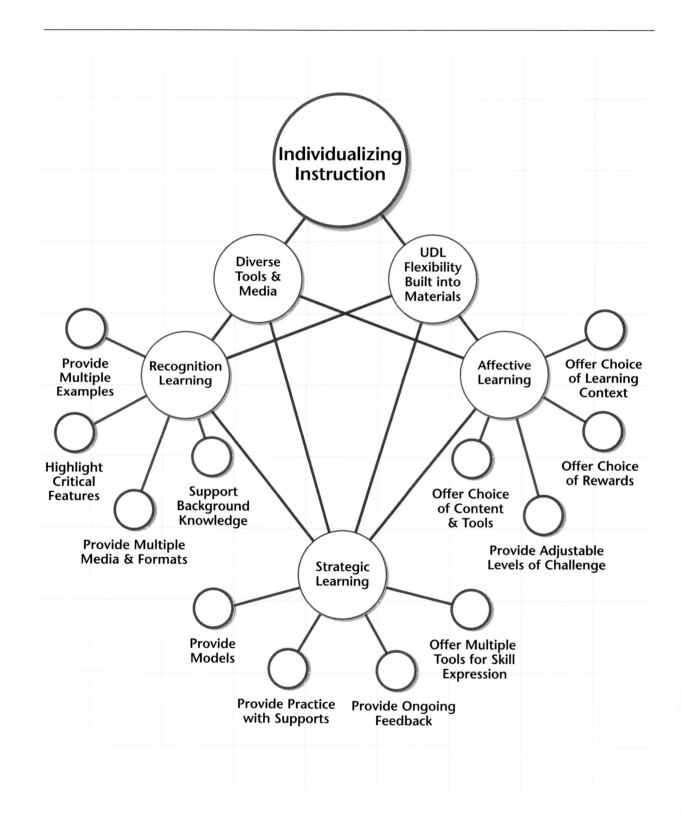

Using UDL to Support Every Student's Learning

6

In this chapter, you will see how UDL can help you provide each student with the appropriate instructional support and challenge.

KEY IDEAS

➤ Knowing how the three brain networks function suggests different approaches for teaching information (*what*), for teaching skills and strategies (*how*), and for teaching students to love learning (*why*).

➤ Individualizing the ways that students work toward goals is feasible if a variety of tools and media are available.

➤ Another approach to individualizing is to build flexibility directly into the curriculum, using embedded, flexible supports. CAST is researching and developing such responsive tools and materials.

A high school teacher stands at the blackboard, about to assign a chapter on the American Revolution from the district-required textbook. As she looks out over the class, she can predict which of her students will master the material and how each of them will perform on the test at the end of the chapter. She feels pessimistic about her ability to improve the achievement of her low-performing students. Considering the time and resources she has available, providing adequate support and differentiating it appropriately to individual needs, while at the same time teaching the content in a way that will stimulate her most prepared students, seems an insurmountable challenge.

Successful learning experiences challenge and support each learner appropriately *and* adjust as the learner changes over time. The goal of UDL is to provide every student this kind of customized and responsive experience. Establishing goals is the first step. The next step is to plan instruction so that students have multiple pathways for achieving their goals. How can you use the UDL framework to individualize methods, and how can UDL materials provide the support necessary to make this option feasible and practical?

In our discussion of standards, we noted that tasks can be classified according to the brain network they most engage. This leads to two important questions:

1. Which *methods* of teaching are most compatible with the ways that each brain network actually functions?

2. What kinds of flexibility must instructional *materials* have to make individualization work?

With clearly stated and well-communicated goals and the answers to these questions, you can use the UDL framework to individualize the path to learning.

Using UDL to Individualize Teaching Methods

Our understanding of learning and teaching is constantly reshaped by theory, applied research, and changing media. As our knowledge of the distributed processing in the brain grows, we know that students do not have one kind of intelligence or one way of learning—they have many. To accommodate these many ways of learning, we can use what we know about how each brain network operates to make our teaching methods and curriculum materials flexible in specific ways.

Certain instructional techniques are very effective in supporting students as they learn to recognize patterns; other techniques are better suited to supporting students as they learn strategic skills or as they build engagement with learning. We can accommodate diverse learners by using a repertoire of teaching strategies suited to each of the brain networks. Figure 6.1 lists the critical guidelines.

—FIGURE 6.1—
NETWORK-APPROPRIATE TEACHING METHODS

To support students' diverse recognition networks:
- Provide multiple examples
- Highlight critical features
- Provide multiple media and formats
- Support background context.

To support students' diverse strategic networks:
- Provide flexible models of skilled performance
- Provide opportunities to practice with supports
- Provide ongoing, relevant feedback
- Offer flexible opportunities for demonstrating skill.

To support students' diverse affective networks:
- Offer choices of content and tools
- Offer adjustable levels of challenge
- Offer choices of rewards
- Offer choices of learning context.

Making Individualization Work with Flexible Media and Tools

Teaching through these varied paths would be daunting or perhaps even impossible if our instructional tools were restricted to print materials alone. Analyzing the potential barrier inherent in current curriculum materials can help us plan for the additional media and tools we will need in order to reach all students. **UDL Classroom Template 2**, available in the Appendix (p. 184) and online, provides a structure for analyzing these barriers in light of particular learning goals and students' learning profiles.

Once you have an understanding of the barriers to learning posed by available materials, you can investigate the digital media and networks available to support differentiated teaching approaches. The growing collection of adjustable software tools, digital content, and World Wide Web resources includes

Web Link

CLASSROOM TEMPLATE:
The **Curriculum Barriers Template** helps you identify potential barriers to learning in materials and methods.
Link to it at
http://www.cast.org/ TeachingEveryStudent/ barriers

➤ Multimedia composition tools such as HyperStudio, Kid Pix, and PowerPoint.

➤ Web-capable electronic graphic organizers (see Figure 6.2) such as Inspiration and Kidspiration.

➤ Programs that support the translation of content from one medium to another (e.g., text-to-speech and text-to-image) such as CAST eReader, Pix Reader, Pix Writer, and Intellitalk II.

In many schools around the nation, teachers are finding that collections of digital tools and resources such as these expand their options for presenting information, scaffolding students, and offering choices for student expression.

—**FIGURE 6.2—**
A WEB-CAPABLE ELECTRONIC ORGANIZER

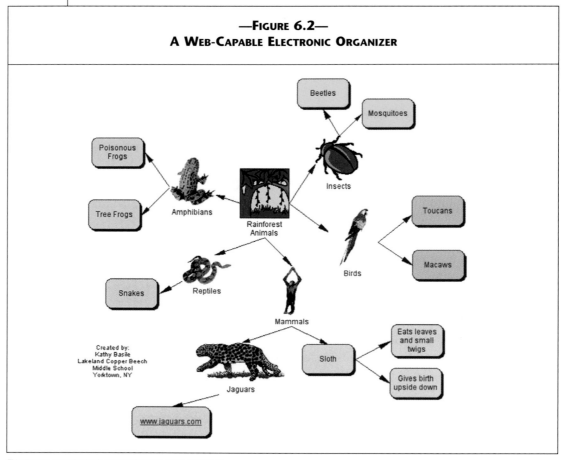

This diagram created using Inspiration Software by Inspiration®, Inc.

In the following sections, we consider the kinds of learning each of the three brain networks specializes in and recommend corresponding UDL-based teaching methods and uses of digital media. We then present more classroom examples to demonstrate how you might apply these methods and materials.

Designing Instruction to Support Recognition Learning

Through education, we convey a vast array of patterns valued by our culture. Although our recognition networks are very efficient, patterns such as alphabetic symbols, the format for writing a research paper, scientific and mathematical theories, and geographical or geological facts require specific study. Because students aren't all on equal footing when it comes to recognizing such patterns, teachers need to provide differentiated instruction. Let's examine how applying insights into recognition networks and new technologies can help us succeed.

Teaching Method 1: Provide Multiple Examples

To learn the key characteristics that define a pattern, whether that pattern be the letter *A*, the structure of a sonnet, or a concept such as *justice* or *sarcasm,* recognition networks need exposure to multiple examples. By seeing, hearing, smelling, or touching many instances of a pattern, recognition networks can extract the critical features that define that pattern and identify new instances that share those features. Thus, exposure to multiple examples supports bottom-up recognition processes.

For example, suppose we tell you that this symbol (~) is a wug. If we then ask you whether this symbol (-) is also a wug, you will have trouble deciding. The second symbol is horizontal like a wug, but shorter, and it's straight instead of wavy. Is it a wug? You don't have enough information to judge.

But if we now show you these examples and tell you that they are also wugs (~, -, _), you can begin to derive the features that define "wugness." You might hypothesize that wugs are horizontal symbols and decide that it doesn't matter whether they are long or short, wavy or straight, or where they are located in space. If we then offer the following counter-examples of things that are *not* wugs (/ and [ ), your hypothesis

Web Link

EXAMPLE:
Computer software offers new opportunities for individualized instruction. A teacher explains how at *http://www.cast.org/ TeachingEveryStudent/ instruction*

is supported. The more examples and counter-examples you see, the more clearly you understand the essence of wugness.

Much of the art of teaching patterns lies in selecting and presenting numerous, effective examples. Digital media and tools can facilitate finding and presenting these examples in the form of text, image, sound, or video. Unlike a printed textbook, in which the examples are limited in number and selected by the publisher, the array of materials available in digital form (online and on multimedia disks) lets us build expansive collections of examples suited to our instructional needs and the needs of our students. These digital resources can be saved and shared from class to class and from year to year. Additionally, because students can edit and manipulate digital materials, they can learn about patterns by interacting with and changing them. Thus, the flexible nature of digital media expands teachers' ability to collect many varied examples that are personally and topically relevant and provides new ways for students to interact with those examples.

Teaching Method 2: Highlight Critical Features

Left to their own devices, recognition networks exposed to multiple examples derive key features and identify patterns. But this is laborious work, and students have much to learn. Good teachers make this process easier by highlighting the critical features of a pattern as a way of directing students' learning.

For example, students of architectural history know that Federal-style buildings may share certain key characteristics, including a central hall plan, stone lintels over windows, a fanlight over the front door, and a Palladian window centrally located on the second story. By viewing enough examples, and some counter-examples for contrast, students can learn to extract the critical features that define the Federal style. But teachers can make the process more efficient by explicitly identifying the critical features in the examples they present. Traditionally, they do this by pointing out these key features in a photographs or a drawing (see Figure 6.3). Bruner and his colleagues (Wood, Bruner, & Ross, 1976) long ago described this "marking of critical features" as one of the key ways to scaffold learning in the tutorial context. Good teaching includes much of this kind of bottom-up scaffolding.

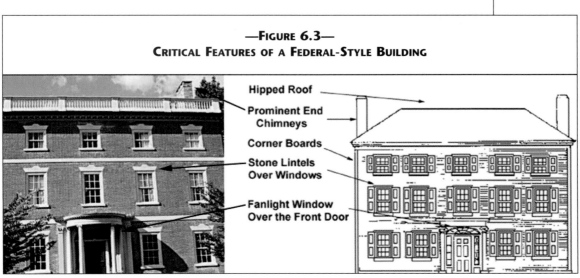

—FIGURE 6.3—
CRITICAL FEATURES OF A FEDERAL-STYLE BUILDING

Image reprinted with permission from *The Salem Handbook, A Renovation Guide for Homeowners.* (1977). Salem, MA: Historic Salem, Inc.

Teachers also highlight critical features when they speak—using pitch, volume, pauses, intonation, pointing, gesturing, and facial expressions. In text, conventions such as italics, bold-faced type, font size, and color highlighting can draw learners' attention to the most important parts. But conventional marking methods—whether visual or auditory—will not work for everyone: textual cues only help those facile with text, spoken words are gone after class, and neither medium may be optimal for working with some kinds of patterns, such as musical themes or geographical features.

Digital media and tools offer teachers a wider variety of ways to highlight key features. Animations, color highlighting, graphic elements that add emphasis, and the capacity to "zoom in" on photographic images are just a few examples. We can also overlay text and images onto video to emphasize particular elements of content. Even more significant for individualizing, with the flexibility of digital tools, we can select different sets of highlighting options for different learners and show or hide these scaffolds depending on the student and his or her particular stage of learning.

Teaching Method 3:
Provide Multiple Media and Formats

Because learners' recognition networks have varying abilities to process visual, aural, olfactory, or tactile patterns, a single means of presentation doesn't work for all students. In the case of the wugs, we presented all examples visually, with textual commentary—an effective format for those able to perceive the marks and decode the words. Presenting the examples through speech alone would provide someone with visual problems access to this information, but would then exclude learners with hearing or language processing disorders.

Providing multiple representations of patterns through a variety of media, formats, organizations, levels of detail, and degree of depth includes more learners by offering both choice and redundancy. Choice enables those with disabilities affecting a particular modality to access the information via another one. It also enables students to find the format or medium that appeals to and works *best* for them—increasing their access to learning. Redundancy offers opportunities to discern patterns in a variety of ways, thereby increasing the understanding about what matters in the pattern. In the words of Howard Gardner, "The best representations are multiple. And so our search should be for the family of representations that can convey core ideas in a multiplicity of ways at once accurate and complementary" (1999, p. 202). Research has shown that teaching in multiple modalities (a technique sometimes called *transmediation*) not only increases access for students with difficulties but also improves learning generally among all students (Siegil, 1995).

Presenting information in multiple formats and media is perhaps the most researched facet of UDL. This is partly because access standards developed for building design have extended into the world of information design. International standards for Web site design specify exactly how to represent information in multiple media for maximum access and usability. With increasing frequency, the kinds of standards and practices that emerged out of the need for access are being applied to educational materials. In fact, citing the need for flexible presentation to serve the learning needs of all students, Florida's 2001–2002 Instructional Materials Specifications for Reading, Grades K–12 and California's Criteria for 2002 Language Arts Adoption call for "universal design" and "universal access" respectively.

Web Link

RESOURCE:
Find guidelines and policies pertaining to access at
http://www.cast.org/ TeachingEveryStudent/ guidelines

The multiple representations that fulfill access requirements are a step in the right direction. But evaluating the suitability of materials or Web sites to support UDL-based teaching requires us to consider a broader set of questions. It's important to evaluate all materials in light of learning goals, the nature of the information, and the characteristics of learners. Do the multiple representations suit the content? Do they tie closely to instructional goals? For example, students studying the impact of interest rate changes on the broader economy could learn about this topic by reading text, hearing a lecture, or viewing images representing that relationship. However, a manipulable, animated graph that dynamically links changes in interest rates to changes in other economic indicators would be a more effective way to explore these interactions. Fortunately, it is becoming easier to find suitable digital materials tied to standards and goals, thanks to ever-increasing online collections of digital resources, which provide high-quality materials ready to integrate into curriculum.

Teaching Method 4:
Support Background Knowledge

When we learn, we incorporate new knowledge into old knowledge. In neural network terms, new learning is integrated into networks that have been shaped by previous learning. Consequently, what the brain already knows can influence what it will learn from a new example or experience.

Of course, as in all other arenas, students differ significantly in the background knowledge they bring to a new situation. For example, those who have learned to recognize several letters of the alphabet learn more readily to recognize a new letter than those who haven't yet mastered their first. Students who have studied other architectural periods and have learned to seek distinguishing architectural elements learn to identify Federal-style buildings more readily than novices to the discipline. And learners who have developed and can articulate an understanding of fair play and mutuality are better prepared to learn about the nature of justice than those who have never learned about these abstract concepts.

Teachers help students tie their background knowledge to new patterns (a top-down recognition process) and help fill in gaps by providing

Web Link

RESOURCE:
Access technology resources, articles, and chapters from Donald Leu and Deborah Diadiun Leu's essential *Teaching with the Internet* at *http://www.sp.uconn. edu/~djleu/third.html*

related information. Some of the familiar ways of doing this are by asking students to reflect on their own experiences that relate to reading material, reviewing key vocabulary prior to reading assignments, and directing students to relevant additional materials.

Digital materials provide an ideal vehicle for supporting background knowledge because they are flexible and because they can be linked to other information resources such as those on the Web. In this context, students can access background knowledge if and when they need to, on their own schedule. Further, digital background supports can be provided in multiple media.

For example, CAST's Universal Learning Edition prototype (see page 171) of Ambrose Bierce's Civil War short story *Occurrence at Owl Creek Bridge* contains links to an online glossary with text, graphics, and video to illustrate unfamiliar vocabulary. It also contains links to a timeline of Civil War events; links to related Web pages; explanations of unfamiliar idioms and language use; a translator to other languages; and links to information about the author and the actual incident upon which the story is based.

Good teachers already practice the four techniques we've described for teaching recognition:

1. Providing multiple examples.
2. Highlighting critical features.
3. Providing multiple media and formats.
4. Supporting background knowledge.

But individualizing these techniques so that each learner finds suitable presentations and supports is nearly impossible without digital content and flexible learning tools. With such resources, teachers can provide diverse pathways to recognition learning and meet the diverse needs of their students. Let's see how Ms. Sablan is doing this in her classroom, with a particular focus on Paula.

Web Link

EXAMPLE:
CAST demonstrates the potential of embedded instructional supports in its Universal Learning Edition prototypes. See an example at *http://www.cast.org/ TeachingEveryStudent/ supports*

Supporting Recognition Learning with UDL

Ms. Sablan has set the following language arts goal for her 3rd graders: *"Students will organize information sequentially from stories and pictures."* To achieve this goal, Paula and her classmates must be able to recognize a story's major structural elements (beginning, middle, and end). This is will be a challenge for Paula, whose reading comprehension is poor.

Because she wants Paula and her peers to focus on story structure, not story content, Ms. Sablan chooses a familiar and popular story, "The Three Little Pigs." She collects three printed versions, including Jon Scieszka's humorous tale told from the wolf's point of the view (see Figure 6.4), two digital versions downloaded from the Web, and a CD-ROM version from Reader Rabbit's Reading Development Library (see Figure 6.5).

The downloaded digital versions provide reading support, further helping to focus the challenge on the learning goal by scaffolding decoding. The CD-ROM provides several versions of the story, including narrations from the perspective of each pig and the wolf. And even more germane to Ms. Sablan's goal, this program uses animation to highlight sentence meaning. As the two screenshots in Figures 6.6 suggest, when a student selects each sentence, the animated characters onscreen perform the action the sentence describes. Because the program scaffolds text-meaning connections in larger chunks than individual words, it helps Paula focus on the meaning of connected text.

Together, the multiple versions of "The Three Little Pigs"—with their varied wording, illustrations, formats, and narrators—provide multiple examples of beginning, middle, and end, helping the students build an implicit understanding of the central features of these structural components. Ms. Sablan reinforces this understanding (and helps students focus attention on these critical

—FIGURE 6.4—
AN ALTERNATE REPRESENTATION OF A FAMILIAR STORY

"Cover" by Lane Smith, Copyright © 1989 by Lane Smith, illustrations, from *The True Story of the Three Little Pigs* by Jon Scieszka, illustrated by Lane Smith. Used by permission of Viking Penguin, an imprint of Penguin Putnam Books for Young Readers, a division of Penguin Putnam Inc.

—FIGURE 6.5—
A DIGITAL ALTERNATIVE WITH SUPPORTS

narrative patterns) by using the eReader high-lighter tool to color-code the beginning, middle, and end of the digital versions of the story. Then, with HyperStudio, she creates a three-page template with color-coded borders, labeled *Beginning, Middle,* and *End.* After reading the stories several times, Paula uses the computer microphone to record her voice as she retells the key segments of the story, then draws images on each page of the template and presents her summary to the class.

By providing the story itself through print, digital text, digital images, and animation, Ms. Sablan can offer multiple media and formats without having to invest a lot of money or time. Finally, because she has used this story with her class before, she knows that everyone shares the necessary background knowledge, enabling them to focus on the goal of the lesson: understanding story structures.

—FIGURE 6.6—
A MULTIMEDIA SCAFFOLD FOR SENTENCE MEANING

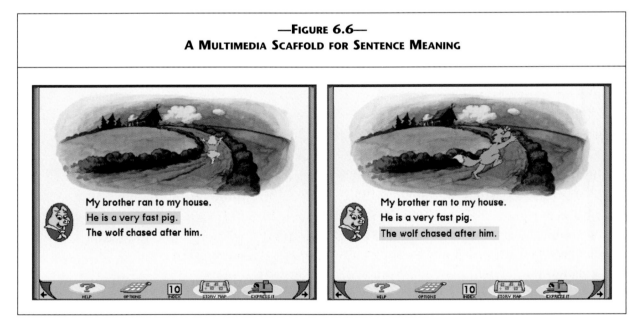

Designing Instruction to Support Strategic Learning

Different learners aiming for the same goal generate different plans and steps for getting there. Because individuals have their own optimal pathways for learning strategic skills, teaching approaches and tools need to be varied. Based on our knowledge of how strategic networks function, we can recommend the following teaching methods to support strategic learning.

Teaching Method 1: Provide Flexible Models of Skilled Performance

Learning to *generate* patterns (*how* to do something) requires developing a mental model of the pattern in question. Developing internal models requires exposure to external models of expert performance and to counter-examples that demonstrate incorrect execution.

Consider learning to play tennis—and for the sake of this example, just learning how to serve. Before the aspiring tennis player can serve well, she must first have a mental model of skilled serving. What does the complete stroke look like when an expert does it? Where must the ball land to be counted "in"? What are the most effective placements and bounces for making the serve difficult to return? Important counter-examples include what a poor serve looks like and what kinds of mistakes contribute to one.

Teachers can present models of processes in a variety of contexts (as one-on-one instruction, in small groups or as a whole class, live or at a distance, online or in person), using a variety of media (video, speech, text, diagram, animation). Exposure to multiple models showing different, effective ways to do something helps learners distill the critical features of a process, different ways it can be accomplished, and where the opportunities exist to inject their own creative means to that end. Think again of Dick Fosbury, who identified the critical features of high jumping and then developed his own new approach for getting over the bar. Or to stick with our tennis example, consider Arthur Ashe, who revolutionized the backhand with an idiosyncratic, powerful, two-handed stroke.

Digital tools and media can extend teachers' ability to present multiple models for strategic teaching. Using the World Wide Web or a local network, we can collect models over time, link these models to a home page, and offer students an increasing array of choices including examples of completed work, steps in a process, demonstrations of skilled execution, or connections to experts willing to share the way they work. We can provide these models in a variety of media to make them accessible and useful for diverse sets of students.

Teaching Method 2: Provide Opportunities to Practice with Supports

To achieve complex strategic goals like playing tennis, driving a car, or writing a research paper, a learner must *automatize*, or over-learn, the individual steps in the process until each is automatic. Only when the subcomponents come automatically can a tennis player concentrate on game strategy, a driver concentrate on destination and route, and a student concentrate on the style and clarity of the research paper. This requires extensive practice.

Because complex strategic patterns are impossible to learn all at once, teachers usually direct students to practice individual subcomponents of the process. But we also know that practicing skills in context is more effective than practicing skills in isolation. To support contextual practice, teachers can scaffold some parts of the process so that learners can focus on strengthening their abilities in other parts. Scaffolds reduce the degrees of freedom in order to focus the learning in specific areas. Examples include the training wheels or parental hand on the back of the bicycle that supports a beginning bike rider's balance; the passenger-side steering wheel a driving instructor can use to monitor a new driver's steering; and a tennis instructor's practice of guiding the arms of the novice server through the motion of the overhead stroke.

Electronic media are ideal for providing scaffolds in the context of learning. Features such as text-to-speech "translation" supports decoding so that learners can focus on strategic reading or content learning; spell checkers support mechanics so that learners can focus on expressing their ideas and improving their writing fluency; built-in calculators scaffold math facts so that learners can focus on mathematical reasoning. Ideally, scaffolds should be optional and assignable to individual students, the better to accommodate individual progress and differences between learners.

Teaching Method 3:
Provide Ongoing, Relevant Feedback

Delivering ongoing, relevant feedback is critical when teaching skills. Learners need to know if they are practicing effectively, and if not, which aspects of the practice process they need to change. If the ball is repeatedly hitting the net, the novice server knows that something is wrong—but what? Is the toss too low? Is the swing too late? Is the step forward too large? Without feedback, the learner doesn't even know if these are the right questions to ask!

Feedback can come in many forms. The aspiring tennis player can watch a video of herself, listen to her coach's observations, watch a demonstration of what she is doing versus the correct approach, or read a write-up of her game in the newspaper. And it is important to point out that feedback is most effective when it is provided in an ongoing fashion—supporting course corrections and building learners' confidence about things that are going well. But even students fortunate enough to have one-to-one instruction don't have their teachers around during every practice session. Thus, helping learners develop self-monitoring skills may be the very best way to ensure ongoing feedback for all practice.

Software tools and digital networks can be an excellent source of ongoing feedback, particularly if students are shown how to take advantage of everything these tools offer. A tool as simple as text-to-speech embedded in a word processor enables students to hear how their writing sounds when read aloud and then to revise as they work. Software programs designed to develop skills such as typing or arithmetic routinely offer specific feedback about performance as students work. And online connections to mentors and peers offer students the chance to seek comments from others outside the classroom.

Teaching Method 4:
Offer Flexible Opportunities for Demonstrating Skill

Another essential part of teaching a strategic skill is providing learners with chances to demonstrate that skill. Demonstration challenges learners to consolidate and apply all parts of the process. It also elicits feedback from a broader audience. The budding pianist performs in recitals; the student gives an oral presentation, displays a poster, or shares a written paper. In this way, demonstrating skills and knowledge can factor powerfully into motivation, helping learners experience the "why" of learning.

Digital media offer widely varied supports and opportunities to help students demonstrate knowledge and skills. Publishing on the World Wide Web or on a class home page invites feedback from an expansive audience and can provide a sense of accomplishment. Presentation tools such as HyperStudio and PowerPoint provide templates and tools for incorporating multiple media and for structuring presentations. Desktop publishing software helps students incorporate images and lay out printed work in a professional manner

In sum, approaches for teaching skills must be flexible and must reflect the way strategic networks learn. As Dick Fosbury and Arthur Ashe demonstrated, there are many ways to skin the strategic cat, and providing options opens the door to creativity and success for diverse learners. By assembling digital content, multimedia software, and Internet resources, teachers can build a collection of options that makes individualization feasible. These resources allow us to vary the media, models, supports, and feedback we offer to our students. To illustrate, let's turn once again to a classroom example.

Supporting Strategic Learning with UDL

Let's imagine Ms. Chen's 5th grade class includes Charlie (the student who has difficulty self-monitoring and staying on task), Jamal (who has good strategic planning skills and a motor disability), and Patrick (who has language-based learning disabilities). Ms. Chen has set the following goal: *"Students will demonstrate competence in the general skills and strategies of the writing process."* Although several of her students have difficulty with text, she keeps the goal focused on writing because she knows that written literacy is critical as her students move on to 6th grade. She also knows that the UDL framework will help her individualize the instruction she provides. Ms. Chen reviews the teaching methods most helpful for strategic learning and considers the multimedia, networked tools, and scaffolds she might use to foster success for all her students.

Concentrating on the skill of writing narratives, Ms. Chen encourages her students to select story subjects they find interesting. To help them envision the stories they will be creating, she provides many models of fiction and nonfiction stories in text, sound, video, and image form. She builds a classroom story collection of printed books, tapes, and videos and uses Inspiration software to create a story home page, with links to a library of digital stories—including some written by former students and some that she has found on the Web. The software also allows her to group these stories into different categories, such as fiction and nonfiction, and even further, into narrative genres such as detective stories, fables, and adventures.

Ms. Chen reads many of these stories aloud for and with her students, leading discussions of what students liked and didn't like and highlighting story elements. She also collects models that call attention to story structures and the writing process, including "famous first drafts" that illustrate the heavily revised beginnings of some well-known works. The story home page provides links to author-focused Web sites so that students can learn from the insights of professional writers who model their working process.

By providing so many different kinds of models, varying in content, medium, and context, Ms. Chen ensures that everyone will find appropriate models to emulate as they begin to develop their own narratives.

All of Ms. Chen's students need to practice at their own level of challenge. To support students at different stages of proficiency, she provides scaffolds such as multimedia story templates, a variety of "clip" media, drawing tools, and tools they can use to digitize images they bring from home or even their own voices. Students who have trouble generating text often begin by creating a series of images or recorded sounds to help them develop their plot and characters; with this foundation, they usually find that text flows more easily. Because this particular learning goal is focused on the writing process, Ms. Chen also encourages students to use scaffolds like spell checkers when editing their work.

Ms. Chen is familiar with the work of Lynne Anderson-Inman and her colleagues at the University of Oregon showing that diverse students benefit from working with graphic organizer software like Inspiration and Kidspiration (Anderson-Inman & Horney, 1996/97). She teaches her students to use these tools, knowing that visualizing story elements as interconnected geometric shapes will help them plan their stories structurally.

Different students in the class rely on scaffolds according to their needs:

• To support Jamal in focusing and condensing his lengthy story, Ms. Chen encourages him to strip it down to its main elements using Inspiration.

• To get Charlie "unstuck" when he can't select a topic, Ms. Chen gives him a deadline, provides him with some rubrics for choosing a topic, and writes out a concrete schedule of steps, each with a mini-deadline.

• To help Patrick through his anxiety about producing text, Ms. Chen provides a multi-media story template and helps him scan in pictures of his favorite baseball player. The series of pictures will form the structure for his story.

To generate ongoing feedback and build students' self-monitoring capabilities, Ms. Chen encourages them to exchange drafts and review each other's work within a structured format that includes constructive suggestions. She also encourages students to use e-mail to solicit opinions from each other and from outside experts. For students who are ready, she suggests submitting drafts to Web sites where they can obtain outside reactions, including the *Stone Soup* site (http://ww.stonesoup.com), which posts student work. Such online connections extend her ability to help students obtain regular, ongoing feedback from a variety of sources.

Ms. Chen also helps her students build their self-monitoring skills by encouraging them to compare their work to external models and compare their drafts to their mental models of their stories. Using a digital microphone, students record themselves telling their stories. Next, they write the text of the story in a word processor and use text-to-speech to listen to how what they've written sounds when read out loud. Comparing the recorded "target" stories with the way their written stories sound provides a supported context for self-monitoring.

To meet the writing standard, Ms. Chen's students need to produce their final story in text. But she encourages them to use other media, supporting alternative modes of expression and skill demonstration in conjunction with text (see Gardner, 1993; Sizer, 1992a, 1992b). Ms. Chen provides a variety of multimedia tools including word processors, HyperStudio, digitizing software, and publishing programs. With these tools, the students enhance the text they produce with images, sounds, and animations. Some students produce artwork on paper or in clay to go along with their stories. By encouraging these diverse expressive pathways, Ms. Chen helps all students reach the text-based goal.

Rich resources and tools enable teachers to diversify strategy instruction. By combining traditional tools, multimedia, and networked resources, teachers can provide every student with customized models, expressive options, supports, and feedback. These options give diverse learners a much better chance to succeed.

Designing Instruction to Support Affective Learning

Affect is the fuel that students bring to the classroom, connecting them to the "why" of learning. The work of Goleman (1995) shares the UDL perspective that motivation is at least as important for school success as the capacity to recognize and generate patterns. Affect goes beyond simple enjoyment, and among other things, it plays a part in the development of persistence and deep interest in a subject. If we emphasize skills and knowledge to the exclusion of emotion, we may breed negative feelings towards learning, especially in students having difficulties. Were we to focus on affect more explicitly in our learning goals, we might be more successful at one of the most important tasks for teachers—developing students who love to learn.

Theodore Sizer (1992a, 1992b), Grant Wiggins (1989), Heidi Hayes Jacobs (1997), and Jacqueline Grennon Brooks and Martin Brooks (1993) are among the many authors who advocate making important and engaging questions central to learning. Their recommendations underscore the importance of connecting learning to students' own lives and interests and giving students choices of content, methods, and materials whenever feasible.

Giving students the flexibility to pursue their interests is an extremely successful teaching technique—and one that can be achieved without sacrificing learning objectives (Hayes Jacobs, 1997). For example, a teacher might relate a unit focusing on the U.S. Bill of Rights to the school's student handbook, thus connecting a distant, abstract subject to students' personal concerns and experiences.

This kind of "hook" makes school subjects more interesting and engaging. But no one hook will work for every student. Over the course of development, unique individuals' constitutions and experiences intermix to create their affective profiles—a combination of what attracts, motivates, and engages them. These differences partially explain why print materials and lectures suit some learners, but leave others yawning. Based on what we know about how affective networks function, which teaching methods are the most effective for reaching diverse learners?

Teaching Method 1:
Offer Choices of Content and Tools

Certain activities are widely appealing—listening to music, watching movies, or getting outdoors. However, few of us love *all* music, movies, and outdoor activities. We are selective in our taste, and, for example, might even prefer silence to music we dislike. In other words, we don't like concerts in general; we like them "in specific."

Giving students choices of content and tools can increase their enthusiasm for learning particular processes. For example, mastering the skill of long division in the abstract may seem uninteresting, but learning to calculate batting averages can be exciting. When affective engagement links background knowledge with strategic or recognition tasks, students are more likely to build skills, sustained interest, and deep understanding. They are also more likely to pursue the extended practice needed for automatization. How can teachers provide content appealing to each of their students? Digital media and materials can offer the needed flexibility.

A staggering array of digital content is available on compact disc and on the Internet. With these kinds of resources at teachers' disposal, creating innovative ways of engaging learners in anything from long division to historical analysis is relatively easy to do. Students might take a QuickTime 3D tour of a pyramid (http://www.pbs.org/wgbh/nova/pyramid/) or learn about the physics behind skateboarding and basketball (http://www.exploratorium.edu/sports/index.html). Through online "WebQuests" they might learn about Ancient Rome from the perspective of a chosen Roman figure—a senator, a child, an Olympian, or a historian (http://www.richmond.edu/~ed344/webquests/rome/frames.html).

Software programs also offer an array of engaging options. Write, Camera, Action! (description at http://www.worldvillage.com/wv/school/html/reviews/write.htm) lets users take on the role of movie producer, developing key writing and language skills in the process. Students who find affective barriers in textbooks or lectures can explore scientific principles through virtual simulations online (see http://www.hazelwood.k12.mo.us/~grichert/sciweb/applets.html). The online game Secrets@Sea (http://www.secretsatsea.org) offers students the opportunity to learn about biology by acting as the detective in an interactive mystery.

At CAST, we have found that working with multimedia and the World Wide Web can break the cycle of discouragement and re-engage learners who are stressed by or indifferent to conventional learning media. We have seen students with writing disabilities use sound or images to develop the key elements of a composition and then spend the next 45 minutes enthusiastically writing text. Enjoyment and competence fuel students' motivation to learn. Suitable programs include Paint, Write and Play; Write, Camera, Action!; HyperStudio; and Kid Pix. In addition, more and more Web sites are dedicated to providing varied content and tools for instruction. The Web site for this book includes an expanding set of online resources for obtaining digital content and tools that fit with a variety of curricula, are easily accessible, and are flexibly presented.

Teaching Method 2:
Provide Adjustable Levels of Challenge

We know that students learn best in their "zone of proximal development" (Vygotsky, 1962), where challenge is just beyond their current capacity but not out of reach. Students' comfort zones—the level of difficulty, challenge, and frustration optimal for them—vary considerably. Teachers who hope to sustain students' engagement must be able to continually adjust the challenge for and among different learners.

Although learning software is not as tightly calibrated as the best electronic games, most products do offer adjustable levels of challenge. For example, 7th Level's Great Math Adventure (description at http://www.worldvillage.com/wv/school/html/reviews/mathadv.htm) offers a variety of math problems and games with five different skill levels. Many of the learning games from Edmark, such as Let's Go Read! An Island Adventure, offer sophisticated management systems that enable teachers to select difficulty levels and specific content for individual students.

Adjustable levels of challenge have advantages beyond the immediate power to engage. Providing such choices for students makes the process of goal-setting explicit and provides a structured opportunity for students to practice setting realistic goals and optimal challenges for themselves. Discovering the consequences of setting goals that are too high or too low helps students develop the meta-skills they need for independent learning. Students with ADHD and other problems with strategic skills,

Web Link

RESOURCE:
Find tips and tutorials on how to obtain digital text and multimedia materials and put them to work in your classroom at *http://www.cast.org/ TeachingEveryStudent/ digitaltext*

who often have difficulty setting appropriate goals, can benefit from practice and experience in a supportive learning context.

Teaching Method 3: Offer a Choice of Rewards

A common way to motivate students is to provide external rewards and punishments. These include deferred rewards like grades, concrete rewards like stickers or money, increased or decreased privileges like recess and field trips, and social rewards like affection and attention.

There are two problems with this practice. First, each student has different ideas about what is or is not a reward. A trip to the ballet, for example, might be a reward to one student and a punishment to another! Fear of punishment (or failure) spurs some students to work hard, but may discourage or frighten others. A true UDL environment solves this problem by offering students choices of rewards—effectively leveling the affective playing field.

Second, external rewards tend to be inappropriate and ineffective in motivating learning over the long term. Research shows that extrinsic rewards can result in unintended negative consequences for learning, such as "turning play into work" (Lepper & Greene, 1978). The answer might be to look a little more closely at play. Most highly motivating video games give no external rewards at all; rather, the motivation they provide comes in the form of immediate feedback and knowledge of results. Building students' meta-awareness of accomplishment and progress—an important tenet of UDL—may be one of the most effective ways to instill intrinsic interest in learning and support students' long-term engagement.

Teaching Method 4: Offer a Choice of Learning Context

Many of us can remember the months of haggling that preceded the Fischer-Spassky world championship chess matches. The combatants negotiated intensely—not only about the geographic location (finally ending up in "neutral" Iceland), but also about virtually every aspect of the setting: the lighting, the size of the room, the placement of the table and chairs, the soundproofing, and the camera locations. These seemingly irrelevant details were crucial to Fischer and Spassky because they understood how important small details of *context* might be in chess matches that would last for months.

The importance of context extends beyond cerebral contests like chess matches. Think about home-court advantages in sports. In basketball, for example, even though the basket is the same height, size, and color on every court, odds makers always assume that members of the home team will be more adept than their visiting opponents at getting the ball through the basket. Although the physical components of shooting a basket are the same at home and away, the knowledge that friends and family fill the gym and the supportive roar of the crowd can activate greater affect and success. These effects of home-court advantage can be attributed to the broad connectedness of our neural networks—almost any aspect of the environment is included when we learn.

In the classroom, factors such as noise and activity in a room or structure in a task contribute to the learning context students experience. By choosing to present a task as an independent in-class assignment or as homework or as a small- or large-group discussion, teachers may inadvertently lend "intellectual home-court advantage" to certain students who are more comfortable in those learning contexts.

Consider this example: One of us has a son named Nick who, as a high school student, drove his parents crazy by doing all his studying with radio, television, computer, or CD player blaring. (Most aggravating were the times when all four devices were on at once and competing for the highest decibel level!) To Nick's parents this seemed lunacy—an impossible context for learning. But for Nick, the amount of background noise was just right. This cacophony followed him as he became a National Merit Scholar and a Harvard graduate.

Context preferences are individual. An optimal context for one student is not necessarily optimal for another. Some students like to explore ideas and create their own individual approaches. Others would be paralyzed by that degree of freedom. One student might prefer to create a story or painting with minimal direction, whereas another would be unable to start unless provided with a topic and some initial, short-term goals. By offering students a selection of materials from which to choose, each with varying degrees of structure, we can offer *all* students an appropriate learning context. As an example, The Great Math Adventure provides adjustable supports and an optional interactive, animated helper—

allowing students to chose between figuring things out on their own or having their learning experience structured externally. Teacher-designed WebQuests can be individually tailored to a student's structural preferences. For students who like many signposts, we might preselect sites that contain the sought-after information. For students who prefer to locate information on their own, we could remove these signposts.

It is even possible to provide electronic options for distracters and background noise. When CAST was newly founded, we operated a Learning Lab where students experimented with educational software. One of these was an Apple II program called Dragon's Keep, where students built vocabulary by "exploring" a big house and summoning the names of the items they found with a mouse click. The program's one unexpected event—or distracter—was the occasional, random entrance of a fire-breathing dragon, which signaled the player to beat a rapid retreat to another room.

One day we tried Dragon's Keep with an autistic youngster. Disaster! At the first appearance of the dragon, the boy was so startled and terrified that he was afraid to approach the computer for months. This reaction contrasted strongly with the reactions of other students, who not only enjoyed the program, but enjoyed the dragon especially. Some students with ADHD considered the dragon the *only* good thing in the whole game! For them, no dragon meant no engagement . . . and no learning. Had Dragon's Keep been universally designed, the program would have included a built-in option to turn the dragon on and off, and consequently, it could have engaged both of these kinds of learners.

Now let's see how our classroom example teachers are using UDL to offer content and media choices, adjustable challenge, and varying degrees of structure to engage their diverse students in learning.

Supporting Affective Learning with UDL

Students in both Mr. O'Connell's and Ms. Abrams's classrooms are pursuing the Algebra benchmarks provided by the National Council of Teachers of Mathematics (available online at http://www.nctm.org).

Mr. O'Connell's 4th grade class is working toward the following goal: *"Students should recognize a wide variety of patterns and the rules that explain them."* This goal affords a lot of leeway for content choice, and Mr. O'Connell decides to focus on graphic patterns with budding artist Miguel, thus engaging Miguel's interest in art without sacrificing the teaching purpose.

The goal Ms. Abrams is working on with her 6th graders is to *"Understand various representations of patterns and functions and the relationships among these representations."* The negative sentiment Kamla has attached to academic tasks is a concern for Ms. Abrams. To engage Kamla in this pre-algebra task, Ms. Abrams builds some exercises around basketball, Kamla's favorite activity. She challenges Kamla to collect data from her basketball performance and use that data in math class. The use of digital cameras and computer spreadsheets make this an operable plan.

Mr. O'Connell and Ms. Abrams are both eager to offer their students alternative media choices. Mr. O'Connell encourages Miguel to create and duplicate a variety of patterns using paper, textiles, mobiles, and mosaics. Miguel scans these patterns into the computer and then manipulates the digital images, creating new designs and structures that apply the patterns in different configurations. The ability to experiment with patterns he's created himself keeps Miguel focused and on task. Mr. O'Connell adjusts levels of challenge by using templates when more support is needed and by providing an open-ended, creative task when Miguel's confidence is strong.

A break from traditional media is perhaps even more important for Kamla, who associates textbooks and worksheets with low achievement and frustration. Ms. Abrams attempts to break the cycle of negative affect by incorporating new tools into the activity. With her teacher's help, Kamla uses a spreadsheet program to develop Venn diagrams, bar graphs, and other graphic displays of her on-court performance data. Ms. Abrams closely monitors the degree of challenge this presents. She begins having Kamla answer questions that require simple observation of the data ("How many points did you score in February?"). As Kamla's competence and confidence improve, Ms. Abrams keeps pace by posing questions that require Kamla to reconfigure and explore the data ("Against which team do you have the best shooting percentage?").

Web Link

CLASSROOM TEMPLATE:
Use the **UDL Solution Template** to expand your repertoire of materials and methods:
http://www.cast.org/ TeachingEveryStudent/ materials

Print media's domination of classrooms is giving way to new materials that provide new visions and possibilities for flexible learning tools and methods. Students' affective differences demand that we apply this flexibility to vary challenge, media, content, rewards, and learning context as we individualize each student's instruction.

It takes time and thought to build a repertoire of media, content, and techniques to individualize teaching while simultaneously considering instructional goals and individual student characteristics. **UDL Classroom Template 3**, available in the Appendix (p. 189) and online, offers guidance to help you plan and develop an appropriate, useful collection of media, tools, and resources that will give your students the supports they need.

Glimpsing the Future: Curricula with Built-In Flexibility

We have seen how teachers can use new media and electronic tools to create options for their students and accommodate differences in recognition, strategy, and affect. By collecting a variety of good software programs, Web sites, and digital content, teachers can gradually build the capacity to individualize instruction for every student in the class.

These kinds of tools and media will always be essential for successful implementation of UDL, but in our view, another approach represents the future of curriculum design. This is *generating curricula with built-in flexibility that inherently accommodates diverse learners.* Such curricula require designers to consider from the outset the varied learners that might use it and the potential instructional approaches that teachers might take. Since our early work with Gateway Stories, Gateway Authoring System, and WiggleWorks, we at CAST have focused our research and development on meeting this challenge.

Web Link

RESOURCE:
The five reading comprehension strategies associated with Reciprocal Teaching are predicting, clarifying, visualization, questioning, and summarizing. Procedures for introducing them to students are detailed at
http://www.miamisci.org/ tec/introduction.html

Among CAST's relevant research is the "Engaging the Text" project, funded in part by the U.S. Office of Special Education Programs. The goal of this project is to develop readers who are strategic, engaged, and self-aware as learners. Drawing on a body of research-supported techniques in strategy instruction, including Reciprocal Teaching (National Institute of Child Health and Human Development, 2000; Palincsar & Brown, 1984), we are exploring how teachers might combine successful instructional techniques with versatile technologies.

One of this project's outcomes is "Thinking Reader," a research prototype of a supported reading environment that can be customized for different learners. Thinking Reader embeds strategy instruction into digital versions of award-winning children's literature (Dalton, Pisha, Coyne, Eagleton, & Deysher, 2001). Although Thinking Reader is not an actual product, CAST has tested the design in classrooms as part of our research. The results are promising, indicating that on average, students who read the computer-supported novels made greater gains on a standardized reading comprehension achievement test than did peers who read and applied strategies with the print version of the novels.

Curricular tools modeled on the Thinking Reader prototype would work with a variety of genres and types of text, ranging from picture books to science articles or social studies Web pages. The prototype (see Figure 6.7) shows how teachers might use various built-in supports to customize instruction for individual differences in recognition, strategic, and affective networks instead of assembling additional materials.

Web Link

EXAMPLE:
Research documenting the benefits of embedded supports for reading comprehension is available at *http://www.cast.org/ TeachingEveryStudent/ supportedreading*

—FIGURE 6.7—
THINKING READER'S BUILT-IN SUPPORTS FOR CUSTOMIZED SCAFFOLDING

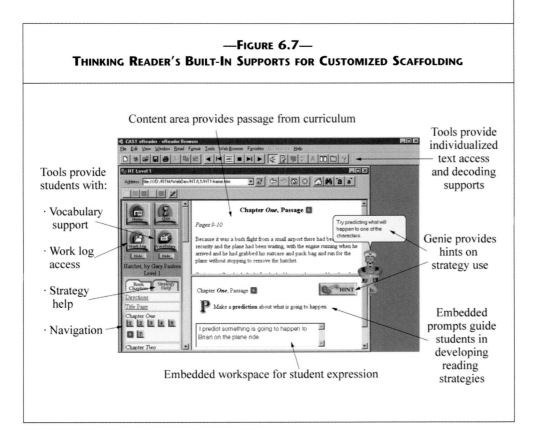

Scaffolds in Thinking Reader can be customized for all three networks:

➤ **Recognition.** Students can use text-to-speech capabilities to hear the text read aloud, and they can change the font size and visual presentation according to their needs. Students can also receive vocabulary support through an online glossary and learn about various strategies through the help section.

➤ **Strategic.** Support for strategic networks is integral to Thinking Reader's design and purpose. While students are reading, they can stop periodically to apply different strategies to predict, question, clarify, summarize, visualize, make a personal connection to the story, or reflect on their progress as readers. Students can ask the Genie for hints or review their saved responses in the work log at any time. There are multiple levels of prompts, hints, and responses available for each strategy, allowing students to begin with extensive support and then reduce it as their performance improves.

➤ **Affective.** Thinking Reader addresses affective networks through the use of age-appropriate, appealing literature, variable levels of challenge and support, student control over access to help, and the focus on learning how to learn.

The Value of UDL in Instructional Design

As teachers, whether we are addressing individual differences in our students' recognition, strategic, or affective networks, we can provide the best support by individualizing pathways to learning. Flexible methods and materials—the heart of the UDL framework and its implementation—make this feasible in the real world. While pursuing a common goal, each student in the classroom can follow his or her own path and obtain a level of performance that represents personal progress.

As long as learning goals are carefully specified, we can provide this flexibility while still preserving the points of resistance necessary to learning. The future promises more digital core curricular materials with a great variety of built-in support options. Demand for this versatility will increase the speed with which it becomes ubiquitous.

➤ ➤ ➤ ➤ ➤

With clear goals and flexible, individual approaches for achieving those goals in hand, how can you apply UDL to get a fairer and more accurate picture of student progress? In the next chapter, we turn to issues of assessment.

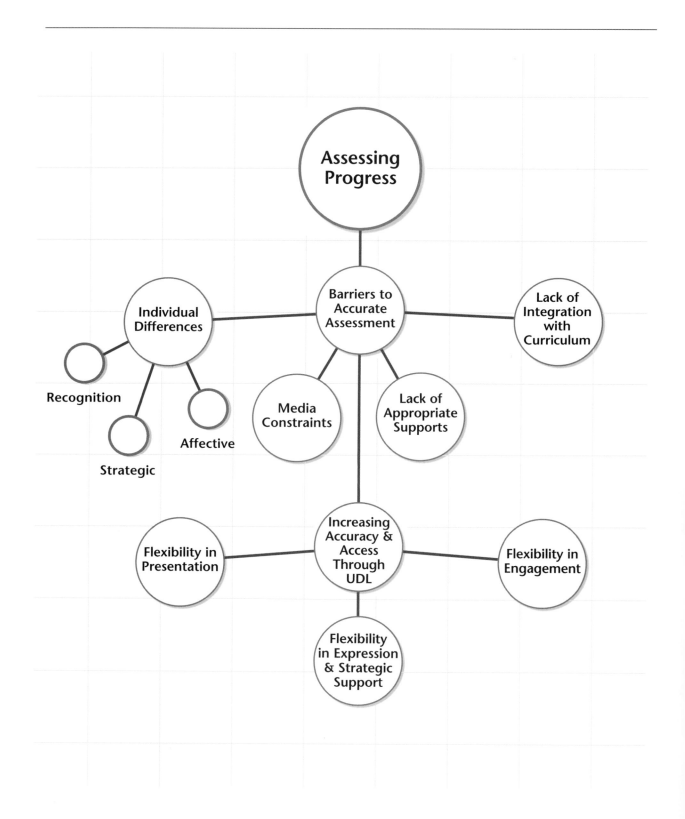

Using UDL to Accurately Assess Student Progress

7

In this chapter, you will learn how UDL can help to increase the accuracy and fairness of classroom assessment.

KEY IDEAS

➤ Giving the same written test to all students is neither fair nor accurate. When a single, inflexible medium is used for testing, students' skills with that medium become hopelessly confused with the skills we intend to measure.

➤ Testing separately from teaching and without the supports that students normally use provides an invalid perspective on what students know and can do.

➤ Digital tools and media make it possible to design ongoing assessments that support individual differences in recognition, strategic, and affective networks, giving us a more accurate measure of students' achievement in relation to the learning goal.

➤ Digital curricula with embedded assessment can track progress and provide ongoing feedback to help students improve performance while they are learning.

Imagine that Patrick is taking a math test with his class. The test comes in two formats: One presents the problems on paper; the other presents the problems on a computer screen and gives test-takers the option of hearing the words read aloud through text-to-speech. According to recent research (Tzuriel, 2000), a student like Patrick, who has difficulty reading and writing, would almost certainly achieve a higher score on the second version than he would on the first. Other students also might benefit from the computer-based format by virtue of the reading supports it offers, their own preference for working with computers, or other factors.

Which version of the test yields the more accurate score? Which provides Patrick's teacher, Mr. Hernandez, with more helpful information? Which is *fairer?* These are questions we seek to answer as we explore how Universal Design for Learning can improve assessment.

Barriers to Accurate Assessment

Teachers evaluate student performance for many reasons: to determine the effectiveness of curriculum materials and methods; to compare achievement levels within and across schools, school systems, districts, and states; and to evaluate students' knowledge and skill. This last type of information is indispensable. Externally, it is used as a criterion for school and college admission. Internally, it helps teachers evaluate the effectiveness of our instruction, so that we can make adjustments necessary to keep students on track.

To be truly useful, assessments must evaluate the knowledge and skills relevant to students' goals—and they must do so accurately. This is more difficult to achieve than it seems, especially when the same test is administered to the entire class. Although using the same assessment tools and procedures for all learners might *seem* to be a fair and equal approach, in reality, this approach yields inaccurate results for many students. Any test that relies on a single medium inevitably, albeit unintentionally, evaluates talents that may not be relevant to instructional goals—talents that are bound up in the medium or methods being used. Thus, students' ability or inability to work with particular media and methods may confound evaluation of their knowledge and skills.

To understand confounding factors in measurement, consider a friendly neighborhood butcher, Al, and his scale. Ms. Smith, one of Al's favorite customers, stops by the butcher shop to purchase some lamb chops. Al neatly trims the fat, places her four chops on his precisely calibrated scale, records the weight, and rings up the price. Fifteen minutes later, another customer appears. Al rolls his eyes. It's Mr. Nyles, who always complains and never appreciates Al's fine meats. Al uses the same accurate scale to weigh the chicken Mr. Nyles has selected, but he "forgets" to remove the chicken from its plastic container and "accidentally" rests his thumb on the scale.

This example illustrates how extraneous factors—a plastic container and a thumb—can corrupt a measurement. Although no one intentionally builds inaccuracies into academic assessments (as Al did with his scale), these inaccuracies do occur. The precision and accuracy of an assessment tool is reliable only to the extent that extraneous factors are removed from the equation. In our view, the traditional model of academic assessment is flawed in four important ways:

1. Student characteristics—individual learning differences—can confound results.

2. Media characteristics can confound results.

3. Withholding student supports can confound results.

4. Poor integration with curriculum limits the value of assessment data.

Let's examine each of these factors, paying close attention to how the three brain networks and their interactions with different kinds of media can help us understand the barriers to and solutions for more accurate and valuable assessment.

Factor 1: Individual Learning Differences

Most current assessments are not designed to accommodate individual differences. Generally, educators have interpreted "fairness" to mean that assessments are uniform in format and administered in a standardized fashion—the same test is given in exactly the same way and under the same conditions for each learner. In some situations, and for some purposes, standardized administration is indeed appropriate, particularly if the format and circumstance of the test exactly match the requirements of a future task. For example, if NASA wants to evaluate aspiring astronauts' ability to react in an emergency, each astronaut under consideration should be presented with the same simulated emergency. In this test, those who can react quickly and perform all of the necessary tasks will truly be the most qualified.

As a counter-example, imagine that you are teaching a middle school science class and are about to administer the textbook-based, multiple-choice test provided in the teacher's edition. You're hoping to find out what each of your students has learned about science over the course of the instructional unit—and by extension, how effective your teaching has been. You duplicate 25 copies of the test and pass them out, announcing to students that they will have 15 minutes to complete the test. Now imagine that among the students about to begin the test are Paula, Patrick, Kamla, Charlie, Jamal, Sophia, and Miguel.

Will the timed, multiple-choice, paper-and-pencil test yield the information you seek—a "fair" determination of what each of these students has learned in your science class? For most of the students we have been following, the likely answer is *no*. The method of assessment confounds science knowledge with facility with various aspects of the test itself, making it impossible to disaggregate the causes of success or failure. Individual differences interact with the test format and administration method in ways that can significantly skew the accuracy of the results. To see how, let's consider the standard, print-format science test within the framework of the three brain networks.

Individual differences in content recognition. Paula decodes words well but has difficulty comprehending connected text. This difficulty limits her ability to respond accurately to the test items, even when she understands the concepts. In fact, Paula's great interest in and facility with decoding words could actually be a *disadvantage* on this test, distracting her from focusing on the real task of demonstrating what she has learned about science.

Sophia would have difficulty with the science test for entirely different reasons. Her conceptual knowledge of science is likely to be strong, given her high degrees of engagement and motivation and her ability to obtain meaning from listening. But Sophia's visual deficits would impede her fluent recognition of the printed words. Her desktop magnifier could make the words more recognizable, but the time required to magnify the page could turn the 15-minute time limit into an insurmountable barrier.

Framed in this way, giving everyone the same test seems unfair. Think about how Paula and Sophia might perform if they took the test in an alternate format: Paula with help to keep her focused on the questions and the process of answering, and Sophia with a computer text-to-speech translator reading items aloud. As is, the standard science test inadvertently measures not only science knowledge but also recognition-based facility with the print medium. These extraneous factors act like the butcher's thumb on the scale.

Would it be fairer to administer the test orally to the whole class, thereby skirting the difficulty arising from Paula and Sophia's recognition weaknesses? Not really, because other students in the class may have trouble accessing speech. The simple truth is, the natural variety of recognition strengths and weaknesses within a typical classroom prevents any *single* presentational medium from yielding an unbiased, accurate assessment for the entire class.

Individual differences in strategic expression. Consider how students' variable abilities to plan, execute, and monitor actions and skills might affect the accuracy of this timed textbook test. Jamal, for example, has a physical disability that makes handwriting virtually impossible, and Charlie has trouble at the other end of the strategic spectrum—with planning and self-monitoring.

Jamal would probably fail this test outright, as would any test-taker who could not effectively manipulate a pencil. He would fail regardless of how well he paid attention, how well he studied, how much he really knew, and how well the new instructional approaches worked. Clearly, a physical disability that renders a student incapable of using the required medium of expression can confound assessment accuracy. And although Charlie is physically able to use pencil and paper, his planning and self-monitoring deficits could interfere with his ability to demonstrate his science knowledge on this standardized exam. The test lacks the inherent structure and support Charlie needs to systematically navigate the questions, budget his time, stay on task, and check his work.

The confounding strategic factors Jamal and Charlie present are obvious, and few teachers would seriously conclude that the boys' low scores on this kind of test indicate a lack of science knowledge. But many learners are affected by more subtle issues with modes of knowledge expression. Research is beginning to show how significantly the way students are asked to express what they know affects their performance— and these findings hold true even for students without documented learning difficulties.

Russell and Haney (1997, 2000) investigated the effects of different modes of expression (handwriting versus keyboarding) on standardized test scores of regular education students. They found that scores supposedly based on content alone were strongly influenced by the expressive medium. For example, students with experience using computers got much higher scores if they keyboarded rather than handwrote their responses. This research backs up the common-sense conclusions of our

Web Link

BACKGROUND KNOWLEDGE: "Do No Harm: High Stakes Testing and Students with Learning Disabilities," a report by Disability Rights Advocates, is online at *http://www.dralegal.org/ publications/dnh.txt)*

classroom examples. Because individual differences in the skills governed by strategic networks can influence performance in ways that are often unrelated to the skills and knowledge teachers are trying to assess, a single, standard mode of expression definitely is not fair to all students. Rather, it often obscures the true significance of assessment outcomes.

Individual differences in engagement. Students' differing levels of engagement can also influence assessment accuracy. For an assessment to accurately reflect what students know and can do, those students must be giving their best effort. This is partly why educators tend to link assessment to significant extrinsic motivators—rewards and punishments designed to get students to pay attention and work hard. Students often see tests as "high stakes," whether or not that formal designation applies. But making tests all-important is not necessarily the best way to motivate and engage every student. Generally speaking, both very low levels of engagement and very high levels of engagement are counterproductive. We have all felt the disabling effects of anxiety—"choking" on the playing field or during a test. Further, the same amount of external pressure, whether positive or negative, affects learners unequally. We each have our own baselines of anxiety and comfort and find different kinds of tests easy or difficult (Goleman, 1995).

Test formats (e.g., multiple choice, essay, short answer) and administration circumstances (e.g., timed/untimed, individual/group administration, in-class/take home) all impact student performance differently, depending on the individual test-taker's affective makeup. Inevitably, a single test, given in a single way, will affect some students positively and some students negatively.

Our example students present a range of affective issues that could confound results on the standardized science test. Sophia, despite her visual deficits, is supremely self-confident and readily confronts a challenge. Assuming she could use her magnifier to see the test items, her enthusiasm and determination could help her to work quickly and perform reasonably well. In Sophia's case, positive affect could promote higher performance than we might expect, given the kinds of challenges she faces. By contrast, Kamla lacks confidence about academics. Tests make her particularly anxious and increase her fears about being thought a poor student. The timed test is especially likely to intimidate Kamla, and it is easy to predict that anxiety might limit her performance.

When we consider individual differences in recognition, strategic, and affective networks, we realize that a common test format and administration method will always favor some students and hurt others, for a variety of complex reasons. Traditional assessments tend to measure things that teachers aren't trying to measure (visual acuity, decoding ability, typing or writing ability, motivation), thus confounding the results and leading us to make inaccurate inferences about students' learning. As a consequence, we risk making off-base instructional decisions—deciding, for example, to re-teach certain content rather than move on to a new challenge or to change our instructional methods when our test design, not our teaching, is contributing to poor scores.

Factor 2: Media Constraints

Our understanding of media differences sheds light on another set of confounding factors: the interaction between the type of skill or knowledge being measured and the medium in which it is being assessed. For example, consider what the members of the Chicago Cubs could demonstrate about their knowledge of physics if they were given a practical "test" in the ballpark. Their ability to intercept a baseball at the precise place where it falls to earth would clearly demonstrate that they understand things like velocity and trajectory. But were we to give the ballplayers a paper-and-pencil test on the principles of physics (and no formal instruction), they probably would not score as well. The written test does a good job of measuring explicit knowledge—the ability to describe physics concepts—but to assess the Cubs' hands-on knowledge, the field test would be a much fairer and more accurate measure of their understanding.

This rather far-fetched example illustrates a point with strong implications for the classroom. Just as students have varying capacities for using different media, media have different capacities for representing different kinds of ideas. For example, skill with the music of language, drama, or poetry is difficult to demonstrate through text but can be easily demonstrated through speech. An aspiring actor might do this by acting the part and the aspiring writer, by reading a poem aloud. Likewise, understanding of a particular narrative might be communicated best through recorded speech or the creation of a video or a drama, using a tool like Grolier Interactive's Hollywood. The format of a text-based outline is helpful for demonstrating the relationships between concepts, but in some cases, a visual map (generated through a tool like Inspiration) might be a more effective way to show these relationships.

The demonstration of some kinds of skill and knowledge fall obviously into certain media categories, such as architectural knowledge and drawing, advertising knowledge and animation, and music knowledge and sound. However, we can gain a richer understanding of what people know by crossing media lines and assessing content with media not usually associated with assessment. This is rare in traditional assessments, which usually consist of a single medium (overwhelmingly printed text) chosen primarily on the basis of availability and with little thought to its appropriateness. This reliance on singular media prevents teachers from fully evaluating different kinds of knowing.

Factor 3: Lack of Appropriate Supports

This factor is related to educators' entrenched concern about cheating. Even if students use supports and scaffolds when learning, teachers tend to feel that these supports should be removed for testing in order to determine what students "really know."

Consider that when calculators first appeared in schools, teachers never dreamed of allowing students to use these tools during a test. It was something of a given that to attain mathematical competency, students needed to be able to perform rapid calculations in their heads. Calculators were viewed as a crutch. But today, in advanced mathematical disciplines, teachers commonly allow calculator use during exams. They now realize that scaffolding calculation is reasonable and appropriate when assessing mathematical concepts and reasoning.

Similarly, many teachers once felt it was inappropriate to allow students to use a word processor on a test. Perhaps they feared that typed responses and the availability of a spell checker might obscure students' problems with mechanics, or even that the computer would somehow "think" for the students. The validity of these concerns depends on the goal of the assessment; however, research shows that students accustomed to working with word processors score significantly lower on tests of composition and expression when they are assessed without them (Russell & Haney, 2000).

These examples remind us why it's important to focus on the goal of an assessment and separate out the tangential variables. In our view, as long as the goal *itself* is not being scaffolded by a particular tool, it is foolish to remove a learner's daily supports during assessment. Suppose you take a professional cooking course, and your final exam is to prepare a fruit soufflé within a certain time limit—a simulation of real restaurant conditions. During your training, you have had regular access to all the tools found in a modern professional kitchen: food processors, electric mixers, and ovens that heat quickly and evenly. Now suppose these appliances are disallowed during the test. The clock is ticking, and you have to hand-chop the fruit, hand-whip the eggs, and preheat a slow oven with an inaccurate temperature gauge. Does this test accurately measure your skill at preparing a soufflé in restaurant conditions? Clearly not.

There are many parallel examples in the classroom. Let's suppose Patrick usually relies on digital text with text-to-speech capability to help him obtain social studies content in a timely fashion. He does most of his social studies-related writing with the help of word processing software equipped with word prediction and spell checking tools. Will the results of a handwritten essay exam accurately reflect Patrick's social studies knowledge? Remember, this test's purpose is to measure mastery of social studies content—not Patrick's reading, handwriting, or spelling abilities.

Although some may feel that providing Patrick this reading, writing, and spelling support is unfair, we think the absence of these tools will confound Patrick's assessment results in the same way that the absence of the kitchen appliances would confound your performance on the soufflé test. When the supports do not undermine the central goal of the assessment, it is perfectly reasonable and, in fact, *more accurate* to include them.

Factor 4: Lack of Integration with Curriculum

Even if the first three barriers to accuracy inherent in traditional assessment were overcome, the value of the results they produce would still be in question. There's a simple reason: *Most traditional assessments are detached from instruction and practice.* Students take a spelling test after they have been taught the words or a social studies test at the end of a unit. And even when these performance measures are well constructed, they reveal very little about the learning process and the value of different teaching approaches.

As teachers, we want to know how a student's knowledge and skills are changing during instruction and what is facilitating or hindering the change. We want to measure not only students' knowledge but also students' learning processes. The way to gain insight into learning processes is not by giving an end-of-unit test, but by examining the interaction between a student and curriculum over time—assessing performance and the factors that underlie it. What cues does the student attend to? What strategies does the student use? What motivates the student? This interaction also involves studying the effects of different aspects of curriculum. What changes in the content presentation are helpful? What kinds of feedback and supports help build skills? What content and what kinds of activities are most engaging?

To measure change accurately, teachers need multiple, flexible, ongoing assessments—more like those used by doctors. An ophthalmologist doesn't assess your needs only by testing your visual acuity; she also assesses what interventions will help meet these needs by trying out a series of prescriptive lenses. And the process does not end there: the doctor continues to consult with you on how well the chosen lenses are working as time goes on.

Two excellent ways to learn what is working and what is not are to observe and talk to students. Alternative assessments such as portfolio assessments and self-assessment journals are also effective ways to learn from students over time, thereby gaining a much more comprehensive picture of a student's status. Ongoing assessment allows us to measure not only a student's performance at one point in time, but also the evolution of that learning and the contributing factors.

Increasing Assessment Accuracy and Accessibility through UDL

We have outlined numerous shortcomings inherent in traditional assessments. How can new media and the UDL framework support teachers' ability to improve the evaluation process? Our knowledge of the three brain networks helps us understand the kinds of flexibility needed for the most accurate and most informative ongoing assessments.

Web Link

RESOURCE:
The Interdisciplinary Middle Years Multimedia Project answers frequently asked questions about electronic portfolios online at *http://www.edu.gov.mb. ca/metks4/tech/currtech/ imym/portfolios.html*

Flexibility in Presentation

Technology enables teachers to provide multiple representations of content in the context of ongoing assessment. Varying the media within the representation is one of the most useful options. For example, Mr. Costa can provide text-to-speech support for Sophia during a history or science test so that her visual recognition deficits will not confound the results. But the concept of multiple representations goes well beyond the idea of offering varied media. Different representations can incorporate different supports, such as links to important background information, context-sensitive vocabulary supports, or glossary items. They can also be displayed in different formats—such as a visual concept map, a set of key points, a timeline, or a diagram—to make the content more accessible to certain students.

How can these varied representations and supports help to create accurate, ongoing assessment? First, they ensure that every student's assessment is accessible to him or her. Second, they permit a teacher to select an assessment that provides the supports a student normally uses. For example, Mr. Costa could retain the "read-aloud" feature in the science material when assessing Sophia's science concept knowledge, and Ms. Chen could allow Charlie to use the supports that help him focus on a task. The result will be the truest picture of students' progress, based on what is being evaluated, the supports these students normally use, and the format that is most accessible to each.

Multiple representations also serve teachers by providing information about the learning process. For example, Mr. Costa could provide the test questions in two formats—one in a large font and the other as text-to-speech—and compare Sophia's performance in the two cases to determine which support is most beneficial. If Ms. Sablan wants to determine whether diagrams, images, word definitions, or short summaries help Paula to connect concepts and understand what she is reading, she can present Paula with multiple versions of the content, each with selected supports turned on or off, to find out where Paula is most successful. This is an example of *dynamic assessment* (see Feuerstein, Rand, & Hoffman, 1979; Lidz, 1987).

As these examples show, offering multiple representations enables teachers to disaggregate specific problems linked to students' recognition networks from the learning and achievement factors under evaluation. It gives teachers a much fairer, more accurate, and deeper understanding of student learning.

Flexibility in Expression and Strategic Supports

We have seen how individual differences in strategic networks interact with traditional paper-and-pencil assessments to skew the accuracy of results. Within the context of ongoing assessment, teachers can accommodate differences in strategic networks by providing students with multiple means for expressing what they know, such as the option to respond by writing, speaking, drawing, creating an animation or video, or developing a multimedia presentation. When students are using tools that are familiar and appropriate for their own styles, needs, and preferences, they are not hindered by the medium of expression and are more likely to be able to demonstrate what they know and know how to do.

Few would argue against letting a student with severe motor difficulties take a test in electronic form that allows for alternative keyboard or voice recognition software. Somewhat less obvious is the degree to which students with subtler difficulties would benefit from the multiple expressive options electronic media can provide. Multiple media options are tremendously useful to students who have trouble with writing mechanics and they are also helpful to the many students more accustomed expressing themselves on a word processor screen than on paper (Russell & Haney, 2000).

Technological tools make it easier for a teacher to provide every student with multiple options for expression. Speech recognition systems can record spoken responses and translate them to text. Software such as Hollywood can be used to create animated presentations. HyperStudio, PowerPoint, and other similar tools make it easy to develop multimedia presentations.

Technology also offers the opportunity to assess skill learning in a deeper and more meaningful way. For example, science students might conduct virtual lab experiments, in which their actual manipulations of data, technologies, and substances would demonstrate their understanding of processes, methods, and outcomes more clearly than any written or verbal response could. Tenth Planet's Geometry program, shown in Figure 7.1, illustrates some of the multiple options for expression digital tools can provide. The program's assessment piece offers a multimedia journal in which students can record and play back audio notes, type in comments, or draw images related to what they have learned. Throughout the assessment, students receive scaffolding in the form of review information and prompts to support them as they enter ideas into their journals. With this one program, students can develop a whole portfolio of work that demonstrates their learning in multiple ways and with a variety of strategic supports.

Options for monitoring varied strategic supports are one of the most complex and fascinating areas of UDL assessment. By examining where supports succeed and fail, a teacher can identify how students successfully learn how to learn. For example, throughout the school year, Ms. Chen could experiment with highlighting, underlining, and italicizing tools to identify which best promotes Charlie's ability to stay on track and digest a text.

—FIGURE 7.1—
OPTIONS FOR EXPRESSION IN
TENTH PLANET'S GEOMETRY PROGRAM

SAMPLE STUDENT

I made a pattern. It is red blue red. I had enugh red triangle and blu triangle to fill the window.

Note: Created in the "Stained Glass Windows" activity in BEYOND.

From Tenth Planet's Introduction to Patterns, Sunburst Technology.

With Anne Marie Palincsar and Jeanne Paratore, CAST is investigating how supports for strategic reading embedded in narrative text can help students learn and can help teachers and students monitor ongoing progress (Palincsar & Brown, 1984). For example, CAST's research prototype, Thinking Reader, uses embedded assessment to track and save all student responses to strategy prompts. When reviewing the student record, students and teachers can see the book and date, the prompts or questions, and the students' responses. Figure 7.2 shows how a Thinking Reader work log might look for Kamla.

In addition to collecting student input, the Thinking Reader prototype supports student self-reflection and self-assessment, offering rubrics and tools for determining whether they are satisfied with the predictions, summaries, and questions they have generated. The screen in Figure 7.3 shows a rubric for checking summary construction. Students can review their summaries to see whether they have addressed the key features and then either revise their work or send it on to their student work logs.

These examples are just the tip of the iceberg—the products of only the early stages of development and testing in classrooms. Nevertheless, teachers can combine a variety of tools currently available to set up

---

—FIGURE 7.2—
THINKING READER WORK LOG

Kamla's Work Log

8:59:45 AM 12/4/00
46. Gift Giver, Level 1: Chapter 14, Passage 1, Pages 90-92
What were you feeling as you read the story? Make a personal connection.

I feel scared that Doris is going to get split up like Amir and Sherman.

9:03:55 AM 12/4/00
47. Gift Giver, Level 1: Chapter 14, Passage 2, Pages 92-94
Ask a question about something important to know and remember.

Why does Doris want to be alone so badly?

10:20:34 AM 12/5/00
48. Gift Giver, Level 1: Chapter 14, Passage 3, Pages 94-96
Ask for clarification about something that might be confusing to you or another reader.

Why is Doris cleaning the whole house, when her mom only told her to watch the baby?

Prompts embedded in a digital novel help guide Kamla's strategic reading. The software collects Kamla's responses in the electronic work log, and later, she and Ms. Abrams can use this record to evaluate her ongoing progress as a reader.

strategic supports that track learner progress. For example, Mr. Mitchell might use Inspiration to help Charlie set up a concept map of the steps to follow when completing an assignment. Each bubble on the map could include prompts and reminders to support Charlie's progress, and he could fill in the bubbles with color as he completes each step. Links to useful Web sites could also be embedded in the map.

Assessments featuring multiple, varied strategic pathways result in far more accurate and insightful evaluation. They ensure that no student's skills and knowledge are obscured by expressive difficulties and that each student can benefit from appropriate supports. Further, they foster a much deeper understanding of the teaching methods and materials that are helping students learn.

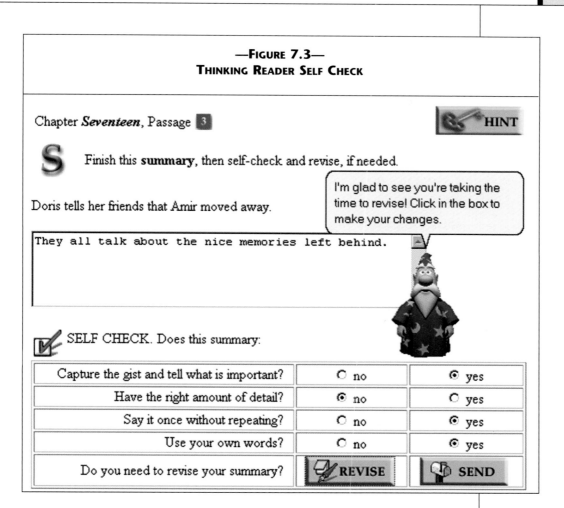

—FIGURE 7.3—
THINKING READER SELF CHECK

Chapter **Seventeen**, Passage 3

HINT

S Finish this **summary**, then self-check and revise, if needed.

Doris tells her friends that Amir moved away.

I'm glad to see you're taking the time to revise! Click in the box to make your changes.

They all talk about the nice memories left behind.

SELF CHECK. Does this summary:

Capture the gist and tell what is important?	○ no	⊙ yes
Have the right amount of detail?	⊙ no	○ yes
Say it once without repeating?	○ no	⊙ yes
Use your own words?	○ no	⊙ yes
Do you need to revise your summary?	REVISE	SEND

Flexibility in Engagement

What if children learned to ride bikes in the same way that they learn academics? After a certain period of instruction, they would take "tests" where they would ride formally in front of a "grader" who would take points off for various deficiencies in execution. Under those circumstances—drained of fun, denied the freedom to topple over, and absent the comfort of a parent's steadying hand—it's a fair bet that most children would be nervous about learning to ride a bike; many would just give up.

The emotional valence of an academic task is critical in determining how well a student will succeed at it—or even how much effort he or she will invest. Students' unique affective networks manifest in their different responses to testing. For some, the stakes are set too high by testing in general and grading in particular, leading to a reduction in performance sometimes called *test anxiety*. For others, anxiety is a function of the particular task's difficulty.

Embedding assessment into ongoing work removes some of the emotional impact of testing and highlights its more positive aspects. For students like Paula and Kamla, who fear academic assessment, freestanding tests loom as an obstacle, a hurdle, a "failure detector." But when assessment is removed from its isolated stature and made a normal, constant part of learning, the feedback for both student and teacher is informative and helpful rather than intimidating.

In a digital environment, embedded assessment can offer additional flexibility to further accommodate students' affect. First, most students find the options available within a multimedia environment—images, sounds, animations, and simulation—fun and appealing. Second, teachers' ability to level and scaffold embedded assessments can ensure that every student is working at a comfortable and appropriate stage of difficulty. For example, the Thinking Reader research prototype offers five levels of support in the form of prompts. The prompts change with each level in response to information recorded as students work. This kind of flexibility means that as students become more skillful with reading strategies, they can be challenged to apply those strategies independently.

Figure 7.4 is a composite screen-shot of the five levels of "summarizing" prompts Thinking Reader might provide for the same section of digital text. Let's quickly examine a few:

➤ The Level 1 prompt provides a high degree of scaffolding; it is appropriate for the student who is just learning the skill and needs to be reminded of which strategy to use and what the key components of that strategy are. At this level, the digital document is an extension of the teacher who is teaching this skill.

➤ The Level 3 prompt provides a medium degree of scaffolding. It is for the student who has basic facility with the strategy but needs reminders and help self-evaluating.

➤ The Level 5 prompt provides minimal scaffolding. It is appropriate

—**FIGURE 7.4**—
THINKING READER PROMPT LEVELS

Level 1 Prompt
A good summary states what is most important to remember.
Choose the best summary below.

Level 2 Prompt
Finish this summary, then self-check and revise, if needed.

Level 3 Prompt
Write a summary, then self-check and revise, if needed.

Level 4 Prompt
Write a summary.

Level 5 Prompt
Choose a strategy and try it out.
*Summary *Prediction *Question *Clarification *Visualization *Feeling
*Reflect on my progress

for learners who know how to use a variety of strategies and how to select among them according to the context, but who may still need reminders to apply strategies consistently.

A third way to increase student engagement with assessment is to vary the content within a particular assessment tool. Standardized tests rarely do this. A test of reading comprehension, for example, is likely to present the same set of text passages for everyone, not taking into account whether each student will find the passages interesting or worth reading. Sophia, the music lover, Kamla, the basketball enthusiast, and Jamal, the expert on tanks and submarines, might all be assessed on the same passage about Mozart. Sophia would most likely be more attentive to the task than the other students, which would give her the best opportunity to show her actual reading skills. Providing multiple content options in a traditional print environment is costly and impractical. But in a digital environment, there is no reason why Kamla couldn't select a passage about sports for her reading comprehension assessment and Jamal, a passage about submarines, as long as both passages are of comparable difficulty.

Possibilities such as these are just beginning to be explored. The research community has paid less attention to issues surrounding affect than to issues relating to recognition and strategy, but this is slowly changing. Teachers and researchers now realize, for example, that student skills may look very different when working with different content. A student may summarize a passage about the Pilgrims poorly but provide an excellent summary for a passage about race cars. This is important information for guiding teaching. Flexible and ongoing assessment can inform teachers about what most interests their students and help them to enlist students' motivation—the essential engine of learning.

The Value of UDL in Assessment

Embedded, flexible, ongoing assessments have the potential to resolve many of the problems with standardized, paper-and-pencil tests, particularly as tools for guiding teaching. It is true that standardized tests can yield valuable information, especially if one is evaluating trends and information about groups, but as accurate assessments of individual students' skills, knowledge, and learning, these assessment tools are severely flawed.

The obvious value of embedded, flexible UDL assessment is its ability to adjust to many individual differences and focus the questions on exactly what teachers are trying to find out. With flexibility in presentation, expression, supports, and engagement, we can reduce the common errors introduced by single-mode fixed assessments. Further, that same flexibility allows teachers to align assessment more closely with teaching goals and methods and thus, to assess students more accurately.

For example, if you are assessing the ability to create a coherent narrative, you can offer a wide assortment of media for that composition including recorded speech, images, video, animation, or dance. If you are assessing the ability to *write* a coherent narrative (i.e., create one in text), you can scaffold spelling, reading, and text entry (either through voice recognition or word processing) and provide additional media, like images and sounds, to scaffold motivation and enhance the narrative. If you are assessing mastery of writing mechanics, you wouldn't scaffold these skills, but you might offer motivational supports such as the use of sound or images, and you might provide prompts to help students self-monitor and build editing skills. The interactive capacity of new technologies allows teachers to provide dynamic assessments that assess the ongoing processes of learning more organically. By tracking the supports a student uses, the kinds of strategies that he or she follows, the kinds of strategies that seem to be missing, and the aspects of the task environment that can bias the outcome, we can gain valuable insights about students as learners.

Assessments in our digital age should be dynamic and universally designed. When we provide a full range of customizations and adaptations as a part of assessments, we are able to more accurately evaluate both student performance and the processes that underlie that performance. The enhanced accuracy comes from the capacity to evaluate performance over time, under varying conditions, including conditions where the student's performance is constrained by barriers inherent in specific modes of representation, expression, or engagement, and conditions where appropriate adaptations and supports are available to overcome those barriers.

Most important, new technologies allow for two-way interactive assessments. With these technologies available in our classrooms, we will be able to create learning environments that not only teach, but also "learn" to teach more effectively. By distributing the intelligence between student and environment, the curriculum will be able to track student successes and weaknesses and monitor the effectiveness or ineffectiveness of its own methods. The result will be a curriculum that becomes *smarter*, not more outdated, over time.

➤   ➤   ➤   ➤   ➤

With clear goals, flexible methods and materials, and embedded, dynamic assessment, we have seen the three major parts of UDL instructional design. How can this vision become real in classrooms across the nation and around the world? In the next chapter, we propose both top-down and bottom-up approaches to making Universal Design for Learning a reality.

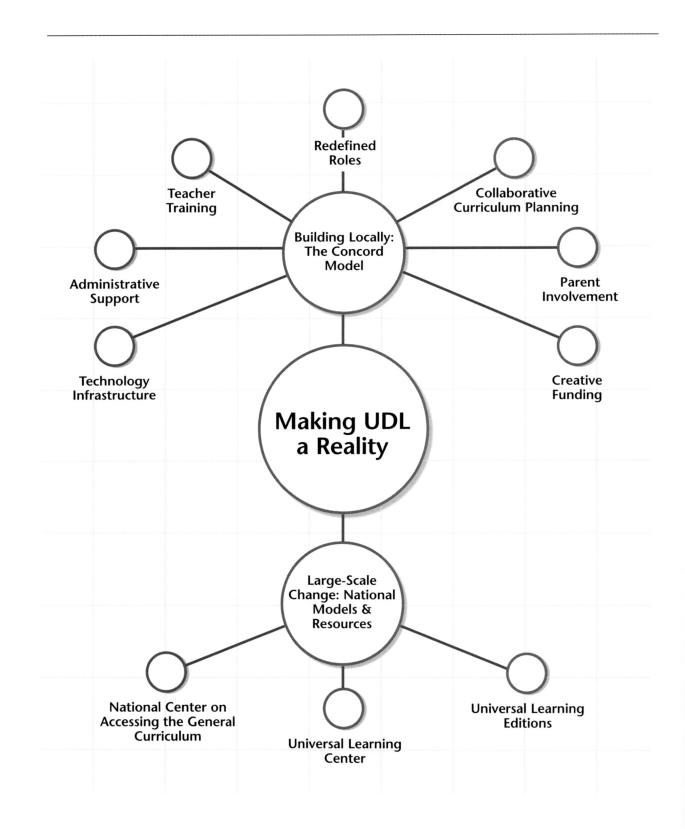

Making Universal Design
for Learning a Reality

8

In this chapter, you will learn useful UDL implementation strategies from a school district that has been implementing UDL since 1995. You will also find out how CAST is collaborating with other organization to bring about larger-scale systemic change.

KEY IDEAS

➤ The major components necessary to implement UDL at the local level within a district are technology infrastructure, administrative support, teacher training and support, redefined roles for special and regular education teachers, a new curriculum planning model, parent and community involvement, and creative funding.

➤ To be practical on a larger scale, UDL requires systemic changes in the following key arenas: policy, curriculum design, teacher training and preparation, consensus building, and parent involvement.

We believe that Universal Design for Learning can help educators harness the power of new media and technologies to remove barriers to learning for all students, including students with disabilities. But how can we move from concept to reality? Taking a cue from brain networks, we know that change needs to happen both from the bottom up and from the top down. In the world of education, bottom-up changes are driven by individual students, parents, teachers, and administrators effecting change in classrooms, teaching methods, homework practices, and curriculum materials. Equally important are top-down changes—systemic changes in educational policies, professional development methods, publishing practices, economic models, and the participation of professional and lay organizations. Together, these two approaches have the power to make UDL a reality in schools worldwide.

CAST is working to bring about both types of change. Together with the Concord, New Hampshire, school system, we are researching and developing working models for school- and district-level implementation. In this chapter we offer lessons from Concord's UDL program, which we have distilled into the beginnings of a model for district change. Further, to exemplify CAST's efforts to elicit systemic change at the regional, state, and national levels, we provide information on the UDL initiatives spearheaded by CAST and the National Center on Accessing the General Curriculum (NCAC).

Building Locally: Concord Works for District Change

Donna Palley, Concord's special education coordinator for the past 15 years, has long been interested in technology's tremendous potential to help learners with special needs. In 1994, when Concord began building its technology infrastructure, Palley seized the opportunity to integrate these kinds of supports. She came to CAST for guidance, and ever since, our organizations have been collaborating to weave the concepts of UDL into the fabric of the entire Concord school district. This has involved work from the bottom up—focusing on one student, one teacher, one unit of curriculum at a time—and from the top down—securing participation and support from the administration and the community.

Early Decisions and First Steps

A critical early decision for Concord personnel was to focus on the limitations of the curriculum rather than the presumed limitations of the students. They replaced the question, "What can't this student do?" with the question, "What barriers will this student encounter when participating in this unit of curriculum?" This approach brought about three significant benefits that proved critical during the program's kickoff stages:

➤ Classroom teachers felt that UDL addressed their work and their curriculum, not just one student.

➤ Special education teachers felt that UDL enabled them to contribute to curricular efficacy for every student, not just for one or two particular students.

➤ Teachers, specialists, administrators, and parents embraced the mindset of expanding and improving curricula.

Donna Palley's discussions with CAST and her personal experience as a technology specialist led her to believe that eliminating curriculum barriers was best supported by a curriculum with embedded technology. The district passed a resolution to "tool up" by installing networked computers in all its schools and supplying the hardware and software necessary to provide text-to-speech and a variety of customizations (for example, Inspiration, Write: OutLoud, CAST eReader, Picture It, PixReader, and MathPad Plus). To facilitate the transition from print-based curricular materials to digital materials, Concord set up a scanning center, where teachers, parents, and community volunteers could digitize curriculum materials and deposit them in the district's newly established digital library.

Concord's decision to increase the availability of digital content and tools expanded learning opportunities for all its students. When the district first began instituting UDL, these opportunities were explored on a limited scale—sometimes as small as one short curriculum unit in one classroom. Donna Palley began by working with individual teachers to assist particular students who did not fit the mold. For example, she pointed out that any text could be digitized, and once digitized, could be read aloud or highlighted for beginning or struggling readers, or for students with learning disabilities, or for students with limited English proficiency. Concord teachers started finding that digital text and images also offered other kinds of flexibility, such as the option to change the appearance of the text or to convert the text to Braille via a Braille printer. And digitized text supported students' ability to take effective notes and made it easier for them to manipulate text for the purposes of composition.

The Model's Evolution

Concord's early experiments in selected classrooms proved to be more globally successful than anyone had hoped. Teachers discovered that the changes benefited not only the children whose needs precipitated them, but others in the class as well. This realization led to contagious enthusiasm. Soon interested teachers from all over the district contacted Palley, wanting in.

Palley built upon this strong teacher support by "infiltrating" the system at several levels. She made presentations highlighting the advantages of UDL to Concord's school board, district administration, and curriculum steering committees. Through workshops, she helped to expand the roles of special education personnel and to develop collaborations between special and regular education teachers. She sought grants to support new initiatives. Throughout these efforts, she worked with CAST to refine ideas and develop new concepts.

What ultimately emerged from work that began with one student, one unit, and one classroom is an entirely new approach to curriculum planning. In the years since 1994, Concord's school system has become living, breathing example of UDL in action. Rather than adapt the curriculum to fit students with particular problems, personnel identify potential barriers to learning at the onset of curriculum planning. By anticipating these barriers, such as those posed by printed text, they are able to construct solutions before problems arise.

Today, Concord is ablaze with new and exciting projects. Teachers are eager to join in. Insights arise daily. Although Donna Palley would be the first to reiterate that the district is still far from its evolving goals, CAST and Concord have learned many valuable lessons. We offer them here as a guide for schools and school systems interested in moving towards UDL.

Making UDL Work in Practice: The Concord Model

Of course, we know it's not possible to import a model wholesale from one context to another. The specific approaches used in Concord will not be appropriate in every school system. For one thing, the Concord Model took shape in the 1990s, and due to considerable technological advances since that time, some of the techniques used may no longer apply. In particular, greater availability of digital content and the ubiquitous presence of the Internet shift the nature of some specific UDL activities. Nevertheless, we have identified seven key components of Concord's UDL implementation (listed in Figure 8.1 and addressed in the subsections that

Web Link

EXAMPLE:
Hear about UDL's impact in one classroom at *http://www.cast.org/ TeachingEveryStudent/ impact*

follow) that, with adaptations, can help any school district begin the change process.

—FIGURE 8.1—
THE CONCORD MODEL: KEY COMPONENTS OF UDL IMPLEMENTATION

- Technology Infrastructure and Support
- Administrative Support
- Teacher Training and Support
- Redefined Roles for Special and Regular Education Teachers
- Collaborative Curriculum Planning
- Parent and Community Involvement
- Creative Funding

Building and Supporting a Technology Infrastructure

Donna Palley admits that she is fortunate to have a close collaborative relationship with the technology specialists in Concord. As she puts it, the two departments speak the same language: *"UDL-ese!"* Both view technology as essential for making curricula flexible. Both agree that consistent tools need to be widely available throughout the system and that computers need to function well. Further, they share a vision of a central library of digital curriculum materials; a collection of varied, flexible software tools for working with these materials; and ongoing, readily available teacher support.

Special education and technology personnel also recognize that without technology to support it, UDL is just an impracticable theory. As Palley notes, "I think that people can have great ideas but they won't succeed if they don't have a feeling that they can get access to the machines, to the software." It is an obvious point, but an essential one, worth stressing: Before teachers can transform UDL theory into practice, they need access to digital materials.

Web Link

EXAMPLE:
Use of electronic tools and learning materials requires technological infrastructure, including support for teachers. Concord staff discuss these supports at *http://www.cast.org/ TeachingEveryStudent/ infrastructure*

The simple act of digitizing materials builds a growing resource for overcoming many of the barriers inherent in printed curricula. This is a valuable first step toward UDL, and one that is increasingly available to educators. In the United States, the 1996 copyright additions (Section 121 of Title 17 of the United States Code) stipulate that educational institutions may transform otherwise proprietary materials into an accessible format for use by individuals with disabilities. This gives teachers new freedom to scan existing print materials into digital format to be used with supportive technologies.

Concord's scanning center, run jointly by volunteers and a part-time staff, is a vital resource in the district's technology infrastructure. As digital materials accumulate in Concord's digital library, and as teachers continue to access these materials on floppy disk and compact disc (and soon, via the district's Web site), the wealth of resources available to the district's students grows richer and richer.

The warm welcome increased technology has received in Concord classrooms is typical of the positive attitude toward technology we are seeing everywhere. In a CAST survey focusing on teachers' current and potential use of adaptive strategies in the classroom, a large percentage of respondents said they would use technological tools to individualize instruction if the tools were available.

Enlisting Administrative Support

Support from the school and district administration has been a critical factor in Concord's success. When a school's principal and the school board buy in to the concept of UDL, it sends a message to faculty and staff that this exploration is worthwhile. It is partly this support that makes UDL satisfying, makes teachers feel they're making a difference, and reassures them that both the time they invest and the risks they take by doing so have the backing of the "higher powers." We believe administrative buy-in is especially important at the middle and high school levels, where teachers have the additional pressure of ensuring students accumulate credits for graduation and pass the necessary high-stakes tests.

In Concord, Donna Palley maintains administrative support by offering UDL training and presentations for the school board, the curriculum steering committee, and the administration. One of the most beneficial outcomes of this administrative support has been the "release time model." As Palley explains it, "For a scheduled number of days each year, the district releases teachers from instructional duties to work on UDL and increase their experience with it. This way, teachers don't feel that they have to stay after school or cut into their personal time to work on UDL. Release time says to teachers that UDL is important." There are really two benefits to this policy. First, it gives teachers *time,* an important resource for actualizing UDL. Second, it signals to them that they should indeed make UDL a priority. In Concord, this dual support has made a huge difference.

Developing Teacher Training and Support

Although support at the upper levels of the school system is vital to UDL's success, Palley uses it to *sustain* rather than initiate UDL. She avoids systemic ultimatums and instead relies on a grassroots approach. When it comes down to it, teachers and their students generate the impetus and energy for UDL.

How does this work? Palley starts with the teachers and curriculum planners. But she doesn't get them all together and present a philosophical argument for UDL; instead, she builds enthusiasm from within the classroom by approaching teachers in small groups, sharing her excitement about UDL, and showing them exactly how it can help them. And Palley's close work with teachers over the years has taught her *never* to present UDL as (another) "great new thing." Her approach is to work with teachers to understand their goals, offer support by identifying potential barriers to reaching those goals, and then collaborate with teachers to develop ways to overcome the barriers. The idea, she says, is not to drastically restructure the way teachers operate but simply to help them continue doing what they normally do while expanding their resources, options, and supports. Palley helps teachers see that UDL serves them, and more importantly, serves their students.

At the curriculum planning meetings Palley attends, she lets participants know that she would like to hear their plan, try to identify potential barriers for students, and devise ways to overcome these barriers using flexible technologies. She focuses on listening well, brainstorming solutions to identified barriers, and ultimately institutionalizing solutions that will really work. This last step, implementation, takes Palley back into classrooms to help teachers meld UDL into their own curricula. Teachers

Web Link

EXAMPLE:
A Concord administrator describes UDL's systemic implementation at *http://www.cast.org/ TeachingEveryStudent/ UDLimplementation*

also have the option of attending ongoing mini-courses and workshops, which are planned at the beginning of each school year. With creative allocation of budget funds, Concord's teachers have release time for planning, collaborations, and curriculum development and so can drop in on numerous training opportunities that address real issues as they arise.

Teacher training in UDL does not have to be a large-scale undertaking. The Concord school system has found that a very effective approach has been to train a small group of teachers (typically special educators) to become UDL mentors. The mentors receive intensive training in UDL concepts and practical skills including digitizing text, images, and sound, and using digital cameras, Internet resources, and a variety of software tools. Once fully trained, each mentor takes on two untrained teachers for collaboration throughout the year. Palley finds that this approach is even more successful when she selects as mentors people who aren't known for their technological skill. Technology novices who develop expertise turn out to be very influential—better at convincing other teachers that they, too, can manage this new technology and new approach.

Part of the beauty of UDL, and a reason that teachers warm to it so quickly, is that it doesn't have to be a separate initiative. Rather, it can be applied to the other things teachers are working on. "My goal," Palley says, "is to get people to have UDL in their minds so that they will apply it regardless of the role they're in—in their teaching lives and in their paraprofessional lives."

Web Link

EXAMPLE:
Learn about Concord's approach to teacher training at
http://www.cast.org/ TeachingEveryStudent/ training

Redefining Teacher Roles

Within traditional models of special education, which usually pull students from regular classrooms for remedial work, special education teachers can feel frustrated at their limited role and isolated from the school's larger educational purposes. Special educators might connect with the general education curriculum only to assist one or two students; this gives them little opportunity to support or affect that curriculum. Yet special educators are nevertheless expected to help students make progress in general education classes—even to help them complete specific assignments. This is particularly true for special educators working in high schools, where students and teachers face immense pressure to keep up with subject area content.

The new and expanded role for special education teachers is one of the most powerful changes UDL has brought to the Concord school system. UDL has formed the basis for a new collaborative effort between special and regular educators *and* technology specialists. Thanks to the excellent rapport Donna Palley has built between these once-insular groups (in part through the mentor-training program), they are now working together on a common agenda. A number of Concord's special education teachers and specialists (such as speech and language pathologists) have joined technology-planning committees and have become part-time technology specialists. Others are officially involved in curriculum design and curriculum planning, working both at the individual-unit level and at the whole-school level. "Our special educators now feel like they have a bigger toolbox," Palley says. "They can sit down one-to-one with a classroom teacher and have something to offer in the conversation about the content. Now they can be influential in the planning. The special educators have a new sense of involvement, and regular teachers are seeing the fruits of collaboration in a much more global way."

Collaborating to Plan, Develop, and Implement Curriculum

Although the idea of developing curriculum sounds potentially overwhelming and time-consuming, several aspects of the Concord Model make it feasible. First, the districtwide commitment to UDL has over time yielded an increasing array of resources to support innovative curriculum ideas. These include

➤ The digital library, with an ever-expanding number of digitized core curricular and supplementary materials.

➤ A repository of software tools and Web sites, with user support.

➤ Consultants for curriculum development.

➤ Release time to work on UDL curricula.

The success of Concord's curriculum development efforts is also due in large part to the district's simple, pragmatic approach. Teachers start with a manageable unit, such as a single project or one segment of a textbook, and then ask the following critical questions:

➤ What are the goals of the unit?

➤ What do students need to do to demonstrate mastery?

Web Link

EXAMPLE:
Teaching every student calls for changing teacher roles. Teachers who welcome these new opportunities discuss their new roles at *http://www.cast.org/ TeachingEveryStudent/ roles*

➤ Where are the barriers for the students?

➤ What tools, materials, and supports might help?

➤ How can I adjust goals, methods, and assessment so that every one of my students can progress?

Once these questions are answered, teachers work collaboratively with curriculum consultants to reconsider the goals, bring in new tools and supports (including digital materials), and individualize that unit for each learner in the class. And once teachers become familiar with the approach and the tools, it becomes easy to apply them to other content.

Concord has found that as more teachers experiment with UDL tools and ideas, the enthusiasm grows and others join in. Gradually, the community has built up a wealth of collective knowledge. Some departments are now planning the whole year by bringing together regular educators, special educators, and technology specialists to review the goals of the entire curriculum. Rather than work from individual students to the curriculum, they work from the curriculum to all students, using their accumulated experience to identify all potential barriers that might occur given the normal diversity of a given class or grade. In Concord, as elsewhere, ideas that make sense are a welcome addition to the curriculum.

Involving Parents and the Community

All educators know that if you want to make an initiative happen, it's a good idea to get parents involved. In Concord, the parents' role is at least twofold. First, as volunteers, they extend the district's capacity to implement UDL. Many parents in the Concord school district contribute by volunteering in various ways. Second, parents continue to promote the progress of UDL simply by becoming informed and encouraging the district to take action.

Palley speaks of parents' power to add the "constructive tension" that helps bring about change. In Concord, parents of students with disabilities are very knowledgeable about UDL and act as catalysts to get teachers and schools involved. The key, Palley says, is to have "parents who expect UDL and require it—parents who will see their children's experiences through the UDL lens. If their children come home with homework they can't do, these parents will go directly to the teacher and say, 'This isn't acceptable. My child can't do that homework.'"

Web Link

EXAMPLE:
Educators talk about incorporating UDL into curriculum planning at *http://www.cast.org/ TeachingEveryStudent/ planning*

Informed parents can bring about change, not just for their own children, but for *all* children in their local schools. When parents raise issues about one student, they raise fundamental issues about every student by compelling teachers to consider carefully the barriers an assignment may pose. Further, involved parents initiate other parents and teachers into the program, creating a powerful impetus for change.

In Concord, Donna Palley constantly seeks new ways to ensure that parents continue to serve as agents for change. For example, one of the district's current grants supports increased parent involvement by providing parents with computers and computer training, allowing students to access online assignments from home. She also recommends making parent and community education about UDL a priority. This might entail building a Web site publicizing the new ideas, illustrating what students have accomplished through UDL at open house night, speaking to the PTO or IEP teams, or making newspaper and public service announcements. As the Concord school system will confirm, these modest efforts can pay off in a huge way.

Developing Creative Funding Practices

Concord has been successful at obtaining a number of grants to pursue UDL work—most in the $10,000 to $20,000 range, but some larger. Grant proposals can originate at the district level, or come from individual schools, departments (such as technology or special education), or groups of teachers. Teachers are both encouraged to take the initiative in finding funding opportunities and invited to respond to UDL-focused requests for proposals within the district. Teachers also have various funded professional development opportunities, including sabbaticals.

Recently, the district was awarded a federal grant to participate in pre-service teacher technology training. Concord will collaborate with 15 institutions of higher education to provide training through digital videos illustrating UDL in action, available on the district's Web site (http://www.concord.k12.nh.us/comm/dropdownindex.html). Some of the newer, smaller projects include an exploration of UDL at home that involves students working on UDL social studies materials via the Web and a project reframing the social studies curriculum.

Web Link

**CLASSROOM
TEMPLATE:**
Use the **Creating
Systemic Change
Template** to apply the
Concord Model to your
district at
*http://www.cast.org/
TeachingEveryStudent/
model*

Through a self-initiated collaboration with CAST, Donna Palley successfully spearheaded a ground-up revamping of the Concord school system.

UDL Classroom Template 4, available in the Appendix (p. 195) and online, is a tool that will help you apply the relevant parts of the Concord Model to your school or district and take the first steps toward building new instructional approaches for teaching every student. We invite you to visit the CAST Web site and contribute your ideas, reflections, and suggestions—tell us how we can help you. We also encourage you to use us as a sounding board as you construct a plan of action.

Working for Large-Scale Change: National Models and Resources

Although change generated from the bottom up is an absolute necessity, there must be systemic change on a regional, state, and even national level if UDL is to be practical. To suggest that every school system digitize its curricular materials would be to propose an unwieldy, costly, and highly inefficient approach. Schools would be (and actually already are) duplicating efforts, misdirecting teacher- and volunteer- resources into a time-consuming undertaking. After a while, digital versions of print-based texts would fall short of their promise; with each school or district occupied with creating its own digital material, there would be limited time to build in the smart supports this flexible medium makes possible.

Digitizing print materials is a start, but it is still anchored in the format and concepts of a print-based world. Clearly, to be practical in the long run for everyone, the shift to providing digital curriculum materials and tools needs to occur from the top down. Educational policy needs to demand UDL curriculum, designers need to create it, publishers need to distribute it, teachers need to be prepared to implement it, and professional and parent organizations need to embrace it.

CAST and The National Center on Accessing the General Curriculum

CAST's National Center on Accessing the General Curriculum (NCAC) is confronting the need for systemic change head-on. Part of a national initiative that emerged from the re-authorization of the Individuals with

Disabilities Education Act (IDEA '97), NCAC was established by CAST in 1999 through a cooperative agreement with the U.S. Department of Education's Office of Special Education Programs. NCAC draws on the talents of five partners, already established leaders in their fields:

➤ CAST, as the lead organization

➤ Harvard University Children's Initiative/Harvard Law School

➤ The Council for Exceptional Children (CEC)

➤ Boston College Lynch School of Education's Department of Teacher Education, Special Education, Curriculum, and Instruction

➤ The Parent Advocacy Coalition for Educational Rights (PACER).

Charged with providing leadership in using the UDL framework to increase access to the general education curriculum for all learners, NCAC is investigating and making recommendations in four major arenas—the areas in which we must effect change if UDL is to become a widespread reality.

1. Policy and legal issues. NCAC is working for shifts in policy and legal matters, such as copyright law and assessment issues including high-stakes testing. The NCAC's Policy Group at the Harvard Law School is examining state special education policies and determining what leeway the new copyright laws allow publishers and third parties in the application of published materials.

2. Curriculum design. NCAC is working for changes in the curriculum itself, starting with provision of digital materials with built-in, flexible supports, built-in goal specification, and built-in assessment tools. CAST is researching and developing new materials with embedded, flexible supports and ongoing assessment.

3. Teacher preparation and training. NCAC advocates new approaches to teacher preparation and ongoing professional development and support, including rethinking the roles of specialists and the curriculum planning process. The Boston College Teacher Practice group has surveyed teachers regarding the frequency with which they adapt their teaching to individual students, the types of adaptations they make, the tools they use in doing so, and additional adaptations that they would like to make. NCAC's Teacher Practice Group has also developed a sample lesson plan outlining the process of developing a UDL lesson.

4. Consensus-building among varied stakeholders. NCAC is generating interest in UDL by reaching out to professional and lay constituencies, including parents and parent organizations; general and special education professional organizations such as the American Federation of Teachers (AFT), the National Association of Elementary School Principals (NAESP), and the National Council of Teachers of Mathematics (NCTM); and organizations such as the International Reading Association (IRA) and the Association for Supervision and Curriculum Development (ASCD). CEC and PACER are working to gather insights, ideas, and feedback from these and other constituents, all of whom are helping to shape UDL.

NCAC is committed to digital media. CAST's work in Universal Design for Learning has now become part of the textbook adoption calls in several states. The California Department of Education has incorporated UDL principles into its Criteria for 2002 Language Arts Adoption, and the Florida Department of Education's Instructional Materials Specifications for Reading, Grades K–12 (2001 adoption) refers publishers to UDL research on the CAST Web site.

Despite this progress, most general curriculum materials, teaching methods, and policies are poorly designed to address individual differences of any kind and fall far short of meeting the challenge of educating students with disabilities. As a result, highly motivated teachers spend a considerable amount of time preparing adaptations and accommodations to their materials and methods. Such retrofitting usually comes at the expense of core preparation and actual instruction. Other teachers continue to use existing materials and methods "as is." The unfortunate result is poor performance from disabled students on large-scale tests, the "warehousing" of these students, and for many, an end to the progress they were making in the general curriculum.

To bring about change, we need to build the awareness that can lead to action.

➤ Teachers need to know that there are alternatives to inaccessible core curricular materials and that finding and using these materials can help them serve the needs of all their students.

➤ Administrators and textbook adoption committees need to require UDL materials and to specify the flexibility those materials and tools should offer.

➤ Parents need to know that they can seek UDL materials and tools so that their children can participate in the general education curriculum at the highest possible level.

Web Link

RESOURCE:
Find online information and links from the National Center on Accessing the General Curriculum at *http://www.cast.org/ TeachingEveryStudent/ ncac*

➤ Publishers need clear and consistent guidelines for how to prepare, disseminate, and protect their materials in accessible digital versions. They need models for how to take advantage of the new technologies to increase access and support for students.

By complementing traditional materials (such as textbooks) with digital versions and providing flexible tools, educators can reduce or eliminate many barriers to learning and set up effective supports.

The Universal Learning Center

CAST, through our leadership of NCAC, has received preliminary funding from the U.S. Department of Education and others to establish an Internet-based service that will provide teachers, administrators, publishers, and parents with just-in-time access to the tools and resources they need for UDL. The Universal Learning Center (ULC) will have four main components:

➤ A Web site, which will serve as a portal to the tools and resources offered by the ULC.

➤ A searchable database of information about digital educational materials available in the ULC and elsewhere on the World Wide Web.

➤ The Content Library and Tools catalogue, housing a centralized collection of digital materials in a secure location.

➤ Consulting and production services to assist publishers and other producers of content.

The Universal Learning Center will help educators and parents obtain accessible digital core curriculum materials; it will give publishers and content providers the capacity to respond to new accessibility requirements so that they can qualify for state adoptions; and it will provide all students with opportunities for success.

Universal Learning Editions

You may be familiar with the Modern Library Editions of classic literature. These handsome volumes offer a high-quality presentation of revered works, adding modern insights, viewpoints, and concepts. CAST is researching and developing a parallel UDL concept: the Universal Learning Editions (ULEs).

Universal Learning Editions, to be available in digital form and online, will include a wide range of supports to scaffold individual learn-

Web Link

RESOURCE:
Visit CAST's Universal Learning Center at *http://ulc.cast.org*

ers and make the content accessible to everyone. ULEs will not only adhere to the Web Accessibility Guidelines developed by the World Wide Web Consortium, but will be further enriched to meet the Universal Design for Learning criteria established by CAST and supported by the National Center on Accessing the General Curriculum.

These editions may include classics from many genres of literature (historical documents, biographies, fiction, poetry, etc.), and music, graphic arts, and film. Textbooks, workbooks, and other forms of instructional media could also be configured to meet Universal Learning Editions criteria, eliminating the need for multiple versions of the same classroom resource. Combining the transformability of digital media with scaffolds for learning goals and customized embedded assessment, ULEs will provide educators, parents, and students with accessible, enhanced, and previously unachievable opportunities for instruction and learning.

The National Consortium on UDL

As part of CAST's approach to systemic change, we have formed the National Consortium on Universal Design for Learning, a community of educators committed to improving learning opportunities for every student by applying UDL principles to classroom practice. Consortium members share information and ideas and together build models and methods that work. For example, the Consortium is working to design and implement new approaches to curriculum planning that capitalize on the collective expertise of regular and special educators to choose, adapt, or design supportive and challenging instructional units for all learners. The Consortium's work connects closely with that of the NCAC: advancing the concept of UDL and exploring promising instructional strategies, curricula, technology tools, and professional development models.

CAST offers UDL-related opportunities to Consortium members. For example, members may participate in occasional instructional workshops held at CAST's Peabody, Massachusetts, offices, and apply through a request-for-proposals process for professional development activities such as UDL fellowships and sponsored attendance at selected conferences. The Fellowship program offers on-site experience at CAST and financial support to further UDL in schools. Consortium members also receive early notice of technologies under development at CAST, with possible participation in beta testing. You will find the Consortium information, forums, and the online newsletter at http://www.cast.org/nationalconsortium.

Conclusion

Teaching has always been a challenging profession. The sense of challenge is particularly acute for teachers today, who face increasingly diverse classrooms and the demands of national and state standards. At the same time, teachers in the Digital Age work in an environment of unprecedented opportunities. Brain research has shed new light on students and how they learn. Technological advances have equipped us with tremendous new instructional resources in the form of computers and digital media. Universal Design for Learning incorporates the insights, tools, and resources born of these developments into a framework that can help teachers respond effectively to 21st-century challenges.

Universal Design for Learning revamps traditional perspectives on education. Within the UDL framework, divisions between ability and disability give way to an understanding that categorical approaches to education obscure the complex and subtle patterns of strength and weakness that affect all learners. We are coming to understand that a learner's true ability lies at the junction of his or her personal capabilities and the capacities afforded by available learning media. By considering the nature of the three brain networks critical to learning and by selecting media and tools wisely, we can extend learners' abilities and open pathways to success for every one.

The UDL framework guides teachers through the process of injecting flexibility into three core elements of teaching: *setting goals, selecting materials and methods to support students in reaching those goals,* and *designing accurate ongoing assessment.* The evolution witnessed with the Concord, New Hampshire, school system offers a glimpse of what teachers, parents, and administrators can accomplish when they apply this new perspective to the carefully considered use of new digital tools and resources. In Concord, regular classroom teachers, special education teachers, and technology specialists are innovating adjustable teaching approaches. In these variable learning environments, students with disabilities are becoming successful and confident members of regular classrooms, while their classmates thrive in ways impossible in the classrooms of the past.

The Concord classrooms illustrate one approach to translating theory from various areas of brain, cognitive, and pedagogical research into effective curriculum and practice. They show that UDL can and does work. Meanwhile, the National Center on Accessing the General Curriculum, the Universal Learning Center, and the Universal Learning Editions promise systemic changes in support of UDL.

➤ ➤ ➤ ➤ ➤

Universal Design for Learning does require change, and change requires activism. Although educational reform efforts are most visible in classrooms where they are being practiced, the most successful ones extend beyond teachers and outside classrooms to involve administrators, parents, and politicians. We hope that this book will encourage you to do your part, to demand Universal Design for Learning within your school system, and to become part of a community that helps make it happen.

Appendix

Appendix:
Classroom Templates

Each learner brings unique qualities to school, including particular challenges, strengths, and interests. With the UDL framework, teachers can apply digital tools and flexible methods to provide adjustable curriculum that works for everyone. These four templates are designed to help teachers apply the UDL framework to reach every learner.

Template 1—Class Learning Profile supports an evaluation of student strengths, weaknesses, and preferences within the three brain networks. This template extends Chapter 2 by offering examples and a framework for collecting insights about students in light of the learning brain.

Template 2—Curriculum Barriers supports evaluation of the curriculum context and analysis of potential barriers in planned methods and materials. It also helps you examine planned curriculum in light of student strengths and weaknesses identified with Template 1. This template extends Chapter 6 by supporting a systematic look at common approaches to teaching and highlighting the ways in which these approaches may limit opportunity for some learners.

Template 3—UDL Solutions supports the use of technology to select and devise methods and materials that will minimize learning barriers and expand opportunities for all students. This template extends Chapter 6 by bringing together a wide variety of techniques and tools you will want to consider when creating UDL solutions.

Template 4—Creating Systemic Change supports district implementation by applying relevant aspects of the approach used by the Concord School District, Concord, New Hampshire. This template extends Chapter 8 by highlighting the key techniques that were successful in Concord, and inviting you to consider these approaches (and new ones) in the context of your own district.

Each template includes an introduction and three parts (Forms A, B, and C):

> **Form A** provides an example of how the template might be used.
> **Form B** offers collected sample items to use in the Blank Template.
> **Form C** offers a framework for applying UDL.

The print version of these templates can be copied and used. The online version is interactive and expandable.

Template 1:
Class Learning Profile

The **Class Learning Profile Template** helps you better understand your students by identifying and noting their strengths, weaknesses, and preferences. The idea is to highlight the particular student talents, weaknesses, or interests that could facilitate or hinder the effectiveness of your teaching.

Develop the profile in the context of particular learning goals, so that you can determine which student qualities may pose challenges or offer special opportunities. For example, if you're addressing a social studies goal requiring work with a textbook and lecture presentations, students who show difficulty with reading fluency, limited English proficiency, or poor listening skills may encounter barriers to learning. Conversely, if a student can draw exceptionally well, and the social studies unit does not tap into this skill, you are missing an opportunity to engage this learner, and possibly others as well. Extending learning options, even for the sake of just one learner, opens new opportunities for the whole class.

Form 1A, the **Model Template,** shows an example of a Class Learning Profile for a particular 3rd grade class, highlighting notable student strengths, weaknesses, and interests that pertain to a science unit on plants. Note that only a few students are described—those whose particular qualities may affect their ability to make use of the curriculum as originally planned.

Form 1B, Examples of Student Qualities, lists examples of student strengths, weaknesses, and interests—structured for each brain network—to help you get started as you create your own Class Learning Profiles.

Form 1C, the **Blank Template,** offers structured support for deriving Class Learning Profiles. Refer to Form 1B for ideas as you consider your students, and add new items as needed.

► Form 1A   Class Learning Profile   Model Template

Grade: 3   **Teacher:** Mrs. G.   **Subject:** Science   **Standard:** 6.23—The Lifecycle of Plants

Goal: *Research and present information on a flower.*

NETWORK	Students—Strengths	Students—Weaknesses	Students—Preferences/Interests
Recognition (Learning "what")	*Elizabeth*—Thorough knowledge of flowers (annuals) *Jorge*—Extensive vocabulary	*Kevin*—Low vision *Brian*—Limited English proficiency *Kiwa*—Difficulty discerning key concepts when reading or listening	
Strategy (Learning "how")	*Bill*—Computer wiz; familiar with electronic encyclopedia and the Web *Marina*—Very good at oral presentations *Jake*—Talented at drawing	*Brian*—Difficulty with organization when doing a project or paper *Sarita*—Poor writing mechanics—spelling, proofreading, handwriting *Phillip*—Fine motor difficulties	
Affect (Learning "why")	*Mandy*—Very confident, strong self-esteem *Phillip*—Extremely persistent through challenges *James*—Leadership/works well in collaborative groups	*Brian*—Easily discouraged, afraid to take risks *Kiwa*—Loses focus and dreams or distracts other kids *Helen*—Personal concerns, often distracted	*Elizabeth*—Loves gardening, horses *Bill*—Loves computer graphics, the Web, any new software program *Jake*—Prefers hands-on activities *Brian*—Thrives with a lot of structure *Jorge*—Plays saxophone very well

▲ Form 1B Examples of Student Qualities

Recognition Strengths

- ☐ Excellent observer
- ☐ Extraordinary spatial ability
- ☐ Excellent interpretation graphs/charts
- ☐ Acute sensitivity to nuance/tone
- ☐ Perfect pitch
- ☐ Extensive musical background
- ☐ Excellent at deriving key points from spoken/written language
- ☐ Extensive vocabulary
- ☐ Extensive content knowledge: (list)

_____

_____

- ☐ Knowledge of multiple languages
- ☐ Advanced reading abilities: (circle)
  word recognition
  word decoding
  text structures/story grammar
  author style
  skimming

_____

- ☐ Facility with hypertext (e.g., Web links, navigation through electronic documents)
- ☐ Skill with rhymes, phonemic awareness, language play

_____

☐ ☐

Recognition Weaknesses

- ☐ Low vision
- ☐ Blindness
- ☐ Poor visual/spatial understanding
- ☐ Color blindness
- ☐ Hearing impairment
- ☐ Deafness
- ☐ Difficulty processing and deriving meaning from spoken language
- ☐ Limited vocabulary
- ☐ Limited content knowledge (list)

_____

_____

- ☐ Limited English proficiency
- ☐ Difficulty with reading: (circle)
  word recognition
  word decoding
  text structures/story grammar
  author style
  fluency

_____

- ☐ Difficulty/confusion with hypertext
- ☐ Tendency to literal interpretation
- ☐ Difficulty finding important information

_____

☐ ☐

► Form 1B   Examples of Student Qualities   *continued*

Strategic Strengths

- ☐ Drawing/artistic talent
- ☐ Talented athlete
- ☐ Skilled with 3-dimensional design
- ☐ Talented singer/musician
- ☐ Excellent at computer graphics
- ☐ Excellent dancer
- ☐ Outstanding speaker/presenter
- ☐ Outstanding written expression skills: (circle)

    poetry
    narrative
    expository writing
    journal
    dialogue/drama
    songs

- ☐ Outstanding concentration/attention
- ☐ Highly organized
- ☐ Highly flexible, adaptable
- ☐ Facility with constructing
    (building, assembling, fixing, designing)
- ☐ Strong problem analysis/solving skills
- ☐ Strong at summarizing, paraphrasing
- ☐ Strong at composing
    (art, dance, multimedia, visual)

    _____

- ☐ ☐

Strategic Weaknesses

- ☐ Fine motor difficulties
- ☐ Gross motor coordination problems
- ☐ Hand-eye coordination problems
- ☐ Poor handwriting
- ☐ Poor spelling
- ☐ Speech impairment
- ☐ Difficulty with oral presentations
- ☐ Written expression problems: (circle)

    selecting/narrowing topic
    planning
    organization
    proofreading
    addressing audience

    _____

- ☐ Restless/fidgety
- ☐ Poor self-monitoring
- ☐ Trouble completing work
- ☐ Over-focused, difficulty with transitions
- ☐ Poor organization
- ☐ Difficulty seeking relevant information
- ☐ Poor memory for spoken information
- ☐ Poor memory for written information
- ☐ Difficulty taking good notes
- ☐ Trouble finding key concepts
- ☐ Trouble prioritizing

    _____
    _____

- ☐ ☐ ☐

➤ Form 1B   Examples of Student Qualities   *continued*

Affective Strengths

☐ Persistent
☐ Optimistic
☐ Highly confident
☐ Outstanding leadership skills
☐ High energy
☐ Deep subject interests
☐ Very independent worker
☐ Deeply caring and considerate
☐ Excellent collaborator
☐ Seeker of challenge
☐ Focused
☐ Good at offering and making use of constructive feedback
☐ Good collaborator
_____
_____
_____
☐ ☐ ☐ ☐ ☐

Affective Weaknesses

☐ Discouraged
☐ Overconfident
☐ Low expectation of success
☐ Difficulty working in groups
☐ Difficulty working in pairs
☐ Fearful
☐ Withdrawn
☐ Domineering
☐ Problems outside of school
☐ Gives up easily
☐ Difficulty with independent work
☐ Tendency to clown
☐ "Turned off" to studying
_____
_____
_____
☐ ☐ ☐ ☐ ☐

Preferences/Interests

☐ Structured tasks
☐ Open-ended tasks
☐ Hands-on activities
☐ Video games
☐ Work with graphics/images
☐ Singing
☐ Drama
☐ Art
☐ Collaborative work
☐ Individual work
☐ Content interests: (list)
_____
_____
_____
_____
☐ Activity interests: (list)
_____
_____
☐ Need to be active
☐ Computer multimedia
☐ ☐ ☐

▲ Form 1C Class Learning Profile Blank Template

Teacher: **Subject:** **Standard:**

Grade:
Goal:

NETWORK	Students—Strengths	Students—Weaknesses	Students—Preferences/Interests
Recognition (Learning "what")			
Strategy			
Affect (Learning "why")			

Template 2: Curriculum Barriers

The **Curriculum Barriers Template** helps you analyze the potential barriers inherent in your planned curriculum materials and methods.

Traditional curriculum materials (such as textbooks, workbooks, and chapter-end questions) and traditional techniques (such as lecturing, writing on the board, and seatwork) pose barriers for some students, limiting their engagement and learning. Newer approaches using computers and the Internet can also be troublesome for some students and need to be thoughtfully applied. Applying the Class Profile you derived from Template 1, use this template to analyze the barriers your students will face in a particular unit of curriculum. The template can help you identify potential barriers based on student weaknesses in the three brain networks, as well as potential missed opportunities based on student strengths and interests. This analysis lays the groundwork for including every learner by developing UDL approaches for teaching.

Form 2A, the **Model Template,** shows how a teacher might examine planned curriculum materials and methods for the science unit on plants planned for the 3rd grade class profiled in Template 1. Each method or material, listed at left, is aligned with student qualities. Form 2A highlights barriers created by the interaction between materials, methods, and student weaknesses and points out missed opportunities created in the intersection between materials, methods, and student strengths or interests.

Form 2B, Examples of Prevailing Methods and Materials, offers examples of common instructional practices. Included are teaching and learning materials, teaching approaches, and student activities.

Form 2C, the **Blank Template,** offers structured support for analyzing potential barriers and missed opportunities in your own curriculum, within the context of your goals and your particular students.

▲ Form 2A   Curriculum Barriers   Model Template

Grade: 3   **Teacher:** Mrs. G.   **Subject:** Science   **Standard:** 6.23—The Lifecycle of Plants

Goal: *Research and present information on a flower.*

Materials and Methods	Student Qualities	Potential Barriers/Missed Opportunities
Printed textbook	*Kevin*—Low vision *Bill*—Loves computer graphics *Brian*—Limited English	Difficulty seeing small text Textbook does not tap into this interest and skill Difficulty decoding and understanding word meaning
Lecture/whole class presentation	*Jose*—Limited English *Helen*—Home problems *Kiwa*—Loses focus, dreams	Difficulty comprehending meaning May not engage with material, distracted from listening May not engage with material, distracted from listening
Library research	*Brian*—Organizational problems *Kiwa*—Trouble with key concepts	May have trouble keeping track of what he is learning May not be able to abstract the important content for project
Written report	*Sarita*—Poor writing mechanics *Jake*—Talented at drawing	Difficulty expressing her ideas effectively Does not tap into Jake's drawing skill
Flower drawing	*Phillip*—Fine motor problems	Drawing is physically arduous—may not engage him
Oral report on flower	*Jorge*—Saxophone player *Brian*—Easily discouraged	Does not tap into Jorge's musical talent May intimidate Brian
Independent project	*James*—Strong leadership and collaboration skills *Helen*—Distracted, personal concerns *Elizabeth*—Deep knowledge of plants	Context won't draw on his leadership and collaboration skills Helen could have difficulty working alone

➤ Form 2B   Examples of Prevailing Methods and Materials

Materials/Media

Printed materials

- ☐ Textbook
- ☐ Workbook
- ☐ Trade book
- ☐ Posters
- ☐ Worksheets
- ☐ Newspapers/magazines
- ☐ _____
- ☐ _____

Computer based materials

- ☐ CD-ROM
- ☐ Internet
- ☐ Interactive software
- ☐ Applications
- ☐ Graphics
- ☐ _____
- ☐ _____

Images

- ☐ Photographs
- ☐ Drawings
- ☐ Timelines
- ☐ Graphs
- ☐ Charts
- ☐ Tables
- ☐ Maps
- ☐ _____
- ☐ _____

Methods/Student Activities

Information presentation method

- ☐ Chalk/white board
- ☐ Overheads
- ☐ Lecture
- ☐ Printed notes/outlines
- ☐ Handouts
- ☐ _____
- ☐ _____

Learning context

- ☐ Small-group discussion
- ☐ Large-group discussion
- ☐ Independent reading
- ☐ In-class assignment
- ☐ Homework
- ☐ _____
- ☐ _____

Instructional formats

- ☐ Small-group instruction
- ☐ Individual seatwork
- ☐ Lecture
- ☐ Collaborative learning
- ☐ 1-to-1 instruction
- ☐ Hands-on activities
- ☐ _____
- ☐ _____

▲ Form 2B   Examples of Prevailing Methods and Materials   *continued*

Materials/Media

Presentation/student response media

- ☐ Video
- ☐ Audio (tape/CD)
- ☐ Slides/overheads
- ☐ Pen/pencil
- ☐ Highlighters
- ☐ Art supplies
- ☐ Computer tools
- ☐ Music
- ☐
- ☐
- ☐ _____
- ☐ _____

Objects

- ☐ Manipulatives
- ☐
- ☐ _____

Methods/Student Activities

Project/presentation formats

- ☐ Term paper/research paper
- ☐ Group project
- ☐ Oral presentation
- ☐ Handwritten paper
- ☐ Drawing/diagram
- ☐ Three dimensional project
- ☐ Oral reading
- ☐ Graphic presentation
- ☐
- ☐
- ☐ _____
- ☐ _____

Student research

- ☐ Library research
- ☐ Online research
- ☐ Data collection
- ☐ Interviews
- ☐
- ☐
- ☐ _____

▲ Form 2C

Curriculum Barriers   Blank Template

Grade: Teacher: Subject: Standard:
Goal:

Materials and Methods	Student Qualities	Potential Barriers/Missed Opportunities

Template 3:
UDL Solutions

The **UDL Solutions Template** helps you select, assemble, or create flexible learning materials and methods including tools, digital content, and Web-based materials to minimize barriers for your students.

Use this template in concert with Template 1 and Template 2 to expand teaching practices and include more students. Consider alternative and additional options for materials, means of presenting information, means for student response, learning context, and instructional content. Note that these approaches and strategies, although chosen to overcome problems for individual learners, open avenues for *all* students in the class.

Form 3A, the **Model Template,** shows examples of UDL solutions to the anticipated barriers and missed opportunities derived using Template 1 and Template 2.

Form 3B, Examples of UDL Solutions, is divided into three segments, addressing the three brain networks: recognition, strategy, and affect. For each, Form 3B offers examples of technology-based tools, media, and methods as well as instructional strategies to expand your repertoire and engage more students. Note that the appropriateness of these solutions and options depends upon your instructional goal. Providing scaffolds such as spell checkers for writing or text-to-speech for reading is appropriate only if the goal of a lesson is focused on process and content, not on writing or reading mechanics.

Form 3C, the **Blank Template,** offers structured support for selecting and designing UDL Solutions for your own class.

▲ Form 3A   Deriving UDL Solutions   Model Template

Grade: 3   **Teacher:** Mrs. G.   **Subject:** Science   **Standard:** 6.23—The Lifecycle of Plants

Goal: *Research and present information on a flower.*

Materials and Methods	Potential Barriers/ Missed Opportunities	UDL Solutions
Printed textbook	*Kevin*—Difficulty seeing small text *Bill*—Doesn't tap his graphics skills *Brian*—Difficulty decoding/understanding word meaning	Electronic text with text-to-speech to read aloud CD-ROM or online encyclopedia; Web page with collections of images Spanish CD-ROM on flowers; link to Spanish Web site
Lecture/whole class presentation	*Jose*—Difficulty comprehending meaning *Helen*—Distracted, may miss info *Kiwa*—Distracted, may miss info	Provide Spanish/English key terms translations with text-to-speech Provide Inspiration concept map of key ideas; eText outline with text to speech that students can access
Library research	*Brian*—May have trouble keeping track *Kiwa*—May not be able to abstract the project's important content	Partially filled-in outlines; Web page with attached resources; collection of online resources, online or CD-ROM encyclopedia, linked to Inspiration outline of key project parts
Create written report	*Sarita*—Mechanics-based difficulty expressing her ideas *Jake*—Format doesn't tap artistic talent	Word processor with spell check; talking word processor Graphics program—Kid Pix
Flower drawing	*Phillip*—Drawing will be physically difficulty	Word processing; selection of graphics to use in report
Oral report on flower	*Jorge*—Format doesn't tap musical talent *Brian*—May be intimidated	Provide option of live or recorded music as part of demonstration Pair Brian with James, who can support him while working
Independent project	*James*—Context won't draw on his leadership and collaboration skills *Helen*—Could have difficulty working alone *Elizabeth*—Deep knowledge of plants	Encourage James to support other students as they work Be sure to find aspect of project of particular interest to Helen and check in frequently; support presentation with notes Pair Elizabeth with Jose to share her knowledge and enthusiasm

▲ Form 3B   Examples of UDL Solutions

Recognition Networks

Multiple Examples

□ Multiple versions of story/math process/content
□ Multimedia collections: (circle)
  Images
  Sounds
  Text
  Video/animation
  Concept maps
□ Links to online examples from Web page
□ Multimedia concept map with online/local links
□ Animation of text meaning (software, Web)
□ □ □

Highlight Critical Features

□ Visual concept maps (Inspiration)
□ Multimedia templates (Hyperstudio, PowerPoint)
□ Color highlighting in word processing
□ Graphic highlighting (circles, arrows, boxes)
□ Links to animations showing key elements
□ Software offering different presentations
□ E-text outline, main points (with text-to-speech translation)
  □ □

Multiple Media and Formats

□ Multimedia glossary, online, CD-ROM or teacher-made
□ Cross-media alternatives: (circle)
  E-text with text-to-speech
  Text and audio descriptions for still images
  Spoken descriptions for video images
  Tactile graphics
  Voice recognition—convert to text
  Image collections in concept maps
□ Text outline, highlighting key concepts
□ Digital photographs from field trips or home
□ Recorded, digitized sounds and stories
□ Adjustable font size/color/background color
□ Adjustable digital images (e.g., maps)
□

Support Background Knowledge

□ Web pages with links to related information
□ Links to author information
□ Key vocabulary (image map, hyperlinks to words)
□ Translation to other languages (online tools)
□ Expansion of information—build multimedia collections
□ Online links to experts
□ Multimedia glossary, encyclopedia
□

▲ Form 3B   Examples of UDL Solutions   *continued*

Strategic Networks

Models of Skilled Performance

☐ Product models—finished versions of target skill
☐ Process models—showing process steps
☐ Collections of completed products (Web links/local): (circle)
☐ Past student work
☐ Work of experts
☐ Teacher generated examples
☐ Students in other settings
☐ Multimedia collections—stories, facts, information
☐ Online links to work of experts
_____
_____
☐ ☐ ☐

Ongoing Relevant Feedback

☐ Digital voice record, play back
☐ Text-to-speech while writing
☐ Links to online mentors
☐ Links to peers/editors (e.g., www.stonesoup.com)
☐ Digital portfolio—review and compare
☐ Prompts to self-reflect, record reflections
☐ Online publishing, local network or Internet
☐ Digital graphing of progress
_____
_____
☐ ☐ ☐

Practice with Supports

☐ Talking word processor (e.g., Write Out Loud)
☐ Templates to structure work as appropriate
☐ Scaffolds, use depending on goal: (circle)
☐ Spell check, grammar check
☐ Built-in calculator
☐ Clip media (all sorts), student projects
☐ Text-to-speech for content reading
☐ Graphic organizers (e.g., Inspiration)
☐ Hyperstudio story or presentation template
☐ Chapter-end answers partially structured
_____
_____
☐ ☐ ☐

Demonstration of Skills

☐ Multimedia presentation tools (Hyperstudio, PowerPoint)
☐ Web-capable graphic organizers (Inspiration)
☐ Publishing software (Hyperstudio, Pagemaker)
☐ Web site design tools (Home Page, Dreamweaver)
☐ Multimedia recording, image digitizing, digital cameras
☐ Media banks—images, sounds, animations, video
☐ Digital recording
☐ Draw tools
_____
_____
☐ ☐ ☐

> Form 3B   Examples of UDL Solutions

continued

Affective Networks

Choice of Content and Tools

☐ Selections of content for learning skills and strategies
☐ Web sites with supplementary, related activities
☐ Multimedia presentation and composition tools
☐ Digital cameras, recording devices
☐ Web page with content options and choices
☐ Selection of stories/nonfiction for learning to read
☐ Tie activities to student's deep subject interests
_____
☐ ☐

Choice of Rewards

☐ Individualized feedback to support student needs
☐ Explicit feedback specific to student progress
☐ Minimal extrinsic "rewards" not tied to work
☐ Build student self-monitoring
☐ Feedback related to explicit student goals
☐ Opportunities for demonstrations
☐ Built-in structured peer feedback
_____
☐ ☐ ☐

Adjustable Support and Challenge

☐ Software/Web sites offering management systems
☐ Optional scaffolds (teacher/student discretion)
☐ Templates supporting process
☐ Templates supporting content
☐ Choice of level, same activity or goal
☐ Optional help (teacher/student discretion)
_____
☐ ☐

Choice of Learning Context

☐ "Web Quest" designs, with varied structure
☐ Software/Web sites, options for feedback and support
☐ Flexible work groups—pairs, small groups, individual
☐ Templates with optional structure and support
☐ Earphones
☐ Embedded hyperlinks, used at student option
☐ Student choice of sources
_____
☐ ☐ ☐

▶ Form 3C   Deriving UDL Solutions   Blank Template

Grade: Teacher: Subject: Standard:
Goal:

Materials and Methods	Potential Barriers/ Missed Opportunities	UDL Solutions				

Template 4:
Creating Systemic Change

The **Creating Systemic Change Template** helps you apply the relevant parts of the Concord Model to your school or district to build new instructional approaches for reaching every learner.

The seven components included in this template have been critical to building systemic change within the Concord school system and creating a districtwide commitment to use flexible curriculum to engage all learners. Because every school and district is unique, it is likely that a subset of these components may be effective or essential for you, and other new components may emerge.

Form 4A, the **Model Template**, lists the seven components of the Concord Model with examples of implementation approaches that have evolved in that district.

Form 4B, Examples from the Concord Model, offers a more comprehensive set of implementation strategies within the seven main components of the model.

Form 4C, the **Blank Template,** offers structured support for selecting those parts of the Concord model that might apply in your district, and adding new components as well as specific implementation strategies.

195

▲ Form 4A   Creating Systemic Change   Model Template

Concord Model Component	Concord Implementation Examples
1. Technology infrastructure	Intranet and Internet installed; teachers as part-time technology experts and mentors; computers in classrooms and labs; software and content availability
2. Administrative support	Advocates present UDL to principals, school board, administrators; Grant writing involving administration; reallocation of funds from various sources to make UDL work for all students
3. Teacher training and support	Ongoing training strands; classroom teachers offered mentoring within building; teachers have option to train for new roles and teach part-time
4. Redefined roles for special and regular education teachers	Special education teachers collaborate with technology staff, acquire technology skills, and bring new techniques to all students in the classroom.
5. Collaborative curriculum planning	Special education teachers, classroom teachers, and technology personnel address curriculum barriers and solutions collaboratively; review potential barriers ahead of working with students
6. Parent and community involvement	Parent volunteers for digitizing and gathering and using other UDL materials; parent participation via the Web in student learning
7. Creative funding	Special funds, including special educations funds, applied to UDL to improve learning for all; small grant opportunities; collaboration with nonprofits

▲ Form 4B Creating Systemic Change Concord Model Examples

Technology Infrastructure

- ☐ Wiring for Internet and Intranet
- ☐ Computers and software, districtwide/networked
- ☐ Technology coordinator staff
- ☐ Commitment to digitizing curriculum
- ☐ Widely available software and digital resources
- ☐ Within-school and within-district servers
- ☐ Classroom connections to Internet and Intranet
- ☐ District Web site; class Web sites
- ☐ Within-building tech support
- ☐ ——————
- ☐ ☐

Teacher Training

- ☐ Multiple, ongoing training strands, required
- ☐ Classroom teachers opportunity to mentor others
- ☐ Teachers have option to train for new part-time roles
- ☐ Teachers as part-time technology coordinators
- ☐ Multiple summer institutes
- ☐ Continuous collaborative support
- ☐ Open atmosphere to share problems and solutions
- ☐ ——————
- ☐ ☐

Administrative Support

- ☐ Advocates present to administrators, school board
- ☐ Some administrators/principals spearhead work
- ☐ Administrators support grant writing
- ☐ Administrators support flexible fund allocation
- ☐ Commitment to UDL from superintendent level
- ☐ ——————
- ☐ ☐

Redefined Roles

- ☐ Special education teachers collaborate with technology staff
- ☐ Special education teachers collaborate with regular education teachers
- ☐ Special education specialists focus on mainstream curriculum
- ☐ Classroom teachers increase flexibility of curriculum
- ☐ Teachers participate in digitizing, creating units
- ☐ ——————
- ☐ ☐

➤ Form 4B Creating Systemic Change Concord Model Examples

Collaborative Curriculum Planning

- ☐ Special education, educational technology, regular education staff plan together
- ☐ Group analyzes curriculum barriers/solutions
- ☐ Focus is on curricular flexibility, not student disabilities
- ☐ Look ahead to potential barriers
- ☐ Pre-build solutions to increase learning for all
- ☐ Commitment shared across disciplines
- ☐ _____
- ☐ _____
- ☐

Creative Funding

- ☐ Reallocation of special education and technology funds to create pool
- ☐ Joint grant applications with nonprofits
- ☐ Small grant applications, state, foundation, federal
- ☐ Districtwide commitment increases willingness to be flexible
- ☐ Commitment shared across disciplines
- ☐ _____
- ☐ _____

Parent/Community Involvement

- ☐ Parent participation in digitizing, resource collection
- ☐ PTO informed and committed to UDL initiatives
- ☐ Parent involvement via Web in classrooms and student work
- ☐ Seek buy-in from community to pool resources
- ☐ _____
- ☐
- ☐

► Form 4C   Creating Systemic Change   Blank Template

Concord Model Component	Implementation Examples
1. Technology infrastructure	
2. Administrative support	
3. Teacher training	
4. Redefined roles	
5. Collaborative curriculum planning	
6. Parent/community involvement	
7. Creative funding	
8.	
9.	

References and Resources

Adamec, R. E. (1991). Individual differences in temporal lobe sensory processing of threatening stimuli in the cat. *Physiology and Behavior, 49*, 455–464.

Adams, M. J. (1994). *Beginning to read: Thinking and learning about print.* Cambridge, MA: MIT Press.

Anderson-Inman, L., & Horney, M. (1996/97). Computer-based concept mapping: Enhancing literacy with tools for visual thinking. *Journal of Adolescent & Adult Literacy, 40*(4), 302–306.

Anderson-Inman, L., Knox-Quinn, C., & Horney, M. (1996). Computer-based study strategies for students with learning disabilities: Individual differences associated with adoption level. *Journal of Learning Disabilities, 29*, 461–484.

Asendorpf, J. (1987). Videotape reconstruction of emotions and cognition related to shyness. *Journal of Personality and Social Psychology, 53*, 542–549.

Aylward, E. H., Minshew, N. J., Goldstein, G., Honeycutt, N. A., Augustine, A. M., Yates, K. O., Barta, P. E., & Pearlson, G. D. (1999). MRI volumes of amygdala and hippocampus in non-mentally retarded autistic adolescents and adults. *Neurology, 53*(9), 2145–2150.

Barkly, R. (1997). Attention deficit/hyperactivity disorder self regulation and time: Toward a more comprehensive theory. *Journal of Developmental & Behavioral Pediatrics, 18*(4), 271–279.

Baron-Cohen, S., Ring, H. A., Wheelwright, S., Bullmore, E. T., Brammer, M. J., Simmons, A., & Williams, S. C. (1999). Social intelligence in the normal and autistic brain: An fMRI study. *European Journal of Neuroscience, 11*(6), 1891–1898.

Blythe, T., & Associates. (1998). *The teaching for understanding guide.* San Francisco: Jossey-Bass. Also available: http://learnweb.harvard.edu/alps/tfu/info3d.cfm

Bolter, J. D. (1991). *Writing space: The computer, hypertext, and the history of writing.* Hillsdale, NJ: Lawrence Erlbaum Associates.

Bregman, A. S. (1990). *Auditory scene analysis: The perceptual organization of sound.* Cambridge, MA: MIT Press.

Brooks, J. G., & Brooks, M. (1993). *In search of understanding: The case for the constructivist classroom.* Alexandria, VA: Association for Supervision and Curriculum Development.

Bruder, G. E., Fong, R., Tenke, C. E., Leite, P., Towey, J. P., Stewart, J. E., McGrath, P. J., & Quitkin, F. M. (1997). Regional brain asymmetries in major depression with or without an anxiety disorder: a quantitative electroencephalographic study. *Biological Psychiatry, 41*, 939–48.

Burbaud, P., Camus, O., Guehl, D., Bioulac, B., Caille, J., & Allard, M. (2000). Influence of cognitive strategies on the pattern of cortical activation during mental subtraction. A functional imaging study in human subjects. *Neuroscience Letters, 287*(1), 76–80.

California Department of Education. (2000). *Criteria for 2002 Language Arts Adoption—Curriculum*. Sacramento, CA: Frameworks and Instructional Resources Office. Available: http://www.cde.ca.gov/cfir

Carels, R. A., Sherwood, A., Babyak, M., Gullette, E. C., Coleman, R. E., Waugh, R., Jiang, W., & Blumenthal, J. A. (1999). Emotional responsivity and transient myocardial ischemia. *Journal of Consulting and Clinical Psychology, 67*, 605–610.

CAST eReader. [Computer software]. (1995). Peabody, MA: CAST.

Cole, M. (1996). *Culture in mind*. Cambridge, MA: Harvard University Press.

Cowan, R. S. (1983). *More work for mother*. New York: Basic Books.

Csikszentmihalyi, M. (1997). *Finding flow: The psychology of engagement with everyday life*. New York: Basic Books.

Cummings, E. E. [1956]. maggie and milly and molly and may. In *Selected poems by E. E. Cummings: Introduction & commentary, Richard S. Kennedy* (p. 6). New York: Liveright Publishing Corporation, 1991.

Dalton, B., Pisha, B., Coyne, P., Eagleton, M., & Deysher, S. (2001). *Engaging the text: Reciprocal teaching and questioning strategies in a scaffolded learning environment* (Final report to the U.S. Office of Special Education). Peabody, MA: CAST. Available: http://www.cast.org/EngagingTheTextFinalReport.htm

Damasio, A. (1994). *Descartes' error*. New York: G. P. Putnam's Sons.

de Gelder, B., Bocker, K. B., Tuomainen, J., Hensen, M., & Vroomen, J. (1999). The combined perception of emotion from voice and face: Early interaction revealed by human electric brain responses. *Neuroscience Letters, 260*(2), 133–136.

DeKosky, S. T., Heilman, K. M., Bowers, D., & Valenstein, E. (1980). Recognition and discrimination of emotional faces and pictures. *Brain and Language, 9*, 206–214.

Dempster, F. N. (1993). Exposing our students to less should help them learn. *Phi Delta Kappan, 74*(6), 432–437.

Deshler, D. D., & Schumaker, J. B. (1988). An instructional model for teaching students how to learn. In J. L. Graden, J. E. Zins, & M. J. Curtis (Eds.), *Alternative educational delivery systems: Enhancing instructional options for all students* (pp. 391–411). Washington, DC: National Association of School Psychologists.

Developing Educational Standards: An annotated list of Internet sites with K–12 educational standards and curriculum frameworks documents. [Online]. Available: http://putnamvalleyschools.org/Standards.html [November 15, 2001].

Dimberg, U. (1990). Facial electromyography and emotional reactions. *Psychophysiology, 27*, 481–494.

Electronic Learning Marketplace: An exchange of ideas and information about assessment and the Maine Learning Results. [Online]. Available: www.elm.maine.edu/mlr/math.stm [November 15, 2001].

Etcoff, N., Ekman, P., Magee, J., & Frank, M. (2000). Lie detection and language comprehension. *Nature, 405,* 139.

Federmeier, K. D., Segal, J. B., Lombrozo, T., & Kutas, M. (2000). Brain responses to nouns, verbs, and class-ambiguous words in context. *Brain, 123,* 2552–2566.

Feuerstein, R., Rand, Y., & Hoffman, M. (1979). *Dynamic assessment of retarded performers.* Baltimore: University Park Press.

Fink, R. P. (1995). Successful dyslexics: A constructivist study of passionate interest reading. *Journal of Adolescent & Adult Literacy, 39*(4), 268–280.

Fink, R. P. (1998). Literacy development in successful men and women with dyslexia. *Annals of Dyslexia, 48,* 311–346.

Florida Department of Education. (1999). *Instructional Materials Specifications for Reading Grades K–12, 2001–2002 Adoption.* Available: http://www.firn.edu/doe/cgi-bin/instruct.pl?url=../bin00015/reading.pdf [November 15, 2001].

Fowler, C. A. (1981). Production and perception of coarticulation among stressed and unstressed vowels. *Journal of Speech and Hearing Research, 24,* 127–139.

Frith, C., & Dolan, R. (1996). The role of the prefrontal cortex in higher cognitive functions. *Brain Research: Cognitive Brain Research, 5*(1-2), 175–181.

Funahashi, S. (2001). Neuronal mechanisms of executive control by the prefrontal cortex. *Neuroscience Research, 39,* 147–165.

Gabrieli, J. D., Poldrack, R. A., & Desmond, R. E. (1998). The role of the left prefrontal cortex in language and memory. *Proceedings of the National Academy of Science, 95*(3), 906–913.

Gardner, H. (1993). *Multiple intelligences: The theory in practice.* New York: Basic Books.

Gardner, H. (1999). *The disciplined mind: What all students should understand.* New York: Simon & Schuster.

Gazzaniga, M. S. (1995). *The cognitive neurosciences.* Cambridge, MA: MIT Press.

Gentile, L. M., Lamb, P., & Rivers, C. O. (1985). A neurologist's views of reading difficulty: Implications for remedial instruction. *Reading Teacher, 39*(2), 174–182.

Goleman, D. (1995). *Emotional intelligence: Why it can matter more than IQ.* New York: Bantam Books.

Gopher, D. (1996). Attention control: Explorations of the work of an executive controller. *Cognitive Brain Research, 5,* 23–38.

Graves, D. H. (1983). *Writing: Teachers and children at work.* Exeter, NH: Heinemann.

Graves, D. H. (1990). *Discover your own literacy.* Portsmouth, NH: Heinemann.

Grossman, M. (1999). Sentence processing in Parkinson's disease. *Brain and Cognition, 40,* 387–413.

Hansen, J. (1980). *The gift giver.* New York: Clarion Books.

Harvey, T., Kigar, D., & Witelson, S. (1999). The exceptional brain of Albert Einstein. *The Lancet, 353,* 2149–2153.

Hayes Jacobs, H. (1997). *Mapping the big picture: Integrating curriculum and assessment K–12*. Alexandria, VA: Association for Supervision and Curriculum Development.

Heilman, K., Scholes, M., & Watson, R. (1975). Auditory affective agnosia. *Journal of Neurology, Neurosurgery, and Psychiatry, 38*, 69–72.

Helprin, M. (1991). *A soldier of the Great War.* New York: Harcourt Brace Jovanovich.

Historic Salem, Inc. (1977). *The Salem handbook: A renovation guide for homeowners.* Salem, MA: Author.

Hoff, R., & Maguire, B. (1996). *Say it in six: How to say exactly what you mean in six minutes or less.* Kansas City, MO: Andrews McMeel Publishing.

Individuals with Disabilities Education Act (IDEA) amendments. [Online]. Available: http://www.ideapractices.org/ [November 15, 2001].

Jambaque, I., Dellatolas, G., Dulac, O., Ponsot, G., & Signoret, J. L. (1993). Verbal and visual memory impairment in children with epilepsy. *Neuropsychologia, 31*, 1321–1337.

Johnson, D. W., & Johnson, R. T. (1989). Cooperative learning: What special education teachers need to know. *Pointer, 33*(2), 5–10.

Johnson, D. W., & Johnson, R. T. (1999). Making cooperative learning work. *Theory into Practice, 38*(2), 67–73.

Kalin, N. H. (1999). Primate models to understand human aggression. *Journal of Clinical Psychology, 60*, 29–32.

Kalin, N. H., Shelton, S. E., & Davidson, R. J. (2000). Cerebrospinal fluid corti-cotropin-releasing hormone levels are elevated in monkeys with patterns of brain activity associated with fearful temperament. *Biological Psychiatry, 47*, 579–585.

Kandel, E. R., Schwartz, J. H., & Jessell, T. M., (Eds.). (2000). *Principles of neural science* (4th ed.). New York: McGraw-Hill.

Kendall, J. S., & Marzano, R. J. (1997). *Content knowledge: A compendium of standards and benchmarks for K–12 education.* Aurora, CO: Mid-continent Regional Educational Laboratory. Available: http://www.mcrel.org/standards-benchmarks/

Kinard, E. M. (2001). Perceived and actual academic competence in maltreated children. *Child Abuse and Neglect, 25*(1), 33–45.

King, Jr., M. L. [1963, August 28]. I have a dream. [Address delivered at the March on Washington for Jobs and Freedom.] In J. M. Washington (Ed.), *A testament of hope: The essential writings and speeches of Martin Luther King, Jr.* New York: HarperCollins, 1986. Also available: http://www.stanford.edu/group/King/

Larsen, R. J. (1987). The stability of mood variability: A spectral analytic approach to daily mood assessments. *Journal of Personality and Social Psychology, 52*, 1195–1204.

LeDoux, J. (1998). *The emotional brain: The mysterious underpinnings of emotional life.* London: Weidenfeld & Nicholson.

Lepper, M. R., & Greene, D. (Eds.). (1978). *The hidden costs of reward: New perspectives on the psychology of human motivation.* Hillsdale, NJ: Lawrence Erlbaum Associates.

Leu, D. (2000). The convergence of literacy instruction with networked technologies for information and communication. *Reading Research Quarterly, 35*(1), 108–127.

Levine, B., Stuss, D. T., Milberg, W. P., Alexander, M. P., Schwartz, M., & Macdonald, R. (1998). The effects of focal and diffuse brain damage on strategy application: Evidence from focal lesions, traumatic brain injury and normal aging. *Journal of the International Neuropsychological Society, 4*(3), 247–264.

Lidz, C. S. (1987). *Dynamic assessment: An interactional approach to evaluating learning potential.* New York: Guilford Press.

Lyon, G. R. (1994). *Frames of reference for the assessment of learning disabilities.* Baltimore: Paul H. Brookes Publishing Company.

Madison Metropolitan School District. Madison Metropolitan School District content standards and grade level performance standards. [Online]. Available: www.madison.k12.wi.us/tnl/lang01.htm [November 15, 2001].

Malone, T. W. (1981). Toward a theory of intrinsically motivating instruction. *Cognitive Science, 4*, 333–369.

Marr, M. B. (1997). Cooperative learning: A brief review. *Reading and Writing Quarterly: Overcoming Learning Difficulties, 13*(1), 7–20.

Martino, G., & Marks, L. E. (2000). Cross-modal interaction between vision and touch: The role of synesthetic correspondence. *Perception 2000, 29*(6), 745–754.

Massachusetts Curriculum Frameworks. [Online]. Available: http://www.doe.mass.edu [November 15, 2001].

McGann, J. J. (1991). *The textual condition.* Princeton, NJ: Princeton University Press.

McLuhan, M. (1994). *Understanding media.* (New Edition). Cambridge, MA: The MIT Press.

Meskill, C. (1999). Computers as tools for sociocollaborative language learning. In K. Cameron (Ed.), *CALL: Media, design and applications* (pp.141–164). The Netherlands: Swets & Zeitlinger.

Mid-continent Research for Education and Learning. [Online]. Available: http://www.mcrel.org/ [November 15, 2001].

Morris, R. G., Miotto, E. C., Feigenbaum, J. D., Bullock, P., & Polkey, C. E. (1997). The effect of goal-subgoal conflict on planning ability after frontal- and temporal-lobe lesions in humans. *Neuropsychologia, 35*(8), 1147–1157.

Mountcastle, V. B. (1998). *Perceptual neuroscience: The cerebral cortex.* Cambridge, MA: Harvard Press.

Murphy, S. T., & Zajonc, R. B. (1993). Affect, cognition, and awareness: Affective priming with optimal and suboptimal stimulus exposures. *Journal of Personality and Social Psychology, 64*, 723–739.

Nadeau, S. E. (1988). Impaired grammar with normal fluency and phonology: Implications for Broca's aphasia. *Brain, 111*(5), 1111–1137.

National Commission on Excellence in Education. (1983). *A nation at risk: The imperative for educational reform.* Washington, DC: U.S. Government Printing Office.

National Council of Teachers of English: Standards for the English language arts. [Online]. Available: http://www.ncte.org/standards/standards.shtml [November 15, 2001].

National Council of Teachers of Mathematics. [Online]. Available: http://standards.
nctm.org [November 15, 2001].

National Dance Association. [Online]. Available: http://www.aahperd.org/NDA/nda-
programs.html#standards [November 15, 2001].

National Geography Standards. [Online]. Available: http://www.ncge.org/publications/
tutorial/standards [November 15, 2001].

National Institute of Child Health and Human Development (2000). *Report of the
National Reading Panel. Teaching children to read: An evidence-based assessment of the
scientific research literature on reading and its implications for reading instruction* (NIH
Publication No. 00–4769). Washington, DC: U.S. Government Printing Office.

New York State Learning Standards. [Online]. Available: http://www.nysatl.nysed.gov/
standards.html [November 15, 2001].

O'Donnell, J. J. (1998). *Avatars of the word: From papyrus to cyberspace.* Cambridge, MA:
Harvard Press.

O'Neil, J., & Tell, C. (1999, September). Why students lose when "tougher standards"
win: A conversation with Alfie Kohn. *Educational Leadership, 57*(1), 18–23.

Palincsar, A. S., & Brown, A. L. (1984). Reciprocal teaching of comprehension foster-
ing and monitoring activities. *Cognition and Instruction, 1*, 117–175.

Paulsen, G. (1987). *Hatchet.* New York: Simon & Schuster.

Perkins, D. N. (1998). What is understanding? In Wiske, M. S. (Ed.), *Teaching for understanding: Linking research with practice* (pp. 39–57). San Francisco: Jossey-Bass.

Petersen, S. E., Fox, P. T., Posner, M. I., Mintun, M., & Raichle, M. E. (1988). Positron
emission tomographic studies of the cortical anatomy of single-word processing.
Nature 331, 585–589.

Posner, M. I., & Pavese, A. (1998). Anatomy of word and sentence meaning.
Proceedings of the National Academy of Sciences, USA, 95, 899–905.

Reader Rabbit's Reading Development Library [Computer software]. (1995). Fremont,
CA: Learning Company.

Reiman, E. M., Raichle, M. E., Butler, F. K., Herscovitch, P., & Robins, E. (1984). A focal
brain abnormality in panic disorder, a severe form of anxiety. *Nature, 310,*
683–685.

Roland, P. E., & Zilles, K. (1998). Structural divisions and functional fields in the
human cerebral cortex. *Brain Research Reviews, 26,* 87–105.

Rose, D., & Meyer, A. (2000). Universal design for learning. *Journal of Special Education
Technology, 15*(1), 67–70.

Rosenholtz, S. J. (1991). *Teacher's workplace: The social organization of schools.* New
York: Teachers College Press.

Roswell, F., & Natchez, G. (1977). *Reading disability: A human approach to evaluation
and treatment of reading and writing difficulties.* New York: Basic Books.

Russell, M., & Haney, W. (1997). Testing writing on computers: An experiment comparing student performance on tests conducted via computer and via paper-and-
pencil. *Education Policy Analysis Archives, 5*(3). Available: http://epaa.asu.edu/
epaa/v5n3.html.

Russell, M., & Haney, W. (2000). Bridging the gap between testing and technology in schools. *Education Policy Analysis Archives, 8*(19). Available: http://epaa.asu.edu/epaa/v8n19.html.

Sacks, O. (1985). *The man who mistook his wife for a hat: And other clinical tales.* New York: Summit Books.

Sacks, O. (1995). *Anthropologist on Mars.* New York: Knopf.

Schmoker, M., & Marzano, R. J. (1999, March). Realizing the promise of standards-based education. *Educational Leadership, 56*(6), 17–21.

Scieszka, J. (1989). *The true story of the three little pigs.* New York: Viking Kestrel.

Shaywitz, S. E., Shaywitz, B. A., Pugh, K. R., et al. (1998). Functional disruption in the organization of the brain for reading in dyslexia. *Proceedings of the National Academy of Sciences of the United States of America, 95,* 2636–2641.

Siegil, M. (1995). More than words: The generative power of transmediation for learning. *Canadian Journal of Education, 20*(4), 455–475.

Sizer, T. R. (1992a). *Horace's school: Redesigning the American high school.* Boston: Houghton Mifflin.

Sizer, T. R. (1992b). *Horace's compromise: The dilemma of the American high school.* New York: Mariner Books.

Sizer, T. R. (1996). *Horace's hope: What works for the American high school.* Boston: Houghton Mifflin.

Sizer, T. R. (1999, September). No two are quite alike. *Educational Leadership, 57*(1), 6–11.

Smith, E. E., Jonides, J., Marshuetz, C., & Koeppe, R. A. (1998). Components of verbal working memory: Evidence from neuroimaging. *Proceedings of the National Academy of Science, 95,* 876–882.

State of Maine Learning Results. [Online]. Available: http://janus.state.me.us/education/lres/lres.htm [November 15, 2001].

Stephens, M. (1998). *The rise of the image, the fall of the word.* New York: Oxford University Press.

Sunshine State Standards. [Online]. Available: http://www.firn.edu/doe/cgi-bin/doehome/menu.pl [November 15, 2001].

Tallal, P., Miller, S. L., Bedi, G., Gyma, G., Wang, X., Nagarajan, S. S., Schreiner, C., Jenkins, W. M., & Merzenich, M. M. (1996). Language comprehension in language-learning impaired children improved with acoustically modified speech. *Science, 271,* 81–84.

Thinking Reader. [Computer software]. (2001). Peabody, MA: CAST.

Thorndike, R. L., Hagen, E. P., & Sattler, J. M. (1986). The Stanford-Binet intelligence scale (4th ed.). Chicago: Riverside.

Tomarken, A. J., Davidson, R. J., Wheeler, R. E., & Doss, R. C. (1992). Individual differences in anterior brain asymmetry and fundamental dimensions of emotion. *Journal of Personality and Social Psychology, 62,* 676–687.

Tomlinson, C. A. (1999a). *The differentiated classroom: Responding to the needs of all learners.* Alexandria, VA: Association for Supervision and Curriculum Development.

Tomlinson, C. A. (1999b, September). Mapping a route toward differentiated instruction. *Educational Leadership, 57*(1), 12–16.

Tucker, D. M., Watson, R. T., & Heilman, K. M. (1977). Discrimination and evocation of affectively intoned speech in patients with right parietal disease. *Neurology, 27,* 947–950.

Tzuriel, D. (2000). Dynamic assessment of young children: Educational and intervention perspectives. *Educational Psychology Review, 12*(4), 385–435.

Vygotsky, L. (1962/1996). *Thought and language* (Rev. Ed.). Cambridge, MA: MIT Press.

Ward, J., Stott, R., & Parkin, A. J. (2000). The role of semantics in reading and spelling: Evidence for the 'summation hypothesis.' *Neuropsychologia, 38,* 1643–1653.

Weintraub, S., Mesulam, M. M., & Kramer, L. (1981). Disturbances in prosody. *Archives of Neurology, 38,* 742–744.

Wiggins, G. (1989, November). The futility of trying to teach everything of importance. *Educational Leadership, 47*(3), 44–48, 57–59.

Willis, A. I., & Johnson, J. L. (2000, September). A horizon of possibilities: A critical framework for transforming multiethnic literature instruction. *Reading Online, 4*(3). Available: http://www.readingonline.org/articles/art_index.asp?HREF=/articles/willis/index.html

Wolk, R. (1998, November 25). Education's high-stakes gamble. *Education Week, 18*(15), 48.

Wood, D., Bruner, J. S., & Ross, G. (1976). The role of tutoring in problem solving. *Journal of Child Psychology and Psychiatry, 17*(2), 89–100.

Wood, K. D., & others. (1993). Promoting cooperative learning experiences for students with reading, writing, and learning disabilities. *Reading and Writing Quarterly: Overcoming Learning Difficulties, 9*(4), 369–376.

Yarbus, A. L. (1967). *Eye movements and vision.* New York: Plenum Publishers, Inc.

Zeki, S. (1999). *Inner vision: An exploration of art and the brain.* Oxford, England: Oxford University Press.

Online Resources

Active Learning Practice for Schools (ALPS) Teaching for Understanding. Available: http://learnweb.harvard.edu/alps/tfu/info1b.cfm

The Brain Injury Association of Washington. Available: http://www.bigwg.org

The Children's Literature Web Guide. Available: http://www.ucalgary.ca/~dkbrown

CNN.com Video Vault. Available: http://www.cnn.com/video_vault

Disability Rights Advocates. Available: http://www.dralegal.org

Electric Library. Available: http://www.elibrary.com/

Fluency Through Fables. Available: http://www.comenius.com/fables

MIDI Explorer. Available: http://www.musicrobot.com

NASA Quest. Available: http://www.quest.arc.nasa.gov/

The National Center to Improve the Tools of Educators. Available: http://idea.uoregon.edu/~ncite/

Neuroscience for Kids. Available: http://faculty.washington.edu/chudler/neurok.edu

NOVA Online Adventure. Available: http://www.pbs.org/wgbh/nova/pyramid/

The Online Books Page. Available: http://www.digital.library.upenn.edu/books/

Premier Programming Solutions. Available: http://www.premier-programming.com

Project Gutenberg. Available: http://promo.net/pg/

Public Domain Images. Available: http://www.pdimages.com

ScanSoft. Available: http://www.scansoft.com/products/omnipage/pro/

SearcheBooks.com. Available: http://www.searchebooks.com

Secrets@Sea. Available: http://www.secretsatsea.org/

Smithsonian Institution. Available: http://www.si.edu

Sport! Science at the Exploratorium. Available: http://www.exploratorium.edu/sports/index.html

Stone Soup Magazine. Available: http://www.stonesoup.com

Virtual Labs & Simulations. Available: http://www.hazelwood.k12.mo.us/~grichert/sciweb/applets.html

Web Accessibility Initiative. Available: http://www.w3.org/WAI

WebQuest. Available: http://www.richmond.edu/~ed344/webquests/rome/frames.html

WGBH. Available: http://www.wgbh.org

World Village. Available: http://www.worldvillage.com/wv/school/html/reviews/write.htm

Yahoo Stock Photography. Available: http://www.yahoo.com/Business_and_Economy/Companies/Photography/Stock_Photography/

Referenced Software Products

Bobby™ is a trademark of CAST, Inc.

Cast eReader™ is a trademark of CAST, Inc.

Discover: Kenx® is a registered trademark of Don Johnston, Inc.

Gateway Stories© CAST, Inc.

Gateway Authoring System © CAST, Inc.

Great Math Adventure is a product created by 7th Level.

Hollywood is a product by Grolier Interactive, a division of Scholastic Inc.

HyperStudio® is a registered trademark of Knowledge Adventure.

Inspiration® is a registered trademark of Inspiration Software, Inc.

Intellitalk II® is a registered trademark of IntelliTools.

IntelliKeys® is a registered trademark of IntelliTools.

Introduction to Patterns, a product created by Tenth Planet™, is published by Sunburst Communications.

Kid Pix® is a registered trademark of The Learning Company.

Kidspiration™ is a trademark of Inspiration Software, Inc.

Let's Go Read! An Island Adventure™ is a registered trademark of Edmark.

L&H™ Kurzweil 3000™ is a trademark of Kurzweil Education Systems.

Lode Runner™ is a trademark licensed to Douglas E. Smith. © 1983 Douglas E. Smith,
    © 1994, 1995 Presage Software Development Company.

MathPad™ Plus is a trademark of IntelliTools.

Paint, Write & Play!™ is a trademark of The Learning Company.

Picture It© 1994 Slater Software, Inc.

Pix Writer© 1998 Slater Software, Inc.

Pix Reader© 1996 Slater Software, Inc.

PowerPoint™ is a registered trademark of Microsoft Corporation.

Reader Rabbit's Reading Development Library® is a registered trademark of
    The Learning Company.

TextHELP!® is a registered trademark of TextHELP Systems Ltd.

Thinking Reader is a product of CAST, Inc.

WiggleWorks® is a registered trademark of Scholastic Inc.

Write, Camera, Action!™ is a trademark of Broderbund.

Write: OutLoud® is a registered trademark of Don Johnston, Inc.

Index

Note: An *f* after a page number indicates a figure, a *wl* after a page number indicates a Web link.

affective goals, 86*f*, 94, 94–95, 106*f*
affective learning teaching methods
    assessment and, 142, 151–154
    challenges made adjustable, 127–128, 127*wl*
    choice in content and tools, 126–127, 126*wl*
    classroom application, 35–37, 131
    context individualized, 128–132
    digital media role, 80
    motivation development, 125
    rewards offered, 128
    Thinking Reader, 134
    UDL principles in, 75*f*
affective networks. *See also* emotions; motivation
    defined, 13
    distributed (lateral) processing, 31–32
    hierarchical processing, 32–33
    image perception, 61
    location in the brain, 31, 32*f*, 33
    media supporting multiple, 101
    overview, 10*f*, 29–31
    reading and, 57–58
    speech comprehension and, 50–51
    thinking/feeling connections, 31*wl*
agrammatism, 47
application of UDL. *See* classroom application
assessment
    alternatives, 146, 146*wl*
    confounding factors, 138–139
    overview, 136*f*
    performance criteria and, 97–98

assessment accuracy (barriers to)
    curriculum integration lacking, 145–146
    learner diversity accommodation, 139–143, 141*wl*
    media constraints, 143–144
    overview, 136*f*
    supports removed, 144–145
assessment accuracy (increasing)
    by accessibility, 147–148
    digital media role, 147–149, 152, 153*f*
    by engagement, 151–154
    by flexible learning measurements, 148–150, 149*f*, 152
    by monitoring progress, 146, 149–151, 150*f*, 151*f*
    overview, 136*f*
    scaffolding in, 152–153
    supports allowed, 148–151

Boston College Lynch School of Education, 169
bottom-up/top-down processing. *See* hierarchical processing
brain injury, 23*wl*, 32
brain structure. *See also* affective networks; recognition networks; strategic networks
    the cerebellum, 26*f*
    dyslexic readers, 55
    emotions and, 34–35
    imaging techniques, 11*wl*
    individual nature of, 17–19, 18*wl*, 26–27

About the Authors

In 1984, **David H. Rose** helped found the Center for Applied Special Technology (CAST) in order to expand opportunities for students with disabilities through the innovative development and application of technology. Dr. Rose specializes in developmental neuropsychology and in the Universal Design for Learning technologies. In addition to his role as co-executive director of CAST, Dr. Rose lectures at Harvard University Graduate School of Education, where he applies CAST's work in neural networks and learning to both the design and content of his course. Dr. Rose completed his undergraduate work at Harvard University; he received his master's degree from Reed College and his doctorate from the Harvard University Graduate School of Education.

As a founder and co-executive director of CAST, **Anne Meyer** plays a key role in the design of the organization's multimedia technology. Dr. Meyer applies her interdisciplinary training in education, clinical psychology, and graphic design to develop new approaches and new learning tools to meet the diverse needs of teachers and students in today's classrooms. She draws upon her long-term focus on psychological aspects of learning and learning disability to develop ways to use computers to build and support students' competence and self-esteem. After earning her undergraduate degree from Radcliffe College, Dr. Meyer received her master's degree and doctorate from the Harvard Graduate School of Education. She is also a licensed clinical psychologist.

Nicole Strangman completed her undergraduate degree in biology at Swarthmore College and earned a doctorate in neuroscience from Brown

University, where she studied the neurobiological basis for pain sensitivity. As a writer, she strives to bridge the gap between scientists and nonscientists by demystifying science for the public and developing excitement for scientific discovery. In addition to her work with CAST, Dr. Strangman is the author of numerous peer-reviewed and freelance articles.

Gabrielle Rappolt completed her Bachelor of Science in Neuroscience at Trinity College and her Master's of Education with a concentration in Mind and Brain at Harvard University. She is currently pursuing her doctorate in cognitive science and education at Harvard. In addition to her work with CAST, her research focuses on the neurobiological correlates of resilient behavior.

The authors welcome your comments and feedback on this book and its companion Web site at *http://www.cast.org/TeachingEveryStudent*.